DATE DUE			

A TENNYSON COMPANION

A TENNYSON COMPANION

Life and Works

F. B. PINION

St. Martin's Press   New York

© F. B. Pinion 1984

All rights reserved. For information, write:
St. Martin's Press, Inc., 175 Fifth Avenue, New York, NY 10010
Printed in Hong Kong
Published in the United Kingdom by The Macmillan Press Ltd.
First published in the United States of America in 1984

ISBN 0–312–79107–0

Library of Congress Cataloging in Publication Data

Pinion, F. B.

    A Tennyson companion.
    Bibliography: p.
    Includes index.
    1. Tennyson, Alfred Tennyson, Baron, 1809–1892.
2. Poets, English — 19th century — Biography.   I. Title.
PR5581.P5   1984   821'.8 [B]   84–4786
ISBN 0–312–79107–0

Contents

List of Illustrations   *page* vii

Acknowledgments   viii

PART ONE: TENNYSON'S LIFE

   Chronology   3
1 Somersby to Cambridge, 1809–28   5
2 Arthur Hallam, 1828–34   14
3 Poetic Recovery and Triumph, 1834–50   22
4 Marriage and Farringford, 1850–67   33
5 Aldworth and the Last Twenty-Five Years, 1867–92   47

PART TWO: TENNYSON'S WRITINGS

 6 Adolescent Poetry   63
 7 A Young Man's Fancies   71
 8 Art and Life   83
 9 Darkness and Living Light   93
10 English Idylls   102
11 *The Princess*   113
12 *In Memoriam A. H. H.*   122
13 The 'Locksley Hall' Poems and *Maud*   141
14 Patriotism and Politics   153
15 Three Tales   162
16 *Idylls of the King*   172
17 Epistolary Poems   195
18 Drama   201
19 Popular Dramatic Monologues   210
20 A Miscellany   218

v

vi Contents

21 The Gleam   226
22 Epilogue   233

    Notes   245

    Appendixes
    A. Family Tree   248
    B. Glossary   249
    C. The Story of *The Princess*   252
    D. Select Bibliography   256

    Index   259

List of Illustrations

PLATES

between pages 118 and 119

1 Mary Turner's home, Caistor, and Langton Hall, home of Bennet Langton
2 The rectory and brook at Somersby
3 The church at Somersby, exterior and interior
4 Portraits of Tennyson's grandfather and father
5 His mother and Louth Grammar School
6 The Great Gate and Great Court, Trinity College, Cambridge; Arthur Hallam
7 Tennyson and Hallam on the *Leeds* from Bordeaux to Dublin; Clevedon Church
8 Home of the Sellwoods, Horncastle, and Shiplake Church
9 Chapel House, Twickenham; Edmund Lushington; Park House, home of the Lushingtons
10 Farringford from the lawn, and Tennyson's study at Farringford
11 Tennyson and his family at Farringford
12 Charles (Tennyson) Turner; Thomas Woolner, R.A.
13 F. D. Maurice; Edward FitzGerald
14 Bayons Manor; Aldworth
15 Alfred (Lord) Tennyson
16 *Punch* on Tennyson's peerage, and Lord and Lady Tennyson with Hallam Tennyson

MAP   8
Tennyson Places in Holderness and Lincolnshire

Acknowledgments

My indebtedness to the editing of Professor Christopher Ricks in *The Poems of Tennyson*, Longmans, 1969 (the text of which I have followed), is inestimable; I owe much also to R. B. Martin's *Tennyson: The Unquiet Heart*. Lines from 'To Poesy', 'Tithon', 'The Little Maid', and 'Hail Briton!' are included by agreement with Longman Group Limited. I am grateful to the Spencer Research Library, University of Kansas, for generously enabling me to examine the late William D. Paden's Tennyson collections; and to the Inter-Library Loan Service department of the University of Sheffield. Dr Claudius Beatty of the University of Oslo, Professor Cecil Y. Lang of the University of Virginia, R. E. Elliott of Horncastle, and the Revd Geoffrey Peace of Halton Holgate have very kindly supplied helpful information.

Permission has been granted to reproduce illustrations from the Tennyson Research Centre, Lincoln, by courtesy of Lord Tennyson and the Lincolnshire Library Service (4 left, 4 right, 15), and from the Spencer Museum of Art, University of Kansas (11, the gift of Dr and Mrs William D. Paden). Non-copyright reproductions include the following: from A. J. Church, *The Laureate's Country*, 1891 (1 above, 2 below, 5 right, 7 below, 8 below); George G. Napier, *Homes and Haunts of Tennyson*, 1892 (9 upper left and right, 9 below); H. D. Rawnsley, *Memories of the Tennysons*, 1900 (5 left, 7 above, 8 above); and J. Cuming Walters, *In Tennyson Land*, 1890 (1 below, 2 above, 3 above, 3 below). Plates 6 above left and 6 below are from Le Keux, *Memorials of Cambridge*, 1842; 10 above and below, from *The English Illustrated Magazine*, 1892; 16 right, from *The Bookman*, 1897–8; and 13 left is a copy of F. Holl's engraving after a portrait by Lowes Dickinson.

I am particularly grateful to Roy Wilson, Photographic Unit of the Library, University of Sheffield, for the reproduction of many illustrations from which to make a choice; to Susan Gates and Elizabeth Anne Melrose for their unfailing assistance at the Tennyson Research Centre, Lincoln; to Mrs Julia Steward and Mrs

Valery Rose for encouragement and ready co-operation on behalf of the publishers; and, above all, to my wife for many helpful queries and recommendations arising from a critical examination of the text.

PART ONE

Tennyson's Life

Chronology

1809	(6 August) Alfred Tennyson born at Somersby
1816–20	At Louth Grammar School
1823–4	Writes *The Devil and the Lady*
1827	*Poems by Two Brothers* published by Jacksons of Louth. Enters Trinity College, Cambridge, in November
1828	Arthur Hallam enters Trinity College in October
1829	Tennyson wins the Chancellor's Gold Medal with 'Timbuctoo'. Becomes a member of 'The Apostles' (October). Hallam spends Christmas at Somersby
1830	*Poems, Chiefly Lyrical.* Visits the Pyrenees with Hallam
1831	His father dies, and he leaves Cambridge
1832	After taking his degree, and coming of age, Hallam stays at Somersby (March); he and Tennyson make a tour along the Rhine (July). *Poems* published in December (dated 1833)
1833	Ridicule of *Poems* in *The Quarterly Review*. Death of Arthur Hallam in Vienna (September)
1835	Death of Tennyson's grandfather George
1836	Tennyson falls in love with Emily Sellwood at his brother Charles's wedding
1837	The Tennysons leave Somersby for Beech Hill House at High Beech near Epping. Victoria becomes Queen
1840	Move to Tunbridge Wells
1841	Move to Boxley, near Maidstone (late in the year)
1842	Emily Tennyson marries. Publication of *Poems* in two volumes. Marriage of Cecilia Tennyson and Edmund Lushington
1843	Collapse of the wood-carving business in which Tennyson had invested most of his inheritance. Move to Cheltenham
1845	Granted a Civil List pension
1847	*The Princess*
1850	*In Memoriam A. H. H.*; marriage; Poet Laureateship
1851	Move to Chapel House, Twickenham (March). Holiday in Italy

3

1852	Birth of Hallam Tennyson (August). Death of the Duke of Wellington (September)
1853	Move to Farringford, Isle of Wight, in November
1854	Birth of Lionel Tennyson shortly before the Crimean War begins (March)
1855	*Maud, and Other Poems*
1856	End of Crimean War
1858	Alfred visits Norway
1859	*Idylls of the King* ('Enid', 'Vivien', 'Elaine', 'Guinevere'). Visit to Portugal
1860	Julia Cameron comes to live near Farringford
1861	Tennyson visits the Pyrenees with his family. Death of Prince Albert (December)
1862	Received by the Queen at Osborne
1864	*Enoch Arden, and Other Poems*
1865	Death of Tennyson's mother
1868	The foundation stone of Aldworth, the Tennysons' summer residence on Blackdown, laid in April
1869	*The Holy Grail and Other Poems* (dated 1870)
1872	*Gareth and Lynette, etc.* (i.e. with 'The Last Tournament')
1874	'Balin and Balan' completed (first published in the 1885 volume)
1875	*Queen Mary*
1876	*Harold* (dated 1877)
1879	*Becket* completed; death of Charles Tennyson; *The Lover's Tale* published; *The Falcon* produced
1880	*Ballads and Other Poems*
1881	*The Cup* produced. *The Foresters* completed (first performed in New York, and published, in 1892)
1882	*The Promise of May* produced
1883	Death of Edward FitzGerald
1884	Tennyson takes his seat in the House of Lords. *Becket* published (first performed in 1893)
1885	*Tiresias and Other Poems*
1886	Death of Lionel. *Locksley Hall Sixty Years After, etc.* (including *The Promise of May*)
1889	*Demeter and Other Poems*
1892	(6 October) Tennyson dies at Aldworth. *The Death of Oenone, Akbar's Dream, and Other Poems* published posthumously

I

Tennyson's detestation of prying biographers erupted in bucolic imagery; their treatment of great men was like ripping pigs open for public gaze. He was certain to be ripped open, and thanked God that he and the world knew nothing of Shakespeare but his writings. He expresses his antipathy in 'The Dead Prophet'; Carlyle, 'one of the people's kings', after labouring to lift them 'out of slime' and show that souls have wings, had been stripped bare by his biographer, and exposed to public gaze. At nightfall, while the sun glares at the approaching storm, a vulturous beldam glides in and kneels by the corpse. She makes much of the man's noble qualities, but insists on the need to 'scan him from head to feet, Were it but for a wart or a mole'. Finding little outward blemish, she tears him 'part from part', extracts heart and liver, and pronounces one small and the other half-diseased. Earlier, in 'To——, After Reading a Life and Letters', Tennyson declared it is better for the poet to die unknown than at the temple gates of Glory, where 'the carrion vulture waits To tear his heart before the crowd'.

Holding that 'something should be done by dispassionate criticism towards the reformation of our national habits in the matter of literary biography', George Eliot reinforced her views with a quotation from the second of these two poems:

> Is it not odious that as soon as a man is dead his desk is raked, and every insignificant memorandum which he never meant for the public is printed for the gossiping amusement of people too idle to re-read his books? 'He gave the people of his best. His worst he kept, his best he gave' – but there is a certain set, not a small one, who are titillated by the worst and indifferent to the best. I think this fashion is a disgrace to us all. It is something like the uncovering of the dead Byron's club-foot.

She believed that most people would read any quantity of trivial details about an author whose works they knew very imperfectly, if at all, and that biographies generally were 'a disease of English literature'.

The distinction between the many whose literary interest is mainly biographical and the relatively few who are genuinely devoted to literature remains as valid as ever. Nevertheless, the study of a writer's works benefits appreciably from an understanding of all the factors that made him and his outlook what they were; and it is fortunate that the principal biographies of Tennyson have become increasingly illuminating. His son Hallam's *Memoir*, though a mine of information, is restricted and guarded; his grandson Charles's *Alfred Tennyson* discloses much more, with admirable lucidity throughout; finally we have *Tennyson: The Unquiet Heart* by Robert Martin, a work which presents little short of what we are likely to know, and appraises with an unusual degree of informed detachment the poet's inherited problems, his temperamental idiosyncrasies, and his literary achievements.

The Tennysons, thought to be Danish in origin, seem to have settled first in Holderness, near the Humber east of Hull. Their descendants belonged predominantly to small yeomen and professional classes. One, whose parents migrated to Cambridgeshire in the seventeenth century, became Archbishop of Canterbury, and founded a famous London school. In the eighteenth century Michael Tennyson, an apothecary at Hedon, married the heiress of the wealthy Clayton family, who owned most of Grimsby before its development, and claimed descent from holders of the Baronetcy of d'Eyncourt. Their son George Tennyson became a solicitor, set up practice at Market Rasen, and married Mary Turner of Caistor, to whom tradition ascribes talent in music and painting. George not only inherited his father's wealth and property but transmitted some of the Clayton hotheadedness and instability. As legal consultant on land enclosures for many years he became a shrewd business man; involvement in electioneering at Grimsby for his own ends made him hard-headed and wily; he lost no opportunity of acquiring land on favourable terms, and in this way became owner of the manor estate of Beacons, once d'Eyncourt property, with traces of an old castle, on the edge of the Wolds near Tealby, three miles from Market Rasen. Plans for improving the house, which was thatched and unpretentious, and for clearing and planting the neighbouring hillsides, were soon under way. In accordance with George's ambition, it was given the ancient name of Bayons Manor which he claimed for it in furtherance of his d'Eyncourt pretensions. For the same reason he leased part of Deloraine Court near Lincoln Cathedral; unsuccessful in his social aims, he moved to Grimsby before occupying Bayons about 1801.

George and Mary's two sons were the youngest of four children. Before George Clayton Tennyson, the elder of the two, was of age, his father decided to make his younger son Charles his heir, concluding that he would be steadier and better qualified to achieve family distinction. After seven or eight years at St Peter's Grammar School, York, the elder brother, sensitive but rather uncouth and fractious (possibly as the result of incipient epilepsy), was sent to a private tutor in Huntingdonshire, where he was coached for admission to St John's College, Cambridge. He could have done well at the University, but informed his father that academic success demanded too much exertion, and finished with a pass degree. Destined for the Church against his will, he was ordained deacon in May 1801, before making a mysterious visit to Russia. The story, which his son the poet Alfred Tennyson believed, is that while dining with Lord St Helens, the English representative at the coronation of Czar Alexander in Moscow, he voiced a common English view that the Czar's predecessor had been murdered by a certain count. A hush followed, and he was later informed that the count had been one of the guests. Urged to ride for his life, he fled to the Crimea, where, as he lay ill and delirious, wild rustics danced round with magical incantations. An English courier passed by every three months, and George, having no money, had to wait for him before he could return to England. Whether this account was a fabrication to excuse his prolonged absence or a subsequent fantasy is conjectural, but it is quite inconsistent with the report of his movements which the officer of the ship on which he sailed to St Petersburg sent his father. He was ordained priest in December 1802, becoming rector of Benniworth, with duties also at South Willingham. Eventually he took lodgings in Louth, where he became engaged to Elizabeth Fytche, daughter of the previous vicar. They were married in August 1805, with expectations (realized at the end of 1806) of additional income from the livings of Somersby and Bag Enderby, two small neighbouring villages in the wold country east of Horncastle.

George's elder sister Elizabeth, beautiful and charming, a great reader and a writer of verse, pleased her father, above all by marrying the son and heir of a rich Durham coal-owner, who had

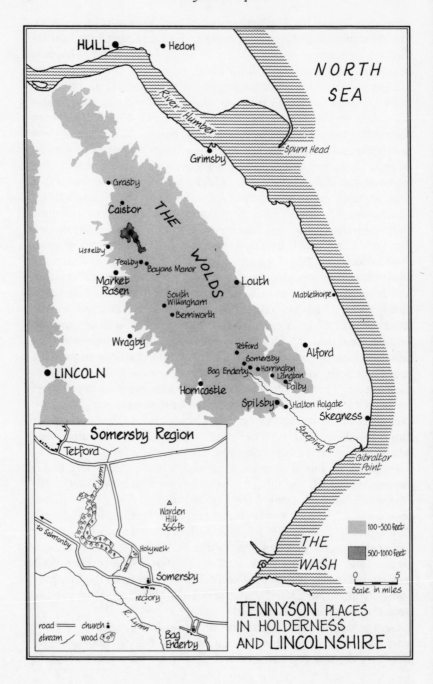

HULL • Hedon

NORTH SEA

River Humber

Spurn Head

• Grimsby

• Grasby

THE WOLDS

Caistor

Usselby •

Tealby • • Bayons Manor

Market Rasen

South Willingham •

• Benniworth

• Louth

Mablethorpe

Wragby

Tetford • • Somersby • Alford

Bag Enderby • • Harrington • Langton Dalby

• LINCOLN

Horncastle

Spilsby • • Halton Holgate

Skegness

Sleeping R.

Gibraltar Point

Somersby Region

Tetford

R. Lymn

△ Warden Hill 366ft

to Salmonby

Holywell

Somersby

rectory

R. Lymn

Bag Enderby

road ═══ church ✝
stream ～ wood ♣

THE WASH

☐ 100–500 feet
☐ 500–1000 feet

0 ─── 5
Scale in miles

TENNYSON PLACES IN HOLDERNESS AND LINCOLNSHIRE

bought Brancepeth Castle and had considerable political power through the acquisition of pocket boroughs. When her father-in-law died, Elizabeth's husband Matthew Russell spent huge sums on restoring and furnishing his castle in medieval style. Charles Tennyson acted as his agent, and in return Matthew used his influence to secure him a place in Parliament, and thereby advance the fulfilment of the elder George Tennyson's ambitions at Bayons Manor. The younger sister Mary, who had sympathized with George against their father, became Calvinistic and married a local dissenting squire, John Bourne of Dalby. Tennyson remembered how she wept to think of God's mercy in making her one of the Elect. 'Has he not damned most of my friends? But *me, me* He has picked out for eternal salvation, *me* who am no better than my neighbours.' She told him one day that she thought of the words of Holy Scripture 'Depart from me, ye cursed, into everlasting fire' when she looked at him.

Delayed by repairs and extensions, George and his family did not enter Somersby rectory until early in 1808. Twelve children were born to him and Elizabeth, ten at Somersby: George, born at Bayons Manor, died within a few weeks in 1806; Frederick was born in 1807 (at Louth), Charles in 1808, and Alfred on 6 August 1809, the fourth anniversary of his parents' wedding; four girls and four boys followed, and accommodation proved inadequate long before the last of the surviving eleven was born in 1819. Three times in his infancy Tennyson was thought to be dead from convulsions. He remembered with affection the woodbine that climbed into the bay-window of his nursery, the Gothic vaulted dining-room with stained-glass windows that, as Charles said, made butterfly souls on the walls, the stone chimney-piece carved by their father, the drawing-room bookshelves, the lawn overshadowed by wych-elms on one side and by larches and sycamores on the other, with a border of lilies and roses, and the garden beyond leading down to the parson's field, at the foot of which flowed the brook described in 'Ode to Memory'. Nor did the seclusion of his native village, 'in a pretty pastoral district of softly sloping hills and large ash trees', with 'a little glen in it called by the old monkish name of Holywell', lose its appeal.

There were fewer than a hundred people in Somersby and Bag Enderby, and most inhabitants of the area were rough, uneducated, and not readily sociable. The Tennysons were not proud, and father and sons were disposed to talk with anyone they met. Fortunately the family had cultural and spiritual resources. George Clayton Tennyson played the harp, wrote talented verse, and was genuinely interested in the arts and architecture. He read widely in English, Greek, and Latin, and had many valuable folio editions, most of which he bought at the sale of a local gentleman's library, that of Bennet Langton, once the friend of Samuel Johnson, whom he succeeded as Professor of Ancient Literature at the Royal Academy. George had a fine voice, and, as a magistrate, was always welcome for his geniality and brilliant conversation at the barristers' mess during Spilsby Sessions. He and his wife were a strikingly handsome couple; in her old age Mrs Tennyson remembered receiving twenty-five marriage proposals. She loved poetry, recited it to her children, and encouraged their verse-writing. Though a pious Evangelical, she had a strong sense of humour, and this and her tender-heartedness endeared her to them. Such was her love of birds and animals that boys deliberately beat dogs near the rectory in the certainty that her plea for mercy would be followed by a bribe.

The Tennysons were far from poor. George did not forfeit his Benniworth benefice; it was worth about £500 a year, out of which he paid a curate £35 for the performance of his duties; Somersby and Bag Enderby brought in about £180, and his father made him an annual allowance of £140. In 1815, two years after purchasing the degree of Doctor of Civil Law, he benefited considerably when his father procured him a Grimsby vicarage. He could now afford a carriage and pair, a groom and a personal servant, in addition to the coachman whom Alfred remembered as half mad, and usually half drunk. Blamed for not keeping the harness clean, he carried it into the drawing-room, threw it down, and shouted 'Clean it thyself then!' The cook vented her indignation against master and mistress in words which Tennyson adapted for 'The Village Wife': 'If you raäked out Hell with a smaäl-tooth coämb you weänt find their likes.'

After attending a school in Holywell glen, the three older boys were sent to the Grammar School at Louth, where they stayed with their grandmother in Westgate Place. Dr Tennyson had taught them Greek and Latin, and made Alfred recite Horace's odes before joining his brothers at the age of seven. Frederick, the most brilliant of the three, left in 1818 for Eton; Alfred was withdrawn before Charles, in 1820, because he was unhappy at school. Learning was enforced by the cane, and masters and boys were often brutal. One of the students who was kind to him was hanged years later for horse-stealing; another who used to punch him in the stomach for being a homesick baby grew up to be generally respected for his kindness and sympathy as a physician. Like Charles, Alfred left with a reputation for poetry. Among his few pleasant memories were the sight of an old weed-covered wall opposite the school windows, and the aural appeal of 'sonus desilientis aquae'. Sounds fascinated him: on a stormy day he would cry out 'I hear a voice that's speaking in the wind'; the words 'far, far away' had such haunting power that, late in life, in a poem of that title, he surmised the source of their charm, singling out 'the mellow lin-lan-lane' of distant evening church bells as the sound dearest to him in his native region.

He was about eight when he wrote Thomsonian lines in praise of flowers for his brother Charles; two or three years later he fell in love with Homer's *Iliad* in Pope's translation, and composed hundreds of lines in 'regular Popeian metre'. From the age of twelve he was busy with 'an epic of six thousand lines à la Walter Scott', and would shout lines fresh from the mint as he wandered about the fields in the dark. He remembered a tender reading of 'The Prisoner of Chillon' by his paternal grandmother, who boasted that all his poetry came from her. Grief at the death of his favourite poet in 1824 made him inscribe 'Byron is dead' on a sandstone face by the brook in Holywell glen. Among the verses he wrote about the age of sixteen is a lengthy account of Napoleon's retreat from Moscow. His father's shelves supplied extensive reading in poetry, fiction, ancient history, and travel; and *The Devil and the Lady*, a sprightly play, testifies to his familiarity with Elizabethan and Jacobean dramatists, and to the breadth of his knowledge, at an even earlier period.

Dr Tennyson was devoted to his elder sons' education, and a governess took charge of the girls. Alfred's high spirits are revealed in a letter addressed to her as his dear Dulcinea, and assuring her that his Quixotic strains contain no 'Ossianic, Miltonic, Byronic, Milmanic, Moorish, Crabbic, Coleridgic' fire. A letter to an aunt at Louth shows precocious learning; its ostentatiousness is not priggish, as it would be from an older writer, but a quaintly pedagogic revelation of conscientiousness steadfastly at work in belated fulfilment of an exacted promise. Tennyson was fast developing his addiction to books and precision in scholarship. He and Charles continued to write poetry.

All was not well at the rectory. Dr Tennyson was becoming more irritable and inflamed by grievances. He suffered attacks of epilepsy and depression, partly temperamental in origin but exacerbated by keen awareness of his restricted prospects at Somersby. His brother Charles's opportunities and political status, with a house and rich wife at Westminster, and close ties with Bayons Manor and Brancepeth Castle, served to fuel the burning indignation that was apt to flare up against his father's injustices. His health suffered, and in 1822 he stayed with his wife at Cheltenham, hoping the waters would effect his cure. His improvement was shortlived. He could be severe as a teacher, and 'more than once Alfred, scared by his father's fits of despondency, went out through the black night, and threw himself on a grave in the churchyard, praying to be beneath the sod himself'.

The older boys played about Baumber's Farm,[1] a red-bricked neighbouring house with a battlemented parapet, fished in the brook, or wandered about the southern Wolds. From Malory's *Morte d'Arthur* came a love of jousting in mock tournaments and, for Alfred, an idealization of King Arthur which remained undimmed all his life. Brothers and sisters composed serial stories collectively for reading at table after dinner. Wellington and Napoleon were the subject of story and verse, as they were for Charlotte and Branwell Brontë. In summer the family left the Wolds and travelled across 'the drain-cut levels of the marshy lea' to the coast for a holiday at Skegness or Mablethorpe.

As the Doctor's health declined he turned to drink and opium; his seizures increased, resulting sometimes in violence, much to the consternation of his wife and children. Charles and Alfred continued to write poems nevertheless, and a selection, with a few by Frederick, was published anonymously at Louth in 1827 with the title *Poems by Two Brothers*. Charles remembered standing on the road with Alfred and his mother, who had encouraged them to write, waiting for the carrier from Louth to appear over Tetford hill with the proofs. Half the £20 offered the two young poets in remuneration had to be taken in books from the publishers' shop, and some of the remainder was spent on hiring a carriage for a day at Mablethorpe, where they 'shared their triumph with the winds and waves'.

There must have been relief in the autumn when Dr Tennyson agreed, for the sake of his health, to stay with an old family friend in Paris, and relief of another kind when Charles and Alfred joined Frederick at Trinity College, Cambridge (to which the latter had been transferred after a year at St John's). After being captain and acquiring a reputation for eccentricity at Eton, he had already

distinguished himself by winning the University medal for the best
Greek ode. His younger brothers, though shy, unsophisticated, and
inelegantly dressed, excited interest and respect as poets. Their
appearance was striking, Alfred's especially. He was tall, strongly
built, with dark wavy hair, aquiline features, olive-dark complex-
ion, and head magnificently set on broad shoulders. He had already
written a Homeric book in Greek hexameters on the Seven against
Thebes. 'That man must be a poet', remarked W. H. Thompson,
the future Master of Trinity, when he first saw him entering the hall.

Writing to his widowed aunt Elizabeth, who realized his genius
and was actively interested in his progress,[2] Tennyson complained
of isolation; the country was 'disgustingly level', the revelry of
Cambridge monotonous, and studies were 'so uninteresting, so
much matter of fact. None but dry-headed, calculating, angular
little gentlemen can take much delight in them.' Intellectual and
cultural appetites were stimulated most in discussions with student
friends or in private reading. The suspicion that his sons were not
making the most of their academic opportunities irritated Dr
Tennyson. When, at the end of 1828, Frederick was rusticated for
three terms, in consequence of refusal to accept impositions for not
attending chapel, followed by apparent insolence in reply to a
demand for an explanation of his indiscipline, matters inevitably
worsened, even though his father thought him harshly treated.
Frederick's aggressive manner annoyed his father, whose increasing
recourse to drink and opiates made him dangerous. A knife and a
gun were found in his room. With the knife he threatened Frederick
in particular; Frederick retaliated with violence, was turned out of
the house, and then allowed £100 per annum to read for the Bar.
Mrs Tennyson, subjected to unfounded accusations, and convinced
that her husband's 'ungovernable violence' made it unsafe for her or
her children to remain, left with the remainder of the family for
Louth, while he was at Bayons Manor with their son Edward, and
Charles and Alfred were at Cambridge. After much sympathetic
persuasion, arrangements were made, chiefly through the agency of
his friend, the Revd T. H. Rawnsley of Halton Holgate near
Spilsby, to release the Doctor from his parochial duties while he
sought cure once again in Paris, after staying first with his father at
Bayons and then in London with his brother Charles.

2

Such developments clouded Tennyson's second year at Cambridge, though his happiness grew, chiefly in friendship with Arthur Hallam. Son of a leading historian, and a close friend of Gladstone at Eton, Hallam had enormous talent; he was an eloquent debater, and a charming enthusiast whose gaiety and idealism were tempered by good sense. More than a year younger than Tennyson, he had spent several months in Italy, where he had fallen under the spell of Italian art and literature, Dante especially, and of an English girl he met at Rome. He entered Trinity in October 1828, and made Alfred's acquaintance in 1829, perhaps through an exchange of their poems. A sonnet written by Arthur at the beginning of the summer term, implying that Tennyson would have been 'first of friends in rank' had not Providence bestowed 'one perfect gem' on the writer's 'early spring', expresses confidence in their friendship. The closing line ('Thou yearner for all fair things, and all true') gives a clue to their mutual attraction.

Tennyson could be a lively companion and conversationalist. He was noted for his mimicry, and his discussions with Hallam were considered magnificent by John Kemble, Mrs Siddons' nephew. The award of the Chancellor's Medal for his poem 'Timbuctoo' in June 1829 set the seal to his Cambridge reputation. He had competed reluctantly under pressure from his father, combining passages from 'Armageddon' (which seems to have been written when he was not more than fifteen) with new material, and capping the whole with an epigraph purporting to come from the works of George Chapman. From Somersby in the summer, too shy to read his prize poem in the Senate House at Commencement, he persuaded his friend Charles Merivale (winner of the medal in 1828) to deputize. Tennyson thought the ode submitted by Hallam much superior. Hallam regarded Alfred as potentially the greatest poet of his generation, possibly of the century; Monckton Milnes thought 'Timbuctoo' equal to 'most parts of Milton'.

Hallam had been elected a member of 'The Apostles' in May;

Tennyson's membership had been proposed at their last meeting before the Long Vacation; and he and Milnes were elected at the next meeting, on 31 October. The group had begun as the Cambridge Conversazione Society at St John's College in 1820. John Sterling had been its most brilliant figure, and F. D. Maurice its spiritual leader. Subjects for discussion ranged from science, literature, and philosophy to theology and politics, at a time when conservatism was continually questioned in consequence of the French Revolution and demands for political reform at home, and when historical and scientific evidences were already casting doubt on time-honoured theological assumptions. The spiritual influence of Coleridge's metaphysics was an inspiration to some of its leaders, who by and large became a force for the regeneration of society; their reforming zeal slowly but inevitably affected the course of Tennyson's poetry. The Society now met in members' rooms at Trinity, where most of its supporters were students. It was dubbed 'The Apostles' when, for practical reasons, its membership was limited to twelve. The sobriquet did not offend, for members enjoyed the prestige of being a light to the Philistines. When Maurice left Cambridge in 1827 he thought that too much levity and discursiveness had entered their discussions. Enthusiasm could lead to high-flown nonsense, as when Kemble said of one of his rare silences, 'The world is one great thought, and I am thinking it.' Friendships grew vigorously within this circle, with frequent meetings for walks and talks, often in the lime-treed avenues of Trinity, or by the Cam, or further afield; but for geniality and wide interests, cliquishness might have been damaging, both to Tennyson with his private sorrows, and to Hallam, who suffered from recurrent headaches and depression.

Weekly meetings were held for the reading and discussion of essays, which each presented in turn. At the Society's debates on whether Shelley's poetry had an immoral tendency and on whether 'an intelligible First Cause' is deducible from 'the phenomena of the Universe' (Hallam's paper), Tennyson voted 'No'; at another, on whether there is 'any rule of moral action beyond general expediency', he voted 'Aye'. He prepared an essay on ghosts, but when the evening (13.ii.30) for reading and discussing it came, was unable to present it, and therefore forfeited membership, though he was allowed to attend subsequent meetings. He had not attended regularly; when he did attend he was content to smoke his clay pipe and strong tobacco (a practice he started when he was fourteen).

Already familiar with the fallibility of reason in the search for truth, he preferred reflection or friendly conversation to the cut and thrust of debate.

Poetry had become his major interest. He was reading Virgil under the desk when the observant mathematics lecturer, his tutor William Whewell, engaged his attention by asking him the compound interest of a penny 'put out' from the early Christian era up to the present. 'A Character' satirizes the unsociably superior manner of Thomas Sunderland, a scholar of distinction and the most brilliant speaker at the Cambridge Union; when told that Tennyson wrote it, he retorted, 'Which Tennyson? The slovenly one?' The slovenly pipe-smoking one loved to recite old English ballads; his readings from Urquhart's *Rabelais* were inordinately entertaining; sometimes, with close friends, he improvised verses or read his poems, including *The Lover's Tale*; his recitation of 'The Ballad of Oriana' in hall after dinner lived long in the memory of Edward FitzGerald. As R. C. Trench realized, there was always the danger that adulation would create damaging overconfidence; it may have emboldened Tennyson to publish a selection of his poems. He and Hallam, whom he regarded as the 'light of those dawn-golden times', had prepared a joint volume, but the latter, accepting his father's advice on the unwisdom of publishing prematurely, withdrew from the venture after the book was in print. Alfred followed his brother's example, his *Poems, Chiefly Lyrical* appearing in June 1830, three months after the publication of Charles's *Sonnets and Fugitive Pieces*.

Meanwhile Dr Tennyson had been on tour in Switzerland and Italy. In Paris, where his hosts had found him a trial, he had met Frederick, who was now conciliatory and tutor to a young nobleman, after having gained re-admission to Trinity for the following year. His father's itinerary and letters suggest a frenzied energy; 'an outcast from England' and his family, he found compensation in Alpine beauty and sublimity, and missed no opportunity of seeing places of interest, from Rousseau's island to classical sites; an eruption of Vesuvius excited his descriptive powers. He returned to Somersby at the end of July 1830, with reports of drawing suspicion and violence upon himself while trying to save a stilettoed man at the Carnival in Rome, and of hairbreadth escapes: he had been almost buried by an avalanche; he would have fallen from giddiness over a precipice had not someone caught him in time; and but for a tree to which he convulsively clung he would have hurtled, with carriage, horses, and driver, to destruction thousands of feet below.

His return to Somersby preceded Alfred's by nearly two months. John Sterling had become friendly with General Torrijos, the leader of Spanish insurrectionaries in London; his cousin Robert Boyd, eager for adventure and with money to spare, agreed to buy and equip a ship lying in the Thames; the support of some of the Apostles was enlisted. In response to the Spanish Government, the Foreign Office intervened and the ship was seized. Sterling escaped, met Torrijos at Deal, and crossed the Channel with him in an open boat. Torrijos met Boyd at Gibraltar, where the conspirators gradually assembled. Tennyson and Hallam left England in July with money and instructions for Pyrenean confederates, the leader of whom soon disenchanted them with threats of cutting the throats of all the curés. They were exhilarated by the mountain scenery around Cauteretz, which Tennyson later put to good use in 'Oenone' and 'The Lotos-Eaters'. After crossing from Bordeaux to Dublin on the *Leeds*, they caught the first train to run (fatally for the statesman Huskisson) from Liverpool to Manchester. Trench and Kemble, who had gone by sea to Gibraltar, stayed on until the early part of 1831; the unfortunate Boyd remained until November, when the Governor had no choice but to order Torrijos and his adherents to leave. Accompanied by Boyd, they slipped out in two small vessels, to be chased by Spanish guardships, captured (after barricading themselves in a farmhouse near the shore), and executed on the esplanade at Malaga.

Arthur Hallam, who had stayed at Somersby during Christmas 1829 and again at Easter, had fallen in love with Alfred's sister Emily; he probably paid a brief visit on his way home from the Pyrenees. Strained family relations and his father's condition made Alfred ill, and his return to Trinity was delayed. Political revolutionary movements in western Europe stirred him less deeply than they did Hallam, who could not make his father understand that, 'after helping to revolutionize kingdoms, one is still less inclined than before to trouble one's head about scholarships, degrees and such gear'. Tennyson's zeal for reform at home may be found in his 'Lines on Cambridge of 1830': its ancient splendours, its doctors, proctors, and deans would be of no avail 'when the Day-beam sports New-risen o'er awakened Albion'. Agitation for Reform led to rioting and the firing of farms and cornstacks; Tennyson helped students to extinguish one such blaze at Coton near Cambridge, and joined an undergraduate defence force when it was rumoured that a mob would attack the University. At the end of term Wordsworth, brother of the Master of Trinity, attended a party in the rooms of James Spedding, an Apostle and son of one of the ageing poet's schoolfellows. A loyal democrat and patriot, alarmed by the demagogy that continually threatened to foment mob violence, possibly worse excesses such as he had known in Paris, Wordsworth chose to speak on revolutions. Tennyson, whose later political views proved to be remarkably similar, was not present; he had left for Somersby with Hallam, who became engaged to Emily. At home that Christmas he imagined her playing the harp he 'used to love so well' or sympathizing with the 'lone desire' of Keats's Madeline or Isabella. The engagement disturbed his father, for Arthur was not yet twenty, and had no settled career in mind. Believing that he could make a more advantageous marriage, Henry Hallam persuaded him not to meet or communicate with Emily before he became of age.

Dr Tennyson was failing rapidly, and unfit to perform any Church duties. Charles and Alfred were called home from Cambridge before he died in March; he was buried at Somersby, contrary to the wishes of his wife, who thought he should be interred at Tealby. George Tennyson of Bayons, however, had withheld consent and persuaded Charles not to attend his brother's funeral; he had little patience with his unpractical Somersby dependants, wished Alfred would enter the Church, and was convinced that events had justified his decision to make Charles, now a Minister of the Crown, his heir. Alfred (who had slept in his father's bed, hoping to see his ghost) did not return to Cambridge, and it was found that the heavy debts which he and his brothers had left behind matched Dr Tennyson's, which included £200 to mercers and £127 to his wine merchant. All these matters were settled by 'the Old Man of the Wolds', who allowed Mrs Tennyson £800 annually, less whatever he spent on supporting and educating her children. As the rectory was not required by the new incumbent, she and her family were allowed to remain.

Alfred's short-sightedness worsened under stress early in 1831, and he feared he was going blind; after a milk diet he recovered. One night he saw moonlight reflected in a nightingale's eye, while her voice vibrated with such passion that the neighbouring leaves seemed to tremble, as he recalled in 'The Gardener's Daughter'. His *Poems, Chiefly Lyrical* had received favourable reviews, including Arthur Hallam's, which, clearly influenced by Keats's poetry, claimed that Tennyson's dedication to beauty or 'sensation' above all else made him 'a poet in the truest and highest sense'. After being encouraged therefore to start preparing for his next volume, Alfred was upset when, in May 1832, Professor John Wilson ('Christopher North'), editor of *Blackwood's Magazine*, attacked commendatory reviewers of his poems, especially Hallam for his praise of Tennyson's allegiance to the Cockney School of poets. Wilson took time to ridicule most of the weaker inclusions, but made judicious amends by admiring poems in which the author's 'fine faculties' appeared.

News late at night of the passing of the Reform Bill created such elation in Tennyson and some of his brothers and sisters that they rang the church bells madly until stopped by the indignant new rector. In London he met Hallam, Spedding, Kemble, and other Apostles (most of whom were familiar with leading poems in his next publication), saw Kemble's sister Fanny in *The Hunchback* at Covent Garden, and dined with the Hallams in Wimpole Street. Benefiting from his aunt Elizabeth's continued allowance, he accompanied Arthur on a tour in the Rhine country. In November, against the wishes of his friends, he instructed his publisher Moxon to withdraw *The Lover's Tale* from his forthcoming volume, though most of the print for this long poem was already set up. He could not resist including a reply to 'Christopher North':

You did late review my lays,
    Crusty Christopher;
You did mingle blame and praise,
    Rusty Christopher.
When I learnt from whom it came,
I forgave you all the blame,
    Musty Christopher;
I could *not* forgive the praise,
    Fusty Christopher.

After beginning his legal studies in London, Hallam found Somersby glorious in its leafy summer pride, but was disquieted by his marriage prospects. He knew that his father could allow him no more than £600 a year, and was disappointed to discover that Mr Rawnsley, inopportunely meeting Emily's grandfather before the latter had recovered from an altercation with his grandson Frederick (on the latter's refusal to adopt a career), had failed to secure her an adequate settlement. Hallam's own attempts to supplement his income through Tennysonian channels proved nugatory. He was at Somersby again at Christmas, and found time to continue his reading of Jane Austen (*Emma* was his favourite, Tennyson's preferences being *Emma* and *Persuasion*). His marriage did not seem assured until the following spring, when Alfred brought his eldest sister Mary to Wimpole Street; the Hallams were so impressed by her beauty and personality that Arthur's engagement was soon accepted, and even the date of his wedding discussed.

Tennyson's *Poems*, the title-page dated 1833, had appeared in December. Most reviewers, taking their cue from Professor Wilson's example, showed their lack of integrity or critical perspicacity by rating the volume lower than its predecessor. Tennyson was charged with affectation, obscurity, and drivel. Worse was to come; Rhadamanthine critics in Edinburgh could operate formidable batteries. 'Christopher', smarting from a rash young poet's squib, engaged his former colleague John Lockhart, author of the notoriously despicable attack on Keats, and now editor of *The Quarterly Review*, to ensure that the onslaught on the latest recruit to the 'Cockney School' continued; the result was J. W. Croker's torrent of ridicule in the April number. Such was the prestige of this periodical that an old Lincolnshire squire described it to Tennyson as 'the next book to God's Bible'. It hardened attitudes against the poet for years, and he repented his indiscreet riposte. A letter to 'Christopher North' in which he admits this, and suggests a truce (in the hope of fending off renewed criticism), reveals the apprehensions of one who had lost confidence and judgment.

Tennyson's self-esteem and enjoyment of life revived nevertheless. He wrote much poetry, and revised it assiduously. He visited Cambridge to meet Hallam and Kemble, and swam and lazed in the hot sunshine at Mablethorpe, recalling no doubt the weather he had experienced there in March, when he probably wrote these lines:

> Here often, when a child, I lay reclined,
>   I took delight in this locality.
> Here stood the infant Ilion of the mind,
>   And here the Grecian ships did seem to be.
> And here again I come, and only find
>   The drain-cut levels of the marshy lea, –
> Gray sandbanks, and pale sunsets, – dreary wind,
>   Dim shores, dense rains, and heavy-clouded sea!

After accompanying his Cambridge friend Monteith to his home near Carstairs, Lanark, while Arthur was with Emily at Somersby, he hurried to London to see Hallam, who had suffered from recurrent headaches and illness, before he set off with his father on their European tour. With Moxon and Leigh Hunt the two friends visited the aged poet Samuel Rogers, and admired a Titian and a Raphael in his picture-gallery; in the library Alfred was chagrined to find a copy of his brother Charles's poems but none of his own.

A lover of freedom, Arthur admired 'the independence and self-respect of the Tyrolese'; he thought Salzburg just the place for Tennyson to live. After visiting Buda, he and his father returned to Vienna, a city he found 'more uniformly handsome' than Paris. His enthusiasm for the paintings he saw, Venetian particularly, is expressed in his last letter to Tennyson; he urges Alfred to write 'as perfect a Danaë' as Titian's. The damp weather chilled him, and he stayed indoors, assuming he had a recurrence of the ague. Two days later, on 15 September, tired after a short walk, he chose to rest on a sofa. His father, returning to the hotel after a further stroll, thought he was asleep; some time elapsed before he discovered his son was dead. A post-mortem showed that Arthur had died of apoplexy, and that, owing to a congenital malformation of the brain, his death could not have been long delayed. Mr Hallam arranged for the body to be shipped from Trieste. When he returned to England, he begged his brother-in-law to write to Tennyson; the letter from Clifton was collected by Alfred's sister Matilda at Spilsby and brought to the rectory after her dancing-lesson. Tennyson conveyed its sorrowful news to Emily and caught her as she fainted. 'She above all is ever a sacred object of my thoughts', Henry Hallam wrote nine days later, and he proved his sincerity by making her an allowance of £300 a year, which he continued after her marriage. The ship carrying Arthur's body reached Dover at the end of the year, and he was buried on 3 January 1834 in Clevedon Church above the Bristol Channel. John Kemble had reported the manner of Hallam's death to his sister, saying it was 'always feared by us as likely to occur'. His loss would most assuredly be felt by their age, 'for if ever man was born for great things he was. Never was a more powerful intellect joined to a purer and holier heart; and the whole illuminated with the richest imagination, with the most sparkling yet the kindest wit.'

3

For a time Hallam's death extinguished the happy, confident expectations of Emily and Alfred Tennyson. Self-prescription of study in languages, science, and theology indicates the determination of the latter to broaden the basis of his poetry. His depression and partial recovery may be seen in 'The Two Voices' and 'Ulysses'. Early lyrics on Arthur's death reveal moods of calm. In July 1834 he visited the Hallams at Molesey Park, and received copies of Arthur's literary remains, edited with a memoir by his father. In the autumn, at Tintern Abbey, he wrote another elegiac poem (*In Memoriam*, xix) and composed 'Tears, idle tears'. During her first visit to the Hallams in October, Emily met Mr Jesse (whom she married in January 1842); she accompanied the Hallams to London for the Christmas and New Year festivities, and was accepted as one of the family. Tired of Lincolnshire society, Tennyson sold his Chancellor's Medal and made a flying visit to Boulogne in February 1835; in the spring he joined the Speddings and Edward FitzGerald, James's old school friend, at Mirehouse on the Skiddaw side of Bassenthwaite Water. Tennyson read aloud his latest poems, including 'Dora' and 'Morte d'Arthur', and several by Wordsworth, whose 'Michael' he was beginning to appreciate. He found Hartley Coleridge congenial company, and was persuaded by Spedding to visit Rydal Mount; whether Wordsworth was at home to meet them is uncertain. The most important outcome of his Lakeland visit was the friendship which Tennyson established with FitzGerald, especially at Ambleside and on Windermere in the absence of Spedding. His pleasure in reading J. S. Mill's favourable review of his poems suffered on finding that his metrical expertise had been questioned by Coleridge in *Table Talk*.

By 1833 'the Old Man of the Wolds' had persuaded his son Charles to give up his political ambition (which had reached a plateau of infertility) and become a county magnate. For this purpose he moved out to Usselby to make room for his heir, who persuaded him to petition for the aristocratic name and arms of 'd'Eyncourt'. His grandson Charles, unlike Frederick and Alfred, had not been averse to ordination, and was now curate at Tealby. Prescribed opium, he became an addict, creating scandal in the parish, embarrassment at Bayons, and additional worry for Tennyson, who suffered on account of his brother Edward's mental affliction (from which there was no recovery) before hearing of Hallam's death. Charles realized his expectations when his great-uncle Samuel Turner died. He inherited estates at Grasby and Caistor; the Grasby living became his; he moved to the house in Caistor market-place where his grandfather had courted Mary Turner, and, in accordance with his benefactor's wishes, adopted the name of Turner. In 1836, after recovering (not altogether, it proved) from his opium addiction, he married Louisa Sellwood, daughter of a well-connected Horncastle solicitor whose wife, a Franklin from Spilsby, had died in 1816, at the age of twenty-eight.

Tennyson had met Louisa's elder sister Emily when she was brought to the rectory in 1830. She had gone for a walk with Hallam, and he had seen them emerging at the turn of a path in the 'woodland ways' of Holywell glen. Struck by her beauty, he asked whether she was a dryad or an oread. She was scholarly, and very devoted to her widowed father. During her sister's wedding at Horncastle, Tennyson thought her lovelier still, as he suggests in 'The Bridesmaid':

> For while the tender service made thee weep,
> I loved thee for the tear thou couldst not hide,
> And prest thy hand, and knew the press returned,
> And thought, 'My life is sick of single sleep:
> O happy bridesmaid, make a happy bride!'

Since his father's death he had been his mother's companion, and become acquainted with the daughters of gentry in the neighbourhood. He was an excellent dancer, and attended assemblies at Horncastle and Spilsby. On one occasion, perhaps at an earlier period, he was horrified to see his partner's white glove blackened when lifted from his shoulder; the servant had used a blacking-brush to clean his coat. For many years he had known Sophy Rawnsley, the attractive and lively daughter of his father's best friend. More recently, as his poems disclose, he had been fascinated by Rosa Baring, stepdaughter of Admiral Eden of Harrington Hall, two miles from Somersby; but there is no evidence that either fell deeply in love with the other.

Mary, Emily, and Cecilia Tennyson found pleasure in writing and discussing poetry, including Alfred's. He often acted as host, and impressed visitors with his courtesy and his care for his mother. With Frederick (soon to set off for Italy, where he was to marry and remain until 1859) he and Mary were guests at Mr Sellwood's dinner in honour of the latter's brother-in-law, the famous Arctic explorer Sir John Franklin, before he sailed to take up responsibilities as Governor of Tasmania. Sir John's niece Catherine observed how tall, dark, and handsome Alfred was, thought Mary the handsomest woman she had ever seen, and all three very remarkable-looking, 'though certainly formidable in their unconventional manner'. All the Tennyson sons and daughters except Frederick had dark complexions, possibly derived, Hallam Tennyson was led to believe, from a Huguenot ancestor related to Mme de Maintenon. Alfred displayed his enormous strength when he astonished two rustics by hurling a crowbar over a haystack, and when he lifted and carried a pet pony on the Somersby lawn; Brookfield, an entertaining Trinity friend, thought it unfair that he should be both Apollo and Hercules.

George Tennyson died at Usselby in the summer of 1835, leaving the greater part of his fortune, his acquired property, to his son Charles, and all his inherited estate to the Somersby Tennysons (with the exception of Charles, who was already well endowed). He bequeathed most of this estate to Frederick (chiefly life interest on the Grimsby property, from which he was to provide his mother an annuity of £200), a manor and small estate at Grasby to Alfred, £3000 in trust for Edward, and a large estate to be sold for the benefit of the seven other children. Soon after his death the licence for the adoption of the d'Eyncourt name and insignia reached Charles, who set out to achieve what had now become the ambition of his life, the rebuilding of Bayons at lavish expense in a variety of period styles suggesting the evolution of a grand old manor from a feudal castle, the ruined keep of which was to be built on a rocky eminence to the rear. His experience at Brancepeth stood him in good stead, and for years he spared nothing in the completion of his elaborate plans, from grander features such as the high flag-tower overlooking the main barbican, the curtains and moat, with drawbridges and portcullises, to such details as sculptured ornament, statues of English kings, stained glass, tapestries, knightly armour, and old pictures selected to give the illusion of d'Eyncourt descent from royalty. Before reaching the main entrance, visitors followed a circuitous drive designed within and around this magnificently sham complex to give every opportunity of admiring its architectural features, the park with its deer and horned sheep, and the amphitheatre of woods and hills above Tealby Vale. There was ample accommodation; the dining-hall could seat two hundred.

The publication of Tennyson's 'St Agnes' Eve' in *The Keepsake* encouraged his friend Monckton Milnes to write at the end of 1836, urging him to contribute to a volume edited by the Marquis of Northampton for charitable ends. After declining, Alfred yielded to persuasion, and sent 'Oh! that 'twere possible', the dormant seed from which *Maud* eventually grew. When it was known that the Somersby rectory was needed by the incumbent, Tennyson spent much time in London, where he met friends and celebrities, hoping to find a home not too far from the heart of the city; he chose Beech Hill House, at High Beech near Epping Forest and three miles from Waltham Cross. There were many farewell visits to be made before he and his family left Lincolnshire in June 1837. One led to a walk with Charles from Caistor to see the rapid progress that had been made in constructing the medieval magnificence of Bayons Manor. He drove Alfred, Mary, and Cecilia very late one evening to call on aunt Mary at Dalby House (destroyed by fire in January 1841); she was astonished when they asked for supper before visiting the Rawnsleys at Halton Holgate.

Tennyson's life was far from secluded. He was at Cambridge in March, and his friend J. W. Blakesley, a former Apostle, now assistant tutor at Trinity, was hardly surprised to find him complaining of nervousness. How could it be otherwise when he smoked 'the strongest and most stinking tobacco out of a small blackened clay pipe on an average nine hours every day'? In London he met friends (including FitzGerald, Spedding, Edmund Lushington, Monteith, Monckton Milnes), was introduced to Gladstone, made Thackeray's acquaintance, and had his portrait painted by Samuel Laurence. Absence made him realize his love of Lincolnshire despite its drawbacks, and he visited Charles and the Sellwoods. He felt 'dim sympathies with tree and hill reaching far back into childhood'. A known landscape was like an old friend, talking continually to him of his youth and 'half-forgotten things'. Suburban society was cold and formal, and he grew tired of looking at the old pond in the park around Beech Hill House, though he

enjoyed skating there with his blue cloak lifted behind him in the
wind. In the autumn of 1838 he was at Torquay, where he wrote
'Audley Court'. The following year he was disappointed not to find
the 'much-sounding' Homeric sea at Aberystwyth; at Barmouth the
breakers were more 'Mablethorpelike', but nothing pleased him as
much as the Llanberis lakes, where he wrote 'Edwin Morris'.

In the High Beech neighbourhood were three mental homes
belonging to Dr Allen, a friend of Thomas Carlyle, though a Scot of
blemished reputation. One of his inmates was the poet John Clare;
for a time Tennyson's brother Septimus was a voluntary patient;
and Alfred himself sought attention in times of nervous stress.
Depression filled him with morbid fear that he was afflicted like
other members of his family, even epileptically like his father and his
uncle Charles. It may have been for this reason, perhaps also from
brooding anxiety about financial independence in the future, that
he allowed his engagement virtually to lapse at a time when relations
between his family and the Sellwoods were strained by the rift
between Charles and his wife Louisa, who had left him because of his
opium addiction. Deep down nevertheless Alfred and Emily
remained mutually attached. Search for relief in the late spring of
1840 took him to his brother at Grasby, to Horncastle (where
Emily's relatives were rude to him), then from Lincoln to Leicester
in an open seatless third-class railway carriage which reminded him
of a cattle-truck. He reached Warwick by mail-coach, caught sight
of FitzGerald on the Leamington road, and with him visited
Kenilworth Castle, Warwick Castle, and Stratford, where he added
his name to countless others on the wall of the room where
Shakespeare was said to be born, and was disappointed by his
whitened bust in the parish chruch. While waiting for a train at
Coventry he mused on the Godiva legend. Before the end of the
summer, in accordance with Mr Sellwood's injunctions, correspondence between Emily and Alfred ceased. ('Love and Duty', it
appears, was the product of the poet's ensuing reflections. It takes
the form of a monologue, as if addressed to Emily. He counsels hope,
not despair; his faith is 'large in Time, And that which shapes it to
some perfect end'. In deciding that love should combine with duty
against love, he has done what is right and manly; he trusts that
through love the drooping flower of knowledge will turn to fruit of
wisdom.)

By this time the Tennysons were living at Tunbridge Wells for the
sake of their mother's health. The place was an abomination to

Alfred, who, unsettled by the break with Emily Sellwood, looked elsewhere for relief. Early in 1841 he was at Mablethorpe, but his whereabouts in the summer was guesswork to his friends. Some weeks were spent in Holland; in September he visited Bolton Abbey, led by some half-remembrance of a note by Wordsworth to the effect that everything desirable in landscape was to be found in Wharfedale around the Abbey ruins. Late in the year his family moved to Boxley, two miles from Park House, Maidstone, the home of Alfred's friend Edmund Lushington, Professor of Greek at Glasgow University. He and Cecilia Tennyson had already met; they were married on her birthday in October 1842. The wedding service was conducted by her brother Charles, and Tennyson celebrated the event with much champagne.

His own prospects were depressing. For years friends had urged him to publish again. The fear that his 1833 poems would be published unrevised in America made him act, and he agreed reluctantly with Moxon to prepare two volumes, the first a revised selection from the 1830 and 1833 volumes, the second a selection from his more recent poems. They appeared in May 1842, and reviews were not very encouraging, though favourable ones came from John Sterling, Monckton Milnes, and later from James Spedding. Tennyson had deeper worries. Lured by the speculative visions of Dr Allen, he had sold his Grasby properties and invested almost all his resources (over £3000) in Pyroglyphs, an enterprise for the production of ornamental wood by machine-carving. Other members of the Tennyson family invested heavily, but Allen's persistent efforts to extract money from Frederick quickened suspicion. 'What with ruin in the distance and hypochondriacs in the foreground I feel very crazy', Alfred wrote to Lushington, while travelling alone to the south-west of Ireland in September 1842. So distracted was he that he had failed to keep his appointment in London with Aubrey de Vere, the Irish poet with whom he intended to make his excursion. The continuance of his worries is probably reflected in the image suggested by one of the caves at Ballybunion, and recalled years later to describe the effect of Vivien's sensual appeal on Merlin: 'So dark a forethought rolled about his brain, As on a dull day in an Ocean cave The blind wave feeling round his long sea-hall In silence.' When the crash came, Tennyson was almost penniless. Fortunately Edmund Lushington took out a policy on Allen's life for £2000, paying the premiums himself; this proved most providential, for Allen died in 1845.

Such was Tennyson's financial distress when Southey died in 1843 that some of his friends tried to persuade the Prime Minister to award him the Laureateship; Sir Robert Peel recommended a grant from public funds, which Tennyson declined. With Emily and Cecilia married, Arthur in Italy with Frederick, Septimus (it seems) still under treatment with Allen, and Edward permanently at York, his family found it expedient to take a smaller house at Cheltenham; Alfred was so ill that he spent months in a hydropathic hospital at the neighbouring village of Prestbury, and even contemplated living in Italy. However, he climbed Snowdon three times in the summer of 1844, before staying at Park House, from which he made a number of visits to London. Through the club founded by Sterling he became friendly with the Carlyles. Thomas, with whom he could smoke freely, described him as 'large-featured, dim-eyed, bronze-coloured, shaggy-headed', a 'most restful, brotherly, solid-hearted man' who 'swims, outwardly and inwardly, with great composure in an inarticulate element as of tranquil chaos and tobacco smoke'. With *The Princess* in mind, Alfred discussed the position and education of women with William and Mary Howitt. In the spring of 1845, when Wordsworth, the Poet Laureate, came to London for presentation to the Queen, Tennyson met him twice before plucking up courage to pay tribute to his works. Wordsworth believed that Tennyson was 'decidedly the first' of contemporary poets, and their continuing friendship was based on genuine but not uncritical admiration.

Henry Hallam, supported by Gladstone and Rogers, used his influence to obtain a Civil List pension for Tennyson, who ultimately accepted the £200 a year he was offered, consoling himself with the reflection that he had in no way solicited it, and that its acceptance imposed no curb on his freedom of expression. His fear of strictures was confirmed when the second part of *The New Timon* appeared. Its pretentious author Edward Bulwer-Lytton, while staying at Bayons Manor, had heard his friend Charles Tennyson d'Eyncourt express surprise that his improvident nephew should receive a pension. Lytton was indignant that the ageing playwright James Sheridan Knowles whom he had recommended had been rejected. In verse imitative of Pope's satire he taunted Tennyson with 'the mock-bird's modish tune'; recalled in 'Let School-Miss Alfred vent her chaste delight On "darling little rooms so warm and bright!"' a poem which, after Croker's derision of it, Tennyson wished he had never written; and expressed a preference for the verse of William Hayley:

> Rather be thou, my poor Pierian Maid,
> Decent at last, in Hayley's weeds array'd,
> Than patch with frippery every tinsel line,
> And flaunt, admired, the Rag Fair of the Nine!

Taking his cue from these lines, Tennyson set to work on a satire of his foppish castigator, with the title of 'The New Timon, and the Poets' over the signature 'Alcibiades'. He left it with John Forster, who could not resist sending it to *Punch*, where it appeared on 28 February 1846. Contrasting the new Timon, 'the padded man – that wears the stays', with Shakespeare's, it refers to Lytton's 'dandy pathos' in prose and his failure as a poet, and concludes:

> What profits now to understand
>   The merits of a spotless shirt –
> A dapper boot – a little hand –
>   If half the little soul is dirt?

> *You* talk of tinsel! why we see
>   The old mark of rouge upon your cheeks.
> *You* prate of Nature! you are he
>   That spilt his life about the cliques.

> A Timon you! Nay, nay, for shame:
>   It looks too arrogant a jest –
> The fierce old man – to take *his* name
>   You bandbox. Off, and let him rest.

The laughs were with Tennyson, but he soon regretted the publication of his retaliatory verses. For self-defence Lytton could think of no better action than to deny his authorship of *The New Timon* and remove the offending lines from further editions.

Tennyson's interest in scientific discovery is evident in some of the sections of *In Memoriam* which he had already read to his friends, and in the request sent to Moxon in November 1844 for a copy of the anonymous *Vestiges of Creation*. Increasingly responding to social and economic injustices, his sympathies ran entirely, but perhaps too ideally, along lines of enlightened progress. In the early months of 1846 he studied Persian with FitzGerald's friend E. B. Cowell, saw much of the Carlyles, and became friendly with Dickens, the young poet Coventry Patmore, and Robert Browning (who thought the way Moxon handled his hazy, naive, unconventionally mannered poet-protégé the 'charmingest thing imaginable'). Dickens invited him to join him in Switzerland, but Tennyson, fearing that he might entreat the novelist 'to dismiss his sentimentality' and thus precipitate a quarrel, declined. He chose to travel to Switzerland with Moxon, after visiting the Isle of Wight, where he stayed with James White of Bonchurch, above the old church outside which John Sterling had been buried in 1844. Their route lay through Bruges and Cologne, along the Rhine, where Nonnenwerth and Drachenfels revived sad memories of Arthur Hallam, to Basle and Lucerne. Two weeks later, after travelling by steamer from Geneva, they reached Lausanne, where Dickens provided 'some fine wine, and cigars innumerable', much to Tennyson's delectation. The best scenic impressions he retained were the view of the valley of Lauterbrunnen from their Wengen descent and that of the Bernese Alps; some of them are found in the lyric 'Come down, O maid, from yonder mountain height', which was included in *The Princess* (in the manuscript book of which he kept his journal of the tour). The work was completed after his return to England; its proofs were read at Umberslade Hall near Birmingham (where Tennyson received hydropathic treatment for nervous depression), at Park House (where his 'coming unwashed and staying unbidden' created a problem for the Lushingtons), and at Mablethorpe. Later, in London, he lived with 'fleas and foreigners', according to FitzGerald. *The Princess* was published on Christmas Day 1847.

To escape social engagements, Tennyson contemplated a visit to Italy, then, his interest in Arthurian legend having revived, a flight to Devon and Cornwall, where he could be 'alone with God'. De Vere's promise to show him greater waves and higher cliffs than could be found on English coasts led to their holiday at Curragh Chase, Aubrey's home in County Limerick. Alfred was shocked by the poverty of the peasantry, but his scenic hopes were finally rewarded on the island of Valencia, where he stayed with the Knight of Kerry. On his way home, an echoing horn at Killarney suggested 'The splendour falls'. In London he met Emerson, who was on his way to France. One night at the end of May Tennyson reached Bude in Cornwall and, in his eagerness to find the sea, tumbled over a wall and gashed his leg on the 'fanged cobbles' six feet below. Two days later he was at Morwenstow with Stephen

Hawker, the eccentric parson–poet, who lost his constraint as soon as he knew that he was with the author of 'Morte d'Arthur', told him stories of the sea's cruelty, rapacious wreckers' guile, and smugglers' daring, and lent him several Arthurian books. It was a memorable day for Tennyson, who then studied the castle ruins and their setting at Tintagel, found King Arthur's Stone near Slaughter Bridge, and proceeded via Polperro to Land's End, the Lizard, and Plymouth. After a beneficial course of water treatment at Malvern, he devoted much of his time to his mother at Cheltenham; he was amused by her allegiance to the apocalyptic doctrines of Dr John Cumming, and could not resist teasing about her 'bottles', the seven vials of Revelation. Before the end of the year he was back in London, drinking a bottle of wine a day, smoking as much as ever, and consulting a new doctor, according to the reports of FitzGerald, who was sure Tennyson's physical deterioration would soon return, and had little expectation of heroic poetry from 'a valetudinary'.

Moxon's keenness to publish more of Tennyson's poetry led to his reading the Hallam 'elegies'. Some weeks later, while at Bonchurch early in 1849, Alfred discovered he had left the manuscript book containing them at his London lodgings, where it was retrieved by Coventry Patmore after the landlady had refused his admittance. Tennyson's new acquaintances included Thomas Woolner, Edward Lear, and Francis Palgrave, a friend of the Lushingtons. After a journey to the Monteiths at Carstairs, to the Pass of Killicrankie and Burns's monument at Kirk Alloway, he stayed with friends in Lincolnshire, where he received a letter from Mrs Gaskell begging him to send a copy of his collected poems to Samuel Bamford. He willingly complied, deeming the old Lancashire handloom-weaver's admiration the highest honour he had ever received. Before the end of the year he was in touch with Emily Sellwood, now living with her father near Farnham to escape the cold Lincolnshire winters. *The Princess* in a revised form, with the version of 'Sweet and low' which she preferred, appeared in February 1850.

The 'elegies' were first printed for private circulation, and a copy was sent to Drummond Rawnsley (son of T. H. Rawnsley of Halton Holgate). He was now vicar of Shiplake-on-Thames, and husband of Catherine Franklin, who obtained permission for her cousin Emily Sellwood to see it. There can be no doubt that the religious tenor of Alfred's new poems, especially of the recently added Prologue, his improved financial prospects, and the reconciliation of her sister and Charles Turner, eased the way for the marriage which was suddenly arranged to take place at Shiplake on 13 June, twelve days after the publication of the elegies under the title which Emily had recommended. Seven weeks earlier Wordsworth had died. Though *In Memoriam A. H. H.* was published anonymously (one reviewer concluding it was written by 'the widow of a military man'), its authorship was soon recognised. It earned Tennyson many admirers, including the Prince Consort, and before the end of the year he was made Poet Laureate. Thanks mainly to *In Memoriam*, 1850 was his *annus mirabilis*; it had brought him happiness, and (in his grandson's words) turned 'a recluse' into 'a National Institution'.

4

After visiting Clevedon to view Hallam's memorial (an act which 'seemed a kind of consecration' to Emily) and spending a few days in Devonshire, the married couple called on Mrs Tennyson at Cheltenham. They then made their way to the Lake District, staying first with James Spedding, then until October at Tent Lodge, Coniston, the home of Mrs Marshall, sister of Alfred's Cambridge friend Stephen Spring-Rice. Carlyle, de Vere, Patmore, Lear, and other acquaintances came to meet or stay with them. Monckton Milnes offered a wing at Fryston, Lady Ashburton a house at Croydon, and the Marshalls, Tent Lodge, as a permanent home, but the Tennysons preferred to live with the Lushingtons at Park House while Alfred looked for a residence in London. Their first home, however, was at Warninglid near Horsham; they had hardly settled in when draughts from a howling storm drove them from one room, and a smoking chimney from another to their bedroom, where part of the wall was blown in and rain poured on them in bed. Two weeks later Tennyson drew his pregnant wife in a wheelchair over two miles of rough track to the main road for their journey to Shiplake, where house-hunting was resumed. They were visited by Charles Kingsley, author of *Alton Locke* (which they read), and as fervent in his uxoriousness as in support of F. D. Maurice and Christian Socialism. After borrowing the court dress which Samuel Rogers had lent Wordsworth for such an occasion, Tennyson attended the Queen's *levée* as Poet Laureate on 6 March, the day he signed a contract for a five-year lease of Chapel House, Montpelier Row, Twickenham. It was a spacious Georgian residence, overlooking the Thames and the grounds of Marble Hill. Emily, who had not seen the house, was brought from the Lushingtons' a few days later, and all seemed well, despite Alfred's impatience with muddy walks and cabbage smells from market-gardens, until their baby was born dead, strangled at birth, probably as a result of the fall Emily sustained on their way from Shiplake to Park House. 'He was a grand massive manchild, noble brow and hands, which he had clenched in his determination to be born', Tennyson wrote.

He took Emily to Italy for her convalescence. In their Paris hotel, on the way, after he had spotted Robert in the Louvre, they entertained the Brownings, who advised them to stay at Bagni di Lucca. After three weeks there, they joined Frederick Tennyson in Florence. Alfred's 'usual travelling companions' included Shakespeare, Milton, Homer, Virgil, Horace, Pindar, and Theocritus. On their return they made the acquaintance of an admirer, the young Irish poet William Allingham. A French invasion scare after Louis Napoleon's *coup d'état* (December 1851) roused the Poet Laureate to anti-Gallic militancy in several poems which were published anonymously or pseudonymously. When he accepted the invitation of the vicar of Malvern, one of his Cambridge friends (whose acquaintance he had renewed at Cheltenham), to stay three weeks with him, he had hopes of finding a quiet home in the country. After returning via Cheltenham, where he and Emily stayed with his mother, he went to Whitby, hoping to cure his hay-fever. He was back at Twickenham in August, after calling on his brother Charles at Grasby and visiting Crowland Abbey, just before the birth of Hallam Tennyson.

When the Duke of Wellington died in September the Poet Laureate felt it his public duty to write in honour of one he greatly admired; his ode appeared two days before the grand funeral ceremony in St Paul's, but its reception was disappointing. Continual visitors, and the dampness of the Thames valley, still prompted the Tennysons to seek residence elsewhere; and it was partly with this in mind that, after a brief period at Seaford House, they stayed with the Kingsleys at Eversley in May 1853. Later they went for a holiday, hoping to visit the Highlands, but Emily's illness in Yorkshire made her turn back to Grasby while Alfred travelled with Palgrave, whose solicitous companionship he found most irksome. Hoping to find a house by the sea, he visited James White again at Bonchurch, where he heard that Farringford was to let. A late Georgian house with fifteen rooms and decorative Gothic features, it stood in its own grounds towards the western end of the Isle of Wight, sheltered by trees, with every promise of seclusion, and with extensive views across the Solent and over the English Channel. It had the advantage of being furnished, and of having its own farm. Tennyson sought Emily's approval; they travelled to Brockenhurst by train but missed the steamboat at Lymington, their most memorable solace as they were rowed across the Solent late one November afternoon being the sight of a dark heron against the daffodil sky. Next day they looked through the drawing-room window over wooded park land to Freshwater Bay between the downs, with the blue sea beyond backed by chalk cliffs extending to St Catherine's Point. It was 'a view to live with', and Farringford was leased at £2 a week for three years, with the option of purchase at the end of that period. It became Emily's 'ivied home among the pine-trees'. For Tennyson another attraction was its proximity to High Down, which flanked the Channel, its sheer white cliffs running west towards the Needles, and reaching their highest point, almost five hundred feet, at the Beacon. To this he would make his way from his garden along a lane, and on through trees and scrub to the open slope. In his black cape he soon became a familiar figure on these heights; he loved to gather impressions of the sea, to watch the habits of birds frequenting the cliffs, most of all to stride or run in the breeze. Borrowing an expression from Keats, he would tell his friends that the air was worth sixpence a pint.

1854 opened with the booming of cannon at Portsmouth, where the artillery were preparing for war with Russia, which was declared at the end of March, shortly after the birth of the Tennysons' second son, whom his father named Lionel, as a result of observing, from his study window at the top of the house when the baby was born, that the planet Mars glowed (in the words of *Maud*) 'like a ruddy shield on the Lion's breast'. Jingoistic feelings revived in Tennyson as news of Crimean battles came through; and 'The Charge of the Light Brigade', on the heroic response to what *The Times* leader described as a 'hideous blunder' of generalship, enjoyed immense popularity both at home and with troops on service.

Emily's health was poor, and she had to rest regularly each day; usually in the evening Alfred read to her from his favourite classical authors or the Bible or the English poets, sometimes from Dante, Goethe, or Thackeray. Yet she managed her staff effectively, and encouraged visits from Tennyson's friends. Edmund and Franklin Lushington were two of their earliest guests; FitzGerald, who acted as proxy godfather for Drummond Rawnsley at Lionel's christening, stayed two weeks, and delighted Alfred by playing Mozart and reading Persian with him. Other visitors included Spedding, Arthur Hugh Clough, Benjamin Jowett of Balliol, Patmore, and John Millais, one of the Pre-Raphaelite painters commissioned to illustrate the poet's works. Tennyson became friendly with shepherds, fishermen, and coastguards. Sometimes he rowed Emily and

Hallam as far as Alum Bay; he worked on the lawn, in the gardens, sometimes on the farm, and took great interest in wild flowers, birdlife, and geological evidences.

Among their closest friends was Sir John Simeon of Swainston Hall, eight miles east. A suggestion of his led to the writing of *Maud*, which was completed by January 1855 but not published until July. In the meantime Tennyson had been awarded the honorary degree of D. C. L. by the University of Oxford; he was nervous as he entered the Sheldonian Theatre, but the gallery wag who cried, 'Did your mother call you early, dear?' did not ruffle him, and he long remembered the tumultuous applause he received, just as he did the hostile reception accorded to *Maud* by reviewers, one of whom suggested that either vowel should be omitted from the title. The work was published with minor poems, including 'To the Rev. F. D. Maurice', which extends the hand of friendship to Hallam's godfather, who had been compelled to resign his professorship at King's College, London, after arguing that the word 'eternal' in 'eternal punishment' could not relate to time.

Tennyson was encouraged to visit the Brownings in London by Robert's admiration of *Maud*; he was a delightful guest until the arrival of William and Dante Gabriel Rossetti after dinner, when he began to bemoan his earlier neglect and the criticism from which he was now suffering. Mrs Browning came to his rescue by inviting him to recite *Maud*, which he did in his deep, resonant, Lincolnshire-accented voice, pausing to point out felicitous touches, and sometimes affected to tears, while Dante Rossetti sketched him in awkward posture and short-sighted concentration. Not being fully appreciative, Jane Welsh Carlyle endured the benefit of hearing the poem three times one evening. Letters in praise of it from Ruskin and Jowett were very welcome, but Tennyson could not resist choosing it when invited to read at Lady Ashburton's New Year party of social and literary celebrities. Among them were the Carlyles, Jane very jealous of her hostess's regard for Thomas; once again she heard the poem she had reason not to relish, while her husband went for a walk with Goldwin Smith, whose criticism of it in the first issue of *The Saturday Review* had not been forgotten.

The success of *In Memoriam*, and even of *The Princess*, and Moxon's assurance that the proceeds of the forthcoming illustrated edition of his works would meet his needs, encouraged Tennyson to purchase Farringford in the spring of 1856. Emily was delighted. She found beauty everywhere she turned: blue hyacinths, orchises, primroses, daisies, marsh-marigolds, and cuckoo-flowers in the withy holt; cowslips and blooming furze in the park; the white blossom of wild cherry trees and hawthorn; the 'golden wreath' of elms at the foot of High Down; flowering chestnuts and apple trees about to blossom on the northern side of the house; the rapture of a thrush's song amid the notes of nightingales and other birds; and, at sunset, the golden green of the trees, the turquoise of the sea, and the burning splendour of the distant coast. Shortly afterwards, with the arrival of the Twickenham furniture, and some of the previous owner's awaiting sale, the house was in confusion when Prince Albert unexpectedly called from Osborne; he was very cordial, admired the views, and asked one of his gentlemen to gather a bunch of cowslips for the Queen. The purchase of Farringford and the growing popularity of *Maud* gave Tennyson a feeling of greater security, and he soon turned to the epic subject which he contemplated when he wrote 'Morte d'Arthur'. After finishing the Merlin story he began 'Enid', which he almost completed in Wales, where he studied and read Welsh with Emily, travelled extensively, and climbed Cader Idris in drenching rain.

Great as was his need of seclusion for meditation, reading, and composition, Tennyson periodically craved attention. The urge to read his own poetry approvingly, and secure approval, made it imperative for him to be noticed in London. His usual resort was Little Holland House, the home of Thoby Prinsep, formerly a distinguished Indian civil servant. Thoby's wife was one of seven half-French Pattle sisters, born in India, and all rich and eccentrically exuberant. With Mrs Prinsep as 'Principessa', they formed the 'Pattledom' of a Kensington rural home (once the farm of the Fox family) which had become the rendezvous of distinction in the arts. Of the sisters, the Countess Somers was the most beautiful, and Mrs Julia Cameron the plainest but most lively-minded. Walls were decorated with frescoes by G. F. Watts, who was a permanent guest and loved to sketch ladies in their draperies. Visitors included Browning, Thackeray, Gladstone, Ruskin, George Eliot, Bulwer-Lytton, Patmore, Henry Taylor, Woolner, Spedding, Maurice, Jowett and, among painters, Burne-Jones, Holman Hunt, Rossetti, and Leighton. Tennyson's prestige was so high that, despite his lack of social tact, he was a great favourite; he admired the unaffected style of Thoby Prinsep, accepted the plain truths of benevolent Mrs Cameron, and appreciated adulation.

The 1857 illustrated edition of Tennyson's poetry was a

disappointment to him and to others; he expected the illustrations would represent the text, and objected to the artistic liberties which Rossetti, Hunt, and others had taken. Despite low sales, Moxon paid the balance of the £2000 he had promised the Poet Laureate. Friendship with the Duke and Duchess of Argyll had led to a three months' tour which took the Tennysons to Scotland. While staying with Charles and Louisa at Grasby they spent an afternoon viewing Bayons Manor in its last stages of completion, and meeting Charles Tennyson d'Eyncourt for the last time. They went on to Manchester, partly to hear Dickens reading from *A Christmas Carol*, principally to see the exhibition of paintings which Queen Victoria and Prince Albert had opened. Nathaniel Hawthorne, American consul at Liverpool, was more interested in Tennyson and his companion Woolner than in the pictures; he thought the poet a most picturesque figure, with his dark sensitive face, black frock coat, black wide-awake hat, long black tangled hair, and pointed beard; there was 'nothing white about him except the collar of his shirt', which 'might have been clean the day before'. More than two months were spent at Tent Lodge; Alfred went riding, and climbed Coniston Old Man with Patmore; other visitors included Matthew Arnold, whose dandiacal superiority consorted with neither Tennyson's general appearance nor his temperament, and C. L. Dodgson, the future 'Lewis Carroll', who came to take family photographs and avowed that he had never met boys more beautiful than Hallam and Lionel. Whatever the misunderstanding, the Duke and Duchess of Argyll were absent from Inverary when the Tennysons arrived; yet the Duchess hurried back on a specially charted steamboat, the Duke returned from Balmoral, and honours were done to the Poet Laureate and his family. The Duke and Duchess respected Tennyson highly; they admired his genius, his independent spirit, and his unaffected manners.

Emily's illness on their return had severe effects; she spent much of her time on the red sofa in the drawing-room, but managed Farringford as before, and wrote most of Alfred's letters. He treated her tenderly, read to her as much as ever, built her a summer-house, and wheeled her whenever he could in the invalid chair which Sir John Simeon had given them. Mindful of his own unhappy youth, he devoted much time to his children, anxious to ensure their health and happiness; he played with them, read to them, and tried to instil a sense of the beauty of language at an early age. Emily kept a record of their quaint remarks; during Hallam's first church service, at Coniston, she had to restrain him from dancing during the sermon, only to be asked when 'the man' would let him go, and whether the man in question was a soldier or a policeman.

Sightseers became a menace; one intruder peered through a window and cried, 'You can see him well from here.' Tennyson planted trees to create greater privacy, and even bought houses at Freshwater, where more were being built, to preserve the view. In January 1858 he had a visit from Algernon Swinburne, who lived at Bonchurch and was a student at Balliol; in February he received from Lord Dufferin, a young Irishman who had attended one of his Argyll Lodge readings, a copy of his *Letters from High Latitudes*, an account of a yachting cruise to Iceland and Spitzbergen. 'Guinevere' was completed in March. In July he began 'The Fair Maid of Astolat' ('Lancelot and Elaine') and attended Little Holland House, where Watts began the 'great moonlight portrait' of him. His visit to Norway was not very venturous, and he found little difference between that country and Scotland; most of all he remembered waterfalls and the storm encountered at sea on his way from Hull to Christiania (Oslo). At the end of the year, in response to Mrs Tennyson's appeal, Jowett sent a number of suggestions for poetic subjects.

Watts's portrait was finished in March 1859, when the poet was in London making arrangements for the publication of *Idylls of the King*: 'Enid', 'Vivien', 'Elaine', 'Guinevere'. Moxon had died, and his family successors had been disputatious about his generous allowance for the *Illustrated Edition*, but they came to terms and had no regrets, for the new volume was well received. After a busy period, during which Edward Lear (who thought Emily a saint) and Dodgson were at Farringford, and the Duke and Duchess of Argyll on the first of several annual holidays at Freshwater, Tennyson was ready for a holiday, and chose to go to Portugal and North Africa, with Palgrave a willing companion. Cintra was disappointing; he wished to see Fielding's grave, but the Protestant cemetery was closed. Heat, flies, and fleas at Lisbon made him cancel the rest of the tour. Having time to spare in England, they proceeded to the New Forest, then to Cambridge, where Tennyson showed Palgrave Hallam's rooms, spent an evening with his old Trumpington Street tobacconist, and dined with the publisher Alexander Macmillan.

He was continually plagued by his inability to find a great subject which fulfilled the dual demand of suiting his genius and answering the deep unarticulated call of his era. Jowett's suggestions provided no answer; he thought the age teemed with appropriate subjects, and that, like blackberries, they could be gathered off every hedge. Neither he nor Emily, who tried to help her husband, realized the difficulty of a writer married to his Muse for life in finding topic after topic of such significance that it was capable of rousing his full imaginative response. Ruskin was not very helpful, but he posed the dilemma when he expressed the wish that the nobleness of the *Idylls* had been 'independent of a romantic condition of externals in general'. He appreciated 'word-painting such as never was yet for concentration', but felt that 'so great power ought not to be spent on visions of things past but on the living present'. To indicate 'the true task of the modern poet', he suggested 'the intense masterful and unerring transcript of an actuality, and the relation of a story of any human life as a poet would watch and analyze it'. His words hardly convey an accurate impression of creative art, yet the advice, like Woolner's recommendation of the sailor story he told Tennyson years earlier, did not pass unheeded.

In the spring of 1860 Julia Cameron came with her aged husband to live near Freshwater Bay. A fund of benevolent energy, she eventually became famous as a portrait-photographer. Draped in gorgeous trailing robes, and an Indian shawl or two, she would come to Farringford whenever she fancied; she was extremely generous, and sent the most unusual gifts. One night soon after her arrival, when her guests had retired, she walked down to the beach, and thought the luminous panorama of the sea so magnificent that she sent for Tennyson, and left him there to admire it. When Edward Lear came to Farringford, she arranged for eight men to carry her grand piano there, knowing that Emily's instrument would give him little pleasure. Lear was overwhelmed by her 'odious incense palaver & fuss', but usually Tennyson was too enamoured of Pattledom to take offence, and tolerated from her what he would from few others. Once she provoked him to a cutting remark which sent her home in tears; he soon followed and apologized. A kiss from her, and they were immediately reconciled.

Tennyson hoped to visit the Levant that summer, but finally journeyed to the 'Lyonnesse' region of Cornwall. He had been encouraged to continue the *Idylls*, particularly by the Duke of Argyll, who twice supported Macaulay's recommendation of a work on the Holy Grail, a subject the poet felt could not be handled at the time 'without incurring a charge of irreverence'. The trip began at Oxford, where Tennyson read a new poem which Jowett advised him not to publish. 'If it comes to that, Master,' he replied, 'the sherry you gave us at luncheon was beastly.' Woolner acted as his escort until Palgrave joined them at Tintagel. Remembering Emily's exhortations, Palgrave could not let the poet out of sight without following or shouting after him. At Helston they were joined by two painters, Holman Hunt and Thoby Prinsep's son Val; Woolner returned to London from Penzance, and the other four visited the Scillies. Back in Cornwall, Tennyson lost all patience with Palgrave for contriving to watch him whenever he sought solitude to meditate or compose poetry. Yet this seemingly unpropitious companionship had surprising results, for it was on this tour that Palgrave's idea of *The Golden Treasury*, the most enduring of all anthologies of English poetry, met Tennyson's approval. The selection was submitted to him at the end of the year, and the result reflects his taste, though the volume would have been shorter had he been solely responsible for the choice. As he would not allow the inclusion of any of his own poetry, poems by all living authors were excluded.

Tennyson continued to read widely; he had studied many philosophers, and lost no time in obtaining a copy of Darwin's *The Origin of Species* at the end of 1859. The heated controversy that broke out the following spring over *Essays and Reviews* excited his interest, and he was particularly sympathetic toward Jowett during his victimization at Oxford. Cambridge awarded him an honorary degree, but he was overcome with palpitations on the way, and turned back, determined – as ineffectually as before – to give up smoking. On the recommendation of Granville Bradley, headmaster of Marlborough (who had become one of Tennyson's friends as a result of holidays on the Isle with his family), Graham Dakyns, a classical scholar just down from Cambridge, became the tutor of Hallam and Lionel, who were too accustomed to freedom to submit readily to discipline. Tennyson enjoyed Dakyns' company and, Emily's health having improved, decided to take his family to the Dordogne, the Auvergne, and the Pyrenees, a maid accompanying them, with Dakyns responsible for the boys and general arrangements. It was no easy journey; the children had not recovered from whooping-cough, Emily was not strong, and travelling in the mountain regions was often primitive. Arthur Hugh Clough, who had spent six weeks at Freshwater in the spring, met them at Mont Dore, and again in the Pyrenees. Tennyson walked and climbed among the mountains with Dakyns, but his main object was to see Cauteretz and renew impressions of magnificent scenes indelibly associated with Arthur Hallam. When they came to the valley, Dakyns noticed his absorption, and dropped behind. Time had brought changes; the charming village had become an 'odious watering-place', but nostalgic memories produced the first version of 'In the Valley of Cauteretz'. Tennyson knew that thirty-one years had passed since his first visit; the 'two and thirty years ago' of his haunting lyric exemplifies his readiness to compromise for aural effect.

Within a week of their return news came of Clough's death; in December, that of the Prince Consort. Tennyson prepared a memorial dedication to preface the next edition of the *Idylls*, sought the Duchess of Argyll's advice, and had a copy forwarded for the Queen's approval. To his and Emily's relief, she was deeply touched and, acting on Argyll's suggestion, invited Tennyson to meet her at Osborne, her Isle of Wight residence, in the spring. The poet was nervous, but the Queen, who had found much consolation in *In Memoriam*, was impressed by his warm sympathy and 'greatness' of mind. He thought he had blundered in saying what an excellent king Prince Albert would have made, but the remark pleased her. When, as he was leaving, she asked whether she could help him in any way, he expressed the wish that she would shake his boys by the hand; it might keep them loyal 'in the troublous times to come'.

A holiday with Palgrave in Derbyshire and Yorkshire in the summer of 1862 seems to have passed amicably. After being entranced with Haddon Hall and favoured with most colourful illuminations in the Peak Cavern, they travelled north to Ripon and Wensleydale, visiting Middleham Castle and Bolton Castle before returning via Skipton. Tennyson had already taken Woolner's advice and written the sailor story 'Enoch Arden'. Late in the year 'Aylmer's Field', another subject suggested by Woolner, gave him far more trouble. The forthcoming marriage of the Princess of Denmark and the Prince of Wales prompted him to write, and send to the Queen, early in 1863, 'A Welcome to Alexandra'; his invitation to the wedding, being misdirected, arrived too late, but he celebrated the event with a dance and supper at Farringford and a bonfire on the neighbouring down. In May he took his wife and boys to be received by the Queen at Osborne; Emily was overcome, but Tennyson talked on many subjects, not forgetting the injustices Jowett still suffered at Oxford for his progressive beliefs.

An excursion to Little Holland House with Mrs Cameron in the summer ended unhappily. At her insistence he had submitted to vaccination, and *post hoc propter hoc*, it seems, soon suffered a high temperature and badly inflamed leg. He went to Palgrave's home, where he received medical attention throughout July, making the acquaintance of the Surgeon-General to the Queen, James Paget, who became a lifelong friend. Spedding, Hunt, Woolner, Froude, Carlyle, and Browning called to see him. Five weeks of convalescence with Emily and his boys followed at Harrogate spa. Palgrave, Allingham, Jowett, and the Bradleys were among their Christmas guests at Farringford, where time was found, especially in the company of Montagu Butler, headmaster of Harrow, to discuss Greek etymology and classical metres. News of Thackeray's death cast a deep gloom on the household. When Mrs Cameron lent Thackeray's daughters a cottage at Freshwater, Tennyson was there in his broad-rimmed hat and heavy cloak to receive them as they arrived in the snow. Everything was done to make them happy, and Farringford became a second home to Annie, who loved walking and talking with Tennyson on the downs. She noticed that he could see further than most people, but liked her to confirm his observations.

His striking figure and dress caught the eye wherever he went, and, despite his disinclination for dinner parties and formal occasions, he enjoyed being the centre of attention, especially in London. The Duchess of Sutherland (mother of the Duchess of Argyll) wished to arrange a meeting between him and Garibaldi at her home, but the poet preferred to meet him at Farringford, where the Italian liberation hero was introduced to the poet–dramatist Henry Taylor, and persuaded to plant, in the presence of many spectators, a wellingtonia reared from a Californian cone by the Duchess of Sutherland. Mrs Cameron (whom he mistook for a beggar because her hands were black with chemicals) knelt down dramatically and besought him unsuccessfully to be photographed at Freshwater. To escape the trippers who came in increasing numbers, the Tennysons spent two summer months visiting Arthurian sites in Brittany. The *Enoch Arden* volume was published with tremendous success; sixty thousand copies were soon sold, and Tennyson was referred to as 'the poet of the people'. With the eponymous poem and 'The Grandmother', 'Aylmer's Field' and 'Tithonus', his first Lincolnshire dialect poem 'Northern Farmer' and the metrical experiment of 'Boädicea', its considerable variety testified to the poet's persisting uncertainty of direction.

His mother died in February 1865 at Rosemount, Hampstead,

which Tennyson had rented for her after the expiry of the Twickenham lease. Wishing to remember her as he last saw her, two or three weeks previously, he would not look at the dead face of one whom he thought 'the beautifullest thing' God ever made. Another unwelcome change came with the departure of Hallam and Lionel to a Dorset boarding-school kept by Kegan Paul, a former Eton chaplain who became Tennyson's publisher. Other tutors had succeeded Dakyns, and Gladstone and Jowett thought the boys needed more discipline. At the end of their first term they were taken on a European tour by their parents, Alfred conducting them over the battlefield of Waterloo. After seeing the Schiller and Goethe homes and memorials at Weimar, they went via Leipzig to Dresden, where they visited the art galleries and returned to look at the Titians and even more at the two Madonnas by Raphael and Holbein; Tennyson took the boys to the zoological gardens. Their return journey lay through Aix-la-Chapelle, which Emily thought magical, with hills and domes of blue and gold in a rich sunset. A few days after reaching Farringford, they received Queen Emma of the Sandwich Islands, for whom a throne had been constructed from an ilex which had grown in the garden; she wished to stay quietly with them while she was on the Isle, but had to attend the banquets and other social functions held to raise funds for her projected Anglican cathedral.

Tennyson's social and cultural interests were too widely spread for his poetic genius to develop significantly in new fields. Edward Lear said of Farringford that one always seemed to live in public there. Despite his short-sightedness the poet had always been an avid reader; he was interested in new poetry, fiction, science, and philosophy, and always found time to return to the great literature of the past; recently he had taken up the study of Hebrew in order to read his favourite Old Testament books, Job, Isaiah, and *The Song of Solomon*, in the original. He spent much time in London, sometimes on publishing matters, more often with friends, among whom Gladstone was now one of the foremost. Others included the physicist John Tyndall, the biologist Thomas Huxley, and three astronomers, Sir John Herschel, Norman Lockyer, and Charles Pritchard; he became a member of the Royal Society in December 1865. It was about this time that differences came into the open. Whether there was any survival of the envy which Gladstone must have felt when Tennyson displaced him as Hallam's first friend must remain uncertain, but tension inevitably arose whenever the leading Liberal statesman and a poet with strong unsubtle patriotic feelings differed on any important question. At Woolner's they disagreed repeatedly on Governor Eyre's savage suppression of Jamaican rioters after the killing of twenty Europeans. On more fundamental issues they were much less divided than were the pagan-minded Swinburne and the Victorian Poet Laureate. Although Tennyson praised his *Atalanta in Calydon*, Swinburne turned his back on him at a meeting arranged by Monckton Milnes (now Lord Houghton), and talked for the remainder of the evening with Palgrave and G. H. Lewes.

In February 1866 Lionel and his mother accompanied Tennyson for a six weeks' stay with her aunt Lady Franklin, widow of the explorer, at Gore Lodge, Kensington. Emily greatly enjoyed meeting Gladstone, Browning, and many other friends of her husband, old and new. They lunched with Dean Stanley and his wife at Westminster, and visited the Abbey to see Thackeray's bust. Alfred took Hallam to Marlborough, his new school, at the beginning of May, and spent an enjoyable week with the Bradleys, during which he visited Silbury and Avebury, conversed with science masters, read 'Guinevere' to the Sixth, accompanied the Bradley children to Wombwell's Circus, and read 'Northern Farmer' and 'The Grandmother' at Mrs Bradley's request. Lionel, whose stammer had worsened, was transferred on Kingsley's recommendation to the school of a speech-therapist at Hastings, and it was after taking him there in September that his parents made inquiries about the possibility of securing a summer retreat in the neighbourhood of Haslemere. Mrs Gilchrist, widow of Blake's biographer, found Grayshott Farm, which they rented for two years. Emily felt the need for a more bracing climate in the warm season, and both were relieved to think they could avoid the trippers and uninvited visitors who intruded on their privacy year after year at Farringford. They visited Queen Victoria again at Osborne in February 1867, and the atmosphere was most cordial. When she said she was not troubled by unwelcome visitors, Tennyson replied, 'Perhaps I shouldn't be, Your Majesty, if I could stick a sentry at my gates.'

On the first of March a telegram arrived from Marlborough, announcing Hallam's serious illness; it was bitterly cold when his parents arrived at the school, and twice the way had to be cleared by a snow-plough before they could reach the sanatorium. Hallam had pneumonia, and survived the crisis. In the spring they took him to

Grayshott Farm, and by May he had sufficiently recovered to accompany his father and Lionel to Gilbert White's Selborne, where they climbed the steep Hanger. Remembering her home near Farnham, Emily was keen to live in the area, and it was while searching for a site on which to build a cottage that Tennyson was addressed by a man at Haslemere station. It was the architect James Knowles, who had dedicated a volume of Arthurian legends to him, visited Farringford in 1866, and been encouraged, because of the poet's short-sightedness, to greet him whenever they met. Tennyson invited him to design the house, and Knowles agreed on condition that he was paid no fee. By the end of June property had been bought on a heathery, wooded slope of Blackdown, room for home and lawn being afforded by a natural terrace just below the crest, about eight hundred feet up, with a superb panoramic view of the Sussex Weald.

5

Gradually Knowles's grander and more fancifully Gothic ideas prevailed over the Poet Laureate's modest intentions, and a decorated stone mansion was planned, with a long first-floor library overlooking the Weald; emblematic devices of Tennyson's favourite non-classical poets – Dante, Chaucer, Shakespeare, Milton, Goethe, and Wordsworth – over the dining-room mantelpiece; arms of the Tennyson d'Eyncourts on the chimney-pieces; and a tiled motto in Welsh, 'The truth against the world', on the floor of the entrance hall. When the general design had been agreed, Tennyson decided to join Palgrave and his family at Lyme Regis. On Yarmouth quay he met Allingham, and persuaded him to accompany him; they reached Dorchester by train, visited Maiden Castle, called on the poet William Barnes, walked to Bridport, and the next day to Lyme, where Alfred wished most of all to see the steps on the Cobb where Louisa Musgrove fell. Allingham had to return to work, while Tennyson set off with Palgrave on a walking-tour in south Devon. His metaphysical interests led him to write 'The Higher Pantheism' on his return; it was followed by 'Lucretius'. Urged on by Knowles, he then applied himself to a continuation of the *Idylls*, beginning preparatory work on 'The Holy Grail' in March; in this he included an image of yew-tree 'smoke' or wafted pollen, a cloud of which appeared like fire in the Farringford shrubbery that spring. On 23 April, Shakespeare's birthday, attended by Sir John and Lady Simeon, Mrs Gilchrist, and his architect, he laid the foundation stone of his summer residence, named Aldworth after the Berkshire village where Emily's ancestors had lived.

That summer forty or fifty neighbours came to tea when Longfellow visited Farringford with a party of ten. After taking Lionel for admission to Eton in July (since 'his health could not endure the cold climate of Marlborough') and visiting the school house where Hallam had boarded, Alfred and Emily turned west to see Tintern Abbey and the Wye Valley. Charles Darwin called soon after their return, and assured him that the theory of evolution did not run counter to Christianity. Tennyson had decided to change his publisher, and reached agreement with Alexander Strahan, who purchased the existing rights at £5000 per annum for five years. The Poet Laureate never forgot his indebtedness to his friend Moxon, and presented £1500 or more to his widow, with an anonymous annuity, first of £300, then £100. Encouraged by friends who had read 'The Holy Grail', he worked on two more Arthurian idylls in the winter. He attended the first meeting of 'The Metaphysical Society', which had been organized by Knowles after discussing it with him and Pritchard; its membership grew to include leading Catholics, Broad Churchmen, agnostics, Rationalists, Positivists, Unitarians, and men of varied distinction such as Gladstone, Ruskin, and Tennyson. Frederick Locker, who had stayed at Grayshott Farm and Farringford, and visited Paris with Tennyson the previous December, found him a delightful, humorous companion, and they spent a month together on a tour to Switzerland in the summer. The enlarged edition of the *Idylls* appeared with other poems at the end of the year, though dated 1870 (when the poet's annual income exceeded £10,000 for the first time).

During their holidays Hallam and Lionel spent many evenings play-reading or acting in Mrs Cameron's little theatre, often in their father's presence. He described old Mr Cameron as 'a philosopher with his beard dipt in moonlight'. With Annie Thackeray 'the queen of all hearts', her cousins (the Ritchie sisters, one singing, the other playing, as if inspired), and 'feats of intellect', especially when Tennyson and Henry Taylor were discussing poetry, life was a continual delight for Mrs Cameron. Emily Ritchie remembered seeing the Poet Laureate for the first time, on the downs with Annie; 'he swooped down the hillside, his large black cloak flying in the wind, and his massive tread seeming to carry him at an astonishing pace'. Nothing was more memorable than his reading of poetry; sometimes it was like an incantation, and 'the power of realizing its actual nature was subordinated to the wonder at the sound of the tones'.

Certain reviewers, after discovering the moral and spiritual import of the new *Idylls of the King*, raised the cry 'Art for Art's sake', which prompted Tennyson to write the lines:

Art for Art's sake! Hail, truest Lord of Hell!
Hail Genius, blaster of the Moral Will!

'The filthiest of all paintings painted well
  Is mightier than the purest painted ill!'
Yes, mightier than the purest painted well,
So prone are we toward that broad way to hell.

Other criticism persuaded him that his *Idylls* required extension and
further co-ordination, work which he planned to begin at Aldworth,
to which he was about to set out on 23 May, when news came of the
sudden death abroad of Sir John Simeon. While waiting for the
funeral procession of his old friend to begin, he recalled two other
lost friends, Arthur Hallam and Henry Lushington, and wrote the
lyrical lament 'In the Garden at Swainston':

Nightingales warbled without,
  Within was weeping for thee:
Shadows of three dead men
  Walked in the walks with me,
  Shadows of three dead men and thou wast one of the three.

Nightingales sang in his woods:
  The Master was far away:
Nightingales warbled and sang
  Of a passion that lasts but a day;
  Still in the house in his coffin the Prince of courtesy lay.

Two dead men have I known
  In courtesy like to thee:
Two dead men have I loved
  With a love that ever will be:
  Three dead men have I loved and thou art last of the three.

At Dickens' funeral in Westminster Abbey, it was the Poet
Laureate who excited most attention; the congregation surged
towards him after the service, and he had to leave by a private door.
FitzGerald, who preferred the beardless Alfred of Laurence's
painting, thought he looked 'rather a Dickens' in the photographs;
the sketch of the dead novelist by Millais brought home to
Tennyson not only the likeness but the tenuity of the partition
between life and his own death. The outbreak of the Franco-
Prussian war was a cause for further depression. It was a relief to
have the opportunity of welcoming friends and relatives for the first

time at Aldworth, among them Charles and Louisa Turner, Cecilia and Edmund Lushington, and Jowett, who had emerged from a long period of discrimination and hostility, and was soon to be Master of Balliol. On the receipt of his edition of Plato at Farringford, Emily cut the pages of the *Phaedo* for Alfred, who 'talked on the subjects nearest his heart, the Resurrection and the Immortality of the Soul'.

'The Last Tournament' was completed in May 1871, soon after Jenny Lind came to sing at Farringford. June at Aldworth saw the visit of Turgenev, who told stories of Russian feudal life with 'a great graphic power and vivacity'. Returning from London by train with G. H. Lewes in July, Tennyson was taken to Shottermill, near Haslemere, to meet George Eliot, who (he thought) resembled a picture of Savonarola; at later meetings that summer he read several of his poems, including 'Guinevere', which made George Eliot weep; he also read *Maud*, unaware that she had been very critical of it in *The Westminster Review*. When Gladstone and his wife were at Aldworth, he read 'The Holy Grail' at their request; the Prime Minister admired it, and Tennyson thought him noble and unaffected. He took Hallam on a walking-tour in North Wales, and then went to stay with the Howards at Naworth Castle near Carlisle. Offered £1000 by a New York editor for a poem even of twelve lines, he sent 'England and America in 1782', which he had written nearly forty years earlier. At Farringford his new study was ready by Christmas, and a new ballroom extended the period of party festivities when it came into use in February, Tennyson dancing as energetically as anyone.

When 'Gareth and Lynette' was finished Tennyson took his family to Paris, where Hallam was left to study French while the others travelled to Grenoble and the Grande Chartreuse, before making a tour in Switzerland; Alfred and Lionel had a fine view of Mont Blanc from the top of the Dent du Chat, and their guide told them they were good mountaineers. The epilogue 'To the Queen' which Tennyson wrote for his new series of *Idylls* in the Library Edition of 1872 brought an appreciative letter from Lord Dufferin, now Governor-General of Canada, who was grateful for a spirited denunciation of those who sought 'to dissolve the Empire'. The Poet Laureate was at Windsor in March 1873, and was taken by the Queen into the mausoleum at Frogmore where Prince Albert was buried. Gladstone offered him a baronetcy, which he declined with the wish that the title could be assumed by Hallam at any age thought suitable. Further work was done on the *Idylls*, to which 'Balin and Balan' was added.

His friends on the Isle of Wight now included the Prinseps, who had left Little Holland House and settled with G. F. Watts near Farringford, and W. G. Ward, who, after being a fellow, tutor, and friend of Jowett at Balliol, had been deprived of his degrees for his conversion to Tractarianism, and received into the Roman Church; he lived with his chaplain west of Farringford. His nimble wit and ample proportions suggested 'a combination of Socrates and Falstaff'. Despite his religious extremism and lack of interest in poetry, his humour and readiness to discuss life after death recommended him to Tennyson, and they often walked together. The poet's willingness to humour Mrs Cameron was illustrated in the spring of 1873, when she persuaded him to join a procession of her friends down to the bay and ceremoniously throw a wreath of red and white flowers into the sea, as if he were the Doge of Freshwater (a whim probably suggested by *Maud*, I.107). In September he took Hallam to the Engadine and the Italian lakes, returning via the Simplon Pass, where he recalled Wordsworth's lines, 'The immeasurable height Of woods decaying, never to be decayed . . . ', but was disappointed in what he saw. When Hallam and Lionel left for Cambridge (both were at Trinity) their parents went to London, where they had agreed to share a house with Lady Franklin for the entertaining of their friends. During their two months' stay, Strahan finding it impossible to continue his contract, Tennyson changed his publisher. Browning came on most Sundays; Carlyle found his old friend wearisome, 'nothing coming from him that did not smack of utter indolence' enlivened by 'boylike naïveté'. At Trinity in November, Tennyson was 'as happy as a boy' with fellows and students.

His interest in the theatre had increased in recent years, and from his London *pied-è-terre* he could now attend the most prestigious performances of the day. Emily's note of 10 April 1874 shows that he was reading Froude on Mary Queen of Scots with a play in mind. So began a change of literary direction which stemmed as much from the desire to score successes at the centre of the metropolitan cultural scene as from the rather arid prospect beyond the *Idylls* which had confronted the poet for some time. In Paris that summer, before proceeding with his family to Tours, he watched a number of plays at the Théâtre Français; from Tours he and Hallam visited the Pyrenees, Cauteretz being inevitably his main objective. Emily collapsed soon after their return to Farringford, and had to give up not only her journal but the heavy secretarial duties which she had long and overconscientiously endured for her husband; her place was taken by Hallam, who was withdrawn from Cambridge at Christmas. Disraeli, on his succession to Gladstone, renewed the offer of a baronetcy, which Tennyson again declined with the hope that it would be conferred on Hallam after his own death.

New ambition energized Tennyson, for *Queen Mary* was published in May 1875. Its temperate anti-Catholicism reflected a Protestant reaction to the irrational assertiveness of the Vatican which Ward upheld. The author's friends, including Ward, were enthusiastic, but critics were cautious, not altogether for polemical reasons; it was long, and qualified for reading rather than the stage, though Tennyson hoped to see it produced with Irving in a leading role. A monument to Emily's uncle Sir John Franklin, discoverer of the Northwest Passage, was unveiled in Westminster Abbey twenty-eight years after his death; for this Tennyson supplied the following lines, which he regarded as the best of his epitaphs:

Not here! the white North has thy bones; and thou,
    Heroic sailor-soul,
Art passing on thine happier voyage now
    Toward no earthly pole.

Later that summer, mainly for his wife's health, he took his family to Pau, where Lionel and Locker's daughter Eleanor became engaged; Tennyson and Hallam enjoyed a tour in the western Pyrenees. After being drastically cut, *Queen Mary* was produced at the Lyceum in the spring of 1876, but audiences soon fell off, and the play was withdrawn after twenty-three performances. At Woodbridge in September, Tennyson and FitzGerald 'fell at once into the old humour', as if they had been parted only twenty days 'instead of so many years'; Hallam observed that 'the old man never got off his own platform to look at the work of modern authors. He had always wanted men like Thackeray and my father to go along with his crotchets, which were many.' The next month Tennyson and his son visited the Gladstones at Hawarden, where the poet read the whole of his second play *Harold*. It was published in November but not publicly performed until 1928. Much to Swinburne's disgust, it was dedicated to Lord Lytton, whose father had written the novel *Harold* and the anonymous attack on 'School-Miss Alfred'.

To complete his historical 'trilogy' Tennyson next set to work on *Becket*. From 1875 to 1882 he was in London more than usual, the period from February to Easter (after Christmas and New Year at Farringford) being spent at various addresses, to rub off the 'country rust' and be near Lionel, who worked at the India Office. He met many friends, Browning and Gladstone particularly, visited Carlyle, and became acquainted with General Gordon and the famous violinist Joachim. So shocked was he at the sight of female forms in a ballet chorus that he left the box and would not return during the performance. Dining with Lord Houghton, he met the archaeologist Schliemann, and could not believe that ancient Troy was no larger than the courtyard of Burlington House. Henry James was present, eager to catch every word from the Poet Laureate, who talked mainly of tobacco and port, a 'monstrous demonstration that Tennyson was not Tennysonian'. Mrs Cameron had left for Ceylon (where she died a few years later) to recoup her fortune, and her place as a forgivable eccentric devotee had been taken by Mrs Greville, a wealthy supporter of the arts, the theatre especially. She would kiss Tennyson's hand whenever they met, and he once addressed her in a letter 'Dear Madwoman'; James liked her but thought her 'on the whole the greatest fool' he had ever known; on one occasion when she was leaving he heard Tennyson tell her she could do anything but kiss him in front of the cabman. At the end of February 1878 hundreds of the poet's friends gathered in Westminster Abbey for the wedding of Lionel and Eleanor Locker.

Tennyson's income had fallen considerably since he turned playwright, as he was reminded when he had to accept a contract with his new publisher Kegan Paul at half the rate he had received from Strahan. He had good reason therefore to be industrious, and he worked to such effect on *Becket* that he found time for a holiday with Hallam in western Ireland, Killarney, Wicklow, and Dublin. The success of 'The Revenge' (which Mrs Greville recited before royalty) made him think of a new volume of poetry, for which he wrote 'The Defence of Lucknow' in March 1879. Then came news in quick succession of the death of his favourite brother Charles and of his wife Louisa, with whom he and his family had often stayed at Grasby, the parish to which they had devoted their energies and charity, building the schools, the new church, and the new vicarage, at their own expense. Alfred persuaded Spedding to edit Charles's collected sonnets (over three hundred), and wrote the prefatory poem 'Midnight – in no midsummer tune'. A copy of *Becket* was hopefully sent to Irving, who calculated that such an elaborate play would be too expensive to produce. Unpublished until 1884, it was a great theatrical success in 1893, just after Tennyson's death, with Irving as Becket and Ellen Terry as Rosamund.

The Falcon, however, enjoyed a moderately successful run at St James's Theatre in the winter of 1879–80. Tennyson was asked to accept nomination for the Lord Rectorship of Glasgow University, but declined the invitation when he understood his candidature was supported by only the Conservative student group. His third rejection of a baronetcy, with the usual proviso, when Gladstone returned to office, suggests that he had hopes of higher distinction. In May 1880 he extended a visit to Stonehenge, which he suddenly decided to take with the historian Lecky from Farringford, to a tour which also included Salisbury Cathedral, George Herbert's church at Bemerton, Amesbury (the last home of Guinevere), and the Vandykes at Wilton. So much did he suffer from a liver complaint and voices in the head about this time that his specialist advised him to take a holiday in North America or Venice; as no berths were available for Canada, he and Hallam travelled via Munich to Lord Acton's at Tegernsee, and on to Venice via Innsbruck and Titian's birthplace near Cortina. In Venice they travelled by gondola 'day and night', climbed the Campanile, and saw many paintings; Tennyson found them badly illuminated in the churches, and preferred his solitary walks on the Lido. On the return journey, after being delighted with Verona, they roamed over Sirmio, the beloved peninsula of Catullus, where memories of the Latin poet's delight and sorrow and of Charles commingled to produce Tennyson's loveliest lyric, 'Frater Ave atque Vale':

Row us out from Desenzano, to your Sirmione row!
So they rowed, and there we landed – 'O venusta Sirmio!'
There to me through all the groves of olive in the summer glow,
There beneath the Roman ruin where the purple flowers grow,
Came that 'Ave atque Vale' of the Poet's hopeless woe,
Tenderest of Roman poets nineteen-hundred years ago,
'Frater Ave atque Vale' – as we wandered to and fro
Gazing at the Lydian laughter of the Garda Lake below
Sweet Catullus's all-but-island, olive-silvery Sirmio!

Ballads and Other Poems, published in November, was favourably received, and was followed in the autumn by another short play, *The Cup*, which was very successful at the Lyceum in the summer of 1881.

Among subjects suggested by Irving was one on Robin Hood; he supplied material, and Tennyson began *The Foresters* without delay, visiting Sherwood Forest in the summer. It was not accepted for production, nor was it published. Tennyson then began *The Promise of May*, a bold venture into modern realism which Mrs Greville and others had encouraged. He was depressed by the death of friends, and sought assurance on posthumous survival; contemporary French art disgusted him, though he found a moralist in Baudelaire's *Les Fleurs du Mal*; he could not oppose Gladstone's conviction that the growing lack of uprightness and integrity boded ill for the next half-century. His revision of 'Hands All Round!', at a time when Swinburne did not hesitate to mock him in parody, excited trenchant anti-imperialistic satire. Not surprisingly a request from the Virgilian Academy of Mantua to celebrate the nineteenth centenary of Virgil's birth appealed to his finer sense, poetic consanguinity, and enduring love, yielding lines accordant to their subject. After a visit to Dovedale and Beresford Dale with Hallam, he completed *The Promise of May*, which won scant approval. By the end of 1882 Tennyson's theatrical career had finished.

While staying at Freshwater, the artist, poet, and novelist Mary Boyle became known to Tennyson, who enjoyed her conversation and playful wit; in the spring of 1883 she brought her attractive niece Audrey to Farringford, and she and Hallam became engaged that same year. Alfred was deeply saddened by the death of his old friend and critic Edward FitzGerald in June. When he was at Osborne a few weeks later the Queen noticed his weakened eyesight, thought him '*very shaky on his legs*', and tried to comfort him when he spoke of lost ones and seemingly adverse trends in the contemporary world. He and Hallam joined the Gladstones at Chester in September, accompanying them by train to Barrow for a holiday on the *Pembroke Castle* during its trial cruise. As Sir Donald Currie's ship left, thousands of spectators raised a special cheer for the Prime Minister and the Poet Laureate. Unlike many of the guests, Tennyson was not a supporter of Gladstone's Liberalism; he discussed Arthur Hallam and Dante, Scott's novels, and the translation of Homer, with him, and recited some of his shorter poems as they made their way from point to point along the western coast of Scotland to Orkney, Kristiansand, and Copenhagen, where Tennyson was the toast of the Queen of Denmark. On the way home Gladstone asked Hallam if he thought his father would accept a peerage; Hallam thought he might for the sake of literature, but Tennyson wished to consider it. He was afraid of spiteful comment in the press, which came when his elevation was announced. Would he give up the Civil List pension he had received for thirty-nine years, it was asked; one parodic satire ended:

> You must wake and call me early, call me early, Vicky dear;
> Tomorrow will be the silliest day we've seen for many a year,
> For I'm a lackey and prig, Vicky, that sham and shoddy reveres,
> And I'm to be one of the Peers, Vicky, I'm to be one of the Peers.

As if to triumph over his uncle Charles, Tennyson and his family wished to assume a d'Eyncourt title, until it was proved that he had no such hereditary claim. Introduced by the Duke of Argyll and Lord Kenmare (in the absence of Lord Houghton), he looked a grand figure in the borrowed robes of Lord Coleridge when he took his seat in the House of Lords in March 1884. Gladstone could hardly have been surprised when he refused to take a party seat. Not far off, three months later, another great event for the Tennysons took place when Hallam and Audrey Boyle were married in the Henry VII Chapel, Westminster Abbey.

Dear to his invalid mother and indispensable to his father, Hallam remained at home, an arrangement too intimately and intellectually exclusive at times for his wife's complete happiness. Tennyson was awarded an honorary degree by Edinburgh University, and offered a tour of fifty lectures in the States at $1000 a lecture. At the end of 1885 *Tiresias and Other Poems* appeared, issued by his new publisher Macmillan and dedicated to Robert Browning. This miscellaneous collection included 'Balin and Balan', and was very popular, many readers finding assurances in assertions on God and the hereafter. The titular poem, in which Tiresias voices the poet's wish to consort after death with the men he knew, and find 'the wise man's word, Here trampled by the populace underfoot, There crowned with worship', was preceded by lines to FitzGerald (which he never saw) recalling *inter alia* a vegetarian dream, the narration of which Tennyson introduced with 'I never saw any landscape that came up to the landscapes I have seen in my dreams.'

At the invitation of Lord Dufferin, the new Viceroy, Lionel had gone to India with his wife Eleanor; he caught jungle fever while hunting in Assam, and never recovered from the illness that began in Calcutta. His death on the homeward voyage was a great sorrow to his father, who was comforted by the Queen's sympathy, and much more by his wife's unfailing spirit. To relieve him, she encouraged visitors to Aldworth, among them Edmund Gosse, still smarting from the chastisement administered by Churton Collins for literary inaccuracy. Having been subjected to the same author's fanciful pedantry in articles which purported to prove his innumerable borrowings from classical authors, Tennyson commiserated, describing Collins as 'a louse on the locks of literature'. His despondency continued; poverty and vice in the cities made him fearful of the future, and he expressed his feelings in 'Locksley Hall Sixty Years After'; published significantly with *The Promise of May* at the end of 1886, it roused Gladstone to reply in *The Nineteenth Century*, vindicating Parliament for its reforms since 1842, stressing the subjectivity of Tennyson's poem, and veiling his annoyance in regret that the Queen's Jubilee had been 'marred by tragic notes'. The concluding section of the Poet Laureate's Jubilee ode showed that he was unrepentant.

In the summer of 1887 the Tennysons chartered a yacht for a cruise to Dartmouth and St David's, where school children sang Welsh songs to them, then to Clovelly and Tintagel (where an old woman said she had seen Tennyson there fifty years previously, and began to recite from the *Idylls*), on to Falmouth, Plymouth, and the Channel Islands, where Frederick had lived since 1859. The two brothers talked about their early years, and on revelations of the future life, Frederick being a convinced spiritualist. Hallam took his father to Cambridge in November to see *Oedipus Tyrannus* in Greek and *The Winter's Tale*. In the spring of 1888 there were meetings with the American actress Mary Anderson to discuss the production of *The Cup*; a visit to the New Forest followed with that of *The Foresters* in mind. At the end of summer Tennyson was bedridden with arthritic gout for two months, and thought as he gazed over the Weald that he was looking into eternity. Vivid dreams, such as had probably given colour to many passages in his poetry, continued: he saw firwoods, cliffs, and temples; pagodas reaching up to heaven; Priam of Troy; and himself as Pope, bearing the sins of the world. After being taken on a special train to Lymington, he had a serious relapse at Farringford, and thought he would die. When spring came, he and Emily were carried into the garden to observe the flowers. A cruise in Lord Brassey's sailing yacht along the coast, and some of the rivers, of Devon and Cornwall restored him.

Tennyson's long illness and the celebration of his eightieth birthday had gained him widespread interest and sympathy, which were evident when *Demeter and Other Poems* was announced; 20,000 copies were sold before publication. Dedicated to Lord Dufferin in a poem commemorating Lionel's death and burial at sea, it offered a wide range of appeal, from the humour and melodrama of popular stories to 'Demeter and Persephone' and 'Merlin and the Gleam'. The poem which caught the popular imagination was 'Crossing the Bar'; it had come to Tennyson as he was crossing the Solent from Aldworth, was composed in five to ten minutes, and was shown the same day after dinner to Hallam, who said, 'That is the crown of your life's work.' Whatever delight the poet felt in the success of his latest volume was dashed when he heard that his faithful friend Browning had died in Venice on the day of its publication. His burial in Westminster Abbey, where Tennyson expected to join him soon, was due in no small measure to Alfred's influence on Dean Bradley.

The Poet Laureate remained very active, meeting and entertaining new friends and admirers. He read widely, finding time for his favourite novels by Jane Austen, Scott, and Thackeray, and contemporary ones by Hardy, Henry James, Miss Braddon, Hall Caine, and others, especially Meredith and Stevenson; he was keenly interested in Frazer's *The Golden Bough*. When Princess Louise visited him in February 1891, he climbed the down above Farringford, and raced with her to the Beacon. 'June Heather and Bracken' was composed prospectively as a dedication of his next volume of poetry (his last) to Emily, possibly during the excursion he made with Hallam, first in Colonel Crozier's yacht to Exmouth, then by train to Dulverton, whence they enjoyed outings in the Exmoor region; the hymn to the sun in 'Akbar's Dream' was written on the return voyage. An agreement with Daly and Ada Rehan for the production of *The Foresters* in New York, coupled with Irving's interest in adapting *Becket* for the stage, gave Tennyson much pleasure.

The end did not come quickly. He would sit frequently on his walks to admire the view or flowers or insects at his feet; more than once Hallam heard him quote 'The wan moon is setting behind the white wave, And time is setting for me, oh!' Colonel Crozier lent them his yacht again, and they sailed to the Channel Islands, especially to see Sark but chiefly to spend time with Frederick. In London they met G. L. Craik at Macmillan's and were conducted round a fascinating display of birds' nests at the Natural History Museum which made Tennyson wish he could have seen it when he was young. Back at Aldworth, he received many visitors about the time of his birthday, but was touched most by two letters from working-class admirers, one a Newcastle artisan who ended, 'May your years of influence be many. The age does so need a guiding hand.' Hallam, after visiting Somersby to give him an account of his old home, was shocked to find how much weaker his father was. Jowett found him clear-minded, and pleased him by saying that his poetical philosophy was of higher value than 'any regular philosophy in England'. Discussing Irving's plans for *Becket* with Bram Stoker, Tennyson was amused to recall 'God, the Virgin', the error which the actor had made when copying from the revised script; he had confidence in him, but regretted that justice had not been done to *The Promise of May*. Craik checked the proofs of *The Death of Oenone, Akbar's Dream, and Other Poems* with him, and on 29 September he took his last drive. Inquiries came from the Queen and Princess Louise. Tennyson dreamt that he was showing his trees to Gladstone, and called for his Shakespeare, though he could not read. It fell open at one of his favourite passages, in *Cymbeline*, 'Hang there like fruit, my soul, till the tree die.' Soon afterwards he called for Hallam and blessed Emily, who had lain on her sofa at the foot of the bed during much of his illness. He died during the second hour of Thursday, 6 October.

Until Monday he lay in his open coffin, crowned with a wreath of laurel leaves which Alfred Austin had obtained for this purpose eleven years earlier from the tomb of Virgil, a bunch of roses (his favourite flower) from Emily over his heart, and a copy of *Cymbeline* in his hand. His friend Dean Bradley was asked to choose whether he should be buried in Westminster Abbey or at Farringford. Fittingly he was laid next to Browning, near the monument to Chaucer. The Abbey was crowded, uniformed representatives of the Balaclava Light Brigade, the London Rifle Volunteers, and the Gordon Boys' Home lining the nave in acknowledgment of causes he had sponsored. The Queen sent two wreaths, but no member of the royal family was present; nor was Gladstone. It was a State occasion nonetheless; among the twelve pall-bearers were the Duke of Argyll, Lord Dufferin, Lord Rosebery, Lord Salisbury, the

United States minister, Jowett, Montagu Butler, Froude, and Sir James Paget. The anthems consisted of 'Crossing the Bar' (to Dr Bridge's music) and another late poem, 'The Silent Voices' (to a melody in F minor composed by Emily at Alfred's request). The occasion was grand, but the ceremony seemed too impersonal. Burne-Jones thought it flat, and the Queen unforgivable for not attending; Hardy found the music sweet and impressive, but the funeral 'less penetrating than a plain country interment'. Within two weeks Hallam began collecting the letters, reminiscences, and appraisals from which his *Memoir* was drawn with the help of his mother, who died shortly after its completion in 1896.

PART TWO

Tennyson's Writings

6
Adolescent Poetry

Given a literary background, children can develop remarkable precocity. In more favourable circumstances than the Brontë orphans, Tennyson was able to recite Horace's odes at the age of seven, and write in Thomsonian verse a year or so later. His linguistic aptitude, like that of his elder brothers, was stimulated by hearing poetry and other forms of literature read aloud in the home, even more by frequent composition. His verse-writing was encouraged by his mother and Charles. Like Branwell Brontë, he acquired great facility in imitating Walter Scott, an epic in that style, full of battles and descriptions of sea and mountains, preoccupying him from the age of twelve; he never felt 'more truly inspired'. The earliest of his verse to be preserved, however, may precede this lost work, though it was probably revised before being transcribed for preservation. Translated from Claudian, it follows the style of Pope's *Iliad*, which Tennyson began to admire at the age of eleven; nowhere does it suggest immaturity, and its subject, the rape of Proserpine, had a lasting appeal for the poet.

The Devil and the Lady, his next work to be preserved, is a three-act fragment which illustrates the copiousness to which he had become habituated. Like Jane Austen's *Love and Friendship*, it was written at the age of fourteen, and in its way is the author's liveliest composition. More than the solemn Victorian respectability which persisted into the twentieth century is necessary to explain why this sprightly performance was not published until 1930. When shown it by Hallam Tennyson, Jowett was astonished that 'the whelp could have known such things'. Its exuberance affords sure testimony that there were adolescent periods when he was supremely happy; the fecundity of witty parallelism which characterizes it is punctuated by arresting dramatic intonations and delightful humour. The author appreciates highly 'The combination of images From whose collision springs the brilliant spark Of heaven-born wit'; he is

capable of some novel punning. Most surprising is his familiarity
(II.i) with Berkeleyan metaphysics, and with the incongruity,
which he never ceased to feel, between atomic materialism and
creative Omnipotence. Indebted though the play is to Elizabethan
and Jacobean drama, Milton, classical mythology and literature,
astronomy, and encyclopedic book-learning, it is notable for
original observation. A lengthy passage in which the magician
describes his sea voyage and the tempest which soon drives him back
reveals the power to adapt a remarkable poetic fluency to the
rhythms of dramatic speech.

Basically the story seems to derive from Francis Palgrave's
'Popular Mythology of the Middle Ages' in *The Quarterly Review*,
January 1820. Magus, an aged necromancer, afraid of being
cuckolded by his young wife Amoret when he is about to depart on a
long journey, summons the Devil to act as his safeguard. The Devil,
after sending her to bed, appears in the guise of Amoret as her lovers
approach after midnight: first a lawyer, then an apothecary, later a
sailor, then an astronomer–mathematician, a soldier, and a monk.
Stimulated by Jonsonian humours, Tennyson takes every opportunity to make these rivals express their mutual animosity by
figurative recourse to technical terms in their several callings.
Mistaken for Amoret, the Devil invites them into the cottage, where
he promises to unveil, and favour his fancy-man after each has sung
an amorous ditty; the brawl which immediately ensues is finally
interrupted when a knocking at the door is repeated more loudly.
After ensuring that the lovers are concealed, the Devil emerges and
discloses himself as a 'petticoated Solecism' to Magus, who, assured
that his wife is asleep, decides to post himself by the northern
casement overlooking the mountain lake, where he can hear all that
happens within. The Devil returns to the cottage, calls the suitors
from their hiding-places, and declares that it is time he announced
his favourite. What he intends next is not clear; his thoughts begin to
burn, and a devil's heat glows through him 'to the core'. With 'have
at ye, Sirs', he and the fragment conclude. It is idle to speculate how
it would have ended, and rash to read nascent philosophy in any of
it, however wide Tennyson's knowledge of life and the universe
seems to be. What interested him most was the relatively free play of
wit and expression engendered by successive situations. The play
should be read chiefly for its style, and not too hurriedly, for the
figurative thought sometimes assumes such length and elaboration
that it demands alert attention at every turn.

A prophetic vision being indispensable for the apocalyptic subject of 'Armageddon', it is an irrelevance to consider at this point how far the youthful poet accepted traditional notions of divine inspiration sponsored by Plato or Milton and revived by Shelley; it would be even more misleading to equate the godlike quality which he attributes to his vision with that of Keats in *Hyperion*, where it implies a mature recognition of good and evil in the tragedies of life. The seraph who extends the poet's distinctness of perception into space until he is 'a scintillation of the Eternal Mind' is uncertain whether these extrasensory powers are hereditary or metempsychotic in origin. Tennyson can take the issue little further. He had already assumed the gift of prophecy, and described ominous signs at sunset, the moon being seen like a 'red eruption from the fissured cone Of Cotopaxi's cloud-capt altitude', as he remembered it in Ulloa's *A Voyage to South America* (1758). The poem ends on the brink of the subject, a pulsation being felt as if the soul of the universe heaved tumultuously in expectation of the final battle announcing the Lord's 'great day'.

In ballad form and varying metre, 'The Coach of Death' also ceases, not surprisingly, at an apocalyptic point. Like *Paradise Lost*, it mingles Christian and classical mythology without discrimination. Set in a sunless, cold, occidental waste behind the ominously burning sun, it finds room for a diversionary contrast between the principal coach and the Paradise coach with its lights, heavenly melodies, silver-sounding wheels (of beryl, like the Messiah's chariot in Milton), and occupants arrayed in white. Macabre elements exert their grisly appeal with reference to travellers on the road to Hell: the coach stands in darkness outside a joyless inn as old as Time, where they think of earth, the family fireside, and summer; skeleton horses are yoked by shrivelled, shadowy grooms; an infernal glow sleeps in the coachman's eyeless sockets; and the wheels in motion throw up dust from the pulverized bones of the dead. The fragment ends with a view of Hell from the highest point of the bridge built by Sin and Death, one stanza recalling features in Keats's description of Hyperion's palace, and others suggesting an anticipation of 'The Palace of Art'.

The influence of the more romantic writers is evident in several slighter compositions. 'We meet no more' owes much to balladry; 'The Druid's Prophecies' recalls Gray's 'The Bard'; 'Midnight' contains a paraphrase from *Ossian*, an image from which, 'the great army of the dead returning on the northern blast', inspired 'Oh! ye

wild winds, that roar and rave'. Scott's *The Lady of the Lake* (III.v)
determined both the style and subject of 'The Vale of Bones'. Also
indebted to Scott for detail, 'Inverlee' is spoilt by bold rhyming
monotony, every alternate line echoing the name, which recurs at
four-line intervals. The metrical unsophistication of lines in 'The
Bridal', which summarizes the tragic climax of *The Bride of
Lammermoor*, suggests rather earlier writing.

Few young poets of the immediate post-Romantic era could resist
the anapaestic beat popularized by Byron and Moore. Tennyson
responded in verses which express the melancholy of the exiled or
friendless: 'The Exile's Harp', 'I wander in darkness and sorrow',
and 'Written by an Exile of Bassorah, while sailing down the
Euphrates'. Lulling metrical regularity hardly sustains readability
in the second, where emotional factitiousness sinks to the bathos of
'In this waste of existence, for solace, On whom shall my lone spirit
call? Shall I fly to the friends of my bosom? My God! I have buried
them all!' 'The Expedition of Nadar Shah into Hindostan' (from Sir
William Jones) and 'Babylon' (suggested by Charles Rollin's *Ancient
History*) bear resemblances to Byron's 'The Destruction of
Sennacherib' in both subject and expression. More dramatic is
'Lamentation of the Peruvians', which ends with curses on the
treacherous Pizarro.

Charles Rollin's work in translation supplied much of the detail
with which 'Persia' is loaded; whether in couplets or more varied
rhyme, the octosyllabics vie with Milton in a succession of sonorities
to which the deft manipulation of place-names contributes in no
small measure; the abrupt ending suggests the tediousness of pedantic
ostentation. 'The High-Priest to Alexander' (also drawn from
Rollin) testifies strongly to the ease with which Tennyson could
have produced rousing strains of hymnody had he wished. By
contrast the rhythms of 'Thou camest to thy bower, my love'
(much indebted to Sir William Jones's translation of an Indian love-
song) are lusciously enchanting.

Dramatizations of imaginary and historical situations are presented. 'Remorse' is a confessional in which the speaker looks back
on his mis-spent years, and is sure he was condemned from birth, 'a
hopeless outcast, born to die A living death eternally'. He is one of
Calvin's damned, and Tennyson probably wrote these lines with
some of his aunt Mary's comments in mind. The self-condemned
reprobate sees his soul winging its way wearily to 'yon vast world of
endless woe', those dread depths where 'glimmerings of the

boundless flame' glow forever; he dreads the Day of Judgment. In regular stanzas, the dramatic lyric 'Antony and Cleopatra' sustains competence, and is climactically concluded. 'Mithridates Presenting Berenice with the Cup of Poison' (from Charles Rollin) hardly attains the poignancy it aims at; most of the feminine rhymes which alternate throughout have a weakening effect, and often the verse runs too freely and evenly to evoke dramatic intensity.

'Did not thy roseate lips outvie', enriched with an epigraph from Horace and a note from Ulloa's *Voyage* on 'gay Anana's spicy bloom', has qualities reminiscent of the seventeenth-century courtly lyric but, like so much of Tennyson's early poetry, loses perfection of design through disproportion and lack of restraint. More artistically planned, but less successful in execution, is 'The Maid of Savoy'. Facility in ballad style is illustrated in 'King Charles's Vision', where the story, of historical interest though seemingly super-natural, lacks an exciting climax; the metre observes a regular stress pattern but, varying from iambic to anapaest, is particularly adaptable to narrative. 'The Dell of—', a lament that the moun-tain scene should be despoiled to build warships, is an exercise in melody, occasionally affecting the archaic, but most interesting because it demonstrates the lure of the Spenserian stanza (only partially followed), which Tennyson was to use with spell-binding effect in 'The Lotos-Eaters'. 'How gaily sinks the gorgeous sun within his golden bed' moralizes nature in swinging fourteeners.

Boldness in verse experimentation and subject is demonstrated in two odes published in 1827. The long elaborate stanzas of 'Time: An Ode' follow the style and vision of eighteenth-century writers. Hoary Time is seen silently majestical in his scythèd car, 'Cleaving the clouds of ages that float by, And change their many-coloured sides, Now dark, now dun, now richly bright, In an ever-varying Light'. For the armour of Death who closely pursues on his pale horse, Tennyson acknowledges indebtedness to a 'famous Chorus' in William Mason's *Caractacus*. The regular stanzas of 'On Sublimity' move briskly to match the author's enthusiasm; a note indicates that he had read Edmund Burke on the subject. The scenes which make him feel 'the genuine force of high Sublimity' derive predominantly, if not wholly, from writers of literature or travel. His imagination is stirred, for example, by Milton's 'Il Penseroso' when he thinks of 'some august cathedral' (Lincoln, no doubt) with its richly dight windows and 'more than mortal music'; his blood curdles or thrills at the thought of ghosts and other sensational manifestations in the Gothic literature of the eighteenth century. Nature's wonders include 'Cotopaxi's cloud-capt majesty' (from Ulloa), Niagara Falls, the Kentucky Cavern, Fingal's Cave, 'loud Stromboli', and the 'terrible Maelstrom'.

Whatever promptings the fight for national independence and freedom abroad brought to Tennyson in early manhood, it never became a soul-stirring cause with him as it did with Wordsworth. His anapaestic 'Exhortation to the Greeks' reads too much like a verse exercise evoked by Byron. More commendable is 'Written During the Convulsions in Spain', where the measure gives to some extent a foretaste of 'The Charge of the Light Brigade', and has a rousing appeal.

His astonishment at winning the Chancellor's Gold Medal at Cambridge must have been unfeigned. About half of 'Timbuctoo' had been taken with scarcely a change from one version of 'Armageddon', and to this he had added a beginning and an end. The result was a most unusual essay around the subject, with splendid lines and Miltonic nuances, necessarily in blank verse, though heroic couplets were considered almost *de rigueur* for the occasion. The poet–narrator stands on Calpe's height in the uncertain light of sunset, musing on fabulous Atlantis and Eldorado, legends which had won the heart of all 'Toward their brightness, even as flame draws air'; their being, however, is in the heart of man 'As air is the life of flame'. The opening begins rather loosely, gathers strength, and concludes at its peak with an epic simile: men clung with 'yearning Hope which would not die' to those imaginary realms,

> As when in some great City where the walls
> Shake, and the streets with ghastly faces thronged
> Do utter forth a subterranean voice,
> Among the inner columns far retired
> At midnight, in the lone Acropolis,
> Before the awful Genius of the place
> Kneels the pale Priestess in deep faith, the while
> Above her head the weak lamp dips and winks
> Unto the fearful summoning without:
> Nathless she ever clasps the marble knees,
> Bathes the cold hand with tears, and gazeth on
> Those eyes which wear no light but that wherewith
> Her phantasy informs them.

Where are those legendary worlds whose lowest deeps were filled with 'Divine effulgence', the poet wonders before asking whether Africa contains a city as fair as 'those which starred the night o' the elder World' or whether Timbuctoo is but a dream 'as frail as those of ancient Time'. The seraph then appears as in 'Armageddon', but reveals more in the concluding passage of 'Timbuctoo'. The narrator learns that the seraph's is the mightiest existing spirit to sway the heart of man or 'teach him to attain By shadowing forth the Unattainable'. Just as the waves of yon river reflect the glories of the city it passes through, and the waves which bore those reflections are finally lost in the sands, so the city, the latest throne to which the spirit has been raised as 'a mystery of loveliness', will surrender its glories to *Discovery*; its brilliant towers will darken and shrink into huts, barbarian settlements, 'Black specks amid a waste of dreary sand'. The spirit departs, leaving the poet in complete darkness on Calpe.

'Timbuctoo' reveals a significant development in Tennyson's concept of the imagination. The seraph of 'Armageddon' endowed the poet with a vision which is universal but dominantly prophetic; here the vision is that of the idealizing imagination from which dream-worlds have sprung. The spirit therefore claims to permeate 'the great vine of *Fable*' which is deep-rooted in 'the living soil of truth'. This truth is the reality of human hope which ever aspires to the Unattainable (as Tennyson insisted to the end). The ideal, as in the Platonically inspired writings of Shelley, is Heavenly truth. Even ordinary mortals see this higher reality dimly or 'darkling' (an echo of St Paul's 'through a glass, darkly'); it comes (as in Wordsworth's 'Intimations' ode) from 'Man's first, last home', and the poet hears its lordly music. The 'heavenly voice' of Fancy in the last stanza of 'On Sublimity' is no facile expression; its idealities are akin to Shelley's 'Forms more real than living man, Nurslings of Immortality'. Discovery or science (as Tennyson feared, and Keats made plain in *Lamia*) is inimical to the world of imaginative beauty. Wordsworth took a different point of view; Tennyson returned to his in 'The Hesperides'.

The divine concept of the poet in 'Armageddon' and 'Timbuctoo' seems to be confirmed in the metaphysics of 'The Idealist': man creates or weaves his universe; he is Place and Time; his 'home' (another echo of Wordsworth) is Eternity; he is all things 'save souls of fellow men and very God'. Two 1828 sonnets 'To Poesy', in the second of which Arthur Hallam had a hand, indicate the dawning of a more mature thought: heavenly inspiration is intended not exclusively for aesthetic enjoyment but for the benefit of mankind. The influence and optimism of Shelley are apparent: 'Methinks I see the world's renewèd youth A long day's dawn, when Poesy shall bind Falsehood beneath the altar of great Truth.' Tennyson hopes that his poetry will be altruistic,

> For this is the condition of our birth,
> That we unto ourselves are only great
> Doing the silent work of charities.

7

A Young Man's Fancies

Tennyson remained, however, in the Keatsian 'Chamber of Maiden Thought', intoxicated with its light and atmosphere, and content for the most part to express its pleasant wonders in melodic verse. The musical experimentation of 'Ilion, Ilion' moves towards Gerard Manley Hopkins. 'Leonine Elegiacs'[3] is more successful, and affords splendid examples of euphony combined with the descriptive precision and economy which Tennyson coveted:

> Low-flowing breezes are roaming the broad valley dimmed in the
> gloaming:
> Thorough the black-stemmed pines only the far river shines. . . .
> Over the pools in the burn water-gnats murmur and mourn.
> Sadly the far kine loweth; the glimmering water outfloweth:
> Twin peaks shadowed with pine slope to the dark hyaline.

The gnats' mourning echoes Keats's 'To Autumn'; the '-eth' rhymes are a silly surrender to the archaic for the sake of rhyme, indulgence in which reaches ridiculous excess in the unbroken succession of lisping end-words which ruin the last verse of 'Claribel'.

With its subtle assonance and alliteration, this is the first of a poetic gallery, a series of fanciful sketches of young women, disembodied spirits or types rather than flesh and blood. The elegiac notes of 'Claribel' contrast with the airy-fairiness of 'Lilian', whose tantalizing spirit is conveyed in light trochees and short, sharp sounds (especially 'i's and 't's: 'She'll not tell me if she love me, Cruel little Lilian'). Rather similar in intonation, though the character combines coquetry with staidness, 'Lisette' ends more pleasingly, and makes an almost perfect whole. 'Madeline' presents a girl so love-adept and unpredictable that none can tell which is fleeter or sweeter, her frown or her smile. 'Amy' is a more serious study; a lily high-minded and chaste, she never trembles to 'starts or thrills of love', her motion resembling 'Hill-shaded streams, that move Through the umber glebe and in brown deeps embosom The tremulous Evenstar'; in the end her virtues transcend the poet's powers: 'O splendour Of starry countenance Wherein I lose myself from life, and wander In utter ignorance . . . You love me not as man, You love me with that love which St Cecilia Did love Valerian . . . .' 'Marion' portrays the neither plain nor handsome, the 'ideal unideal' or 'uncommon commonplace' who by peculiar alchemy changes common thought to precious ore, and exerts a gentle, almost imperceptible influence which enriches life. The heroine of 'Adeline' seems to have greater affinity with the poet; she is shadowy, dreaming, and spiritual. In fanciful poeticizing imagery, ending with close observation of the red spots in cowslip bells (like letters of a fairy alphabet, Tennyson wrote), he suggests that her faint smile expresses subtle communications with nature:

> Doth the low-tongued Orient
>   Wander from the side of the morn,
>   Dripping with Sabaean spice
> On thy pillow, lowly bent
>   With melodious airs lovelorn,
> Breathing Light against thy face,
> While his locks a-drooping twined
>   Round thy neck in subtle ring
> Make a carcanet of rays,
>   And ye talk together still,
>   In the language wherewith Spring
>   Letters cowslips on the hill?

Three poems not published until 1832 belong to this series. The subject of 'Margaret' is Adeline's twin-sister, darker and more human, her melancholy 'sweet and frail As perfume of the cuckoo-flower'; the composition is less even and melodious than that of its companion-piece. The 'full-sailed verse' of 'Eleänore' is eloquent with romantic hyperbole which ends in bathos. The adored is stately and divine, her smile ambrosial; the entranced one yearns to gaze eternally on his 'Serene, imperial Eleänore'. Passion becomes passionless in her presence; and Love appears in contemporary art mode, his bow slackened, his wings drooping, as he leans cheek in hand languidly contemplating his beloved. If she but breathed his name, he would faint and die in the Sapphic (or Shelleyan) manner. 'Yet tell my name again to me, I *would* be dying evermore, So dying ever, Eleänore', he concludes. 'Kate' presents her antithesis, a potential feminist who speaks her mind, and loves the bold and fierce. The poet's dream of being inspired by her eyes as he fights valiantly in knightly battle strengthens the case for thinking that the germinal idea for the crucial action in *The Princess* may have lain in this miniature.

'Isabel' has a closer texture, and its adjudicating analysis suggests more penetrating insights. The poem presents an idealized portrait of Tennyson's mother, the 'queen of marriage, a most perfect wife', on whose lips the 'summer· calm of golden charity' perpetually reigned. His father fares less happily: she is 'a clear stream flowing with a muddy one' and absorbing 'the vexèd eddies of its wayward brother'. Most impressive is the conciseness of observations steeped in love:

> The intuitive decision of a bright
>> And thorough-edgèd intellect to part
>>> Error from crime; a prudence to withhold;
>>> The laws of marriage charactered in gold
>> Upon the blanchèd tables of her heart;
> A love still burning upward, giving light
> To read those laws; an accent very low
> In blandishment, but a most silver flow
>> Of subtle-pacèd counsel in distress,
> Right to the heart and brain, though undescried,
>> Winning its way with extreme gentleness
> Through all the outworks of suspicious pride . . . .

Tennyson's fascination with the legendary wonders of the deep appears in 'The Kraken', but it would be an uncritical exercise in fatuity to search for a subliminal correlative of the creative poetic essence in the monster's 'ancient, dreamless, uninvaded sleep', as it lies, and will continue to lie, battening on huge seaworms at an abysmal depth. Far lighter and livelier are 'The Merman' and 'The Mermaid', twin poems in which the amorousness of male and female is distinguished by the playful abandon of the former and the vanities of the latter. 'The Sea-Fairies' transfers a similar high-spiritedness to Homer's sirens, with a hint of 'The Lotos-Eaters' in the weary listening sailors: 'Who can light on as happy a shore All the world o'er, all the world o'er? Whither away? listen and stay: mariner, mariner, fly no more.'

Among the most outstanding of the poems published in 1830 is 'Recollections of the Arabian Nights'. Its stanza is artfully contrived, with a concluding refrain which carries the reader stage by stage through varying scenes of enchantment, preparing the way for the final, focal point which irradiates the whole. Tennyson recalls how, 'When the breeze of a joyful dawn blew free In the silken sail of infancy', the forward-flowing tide of time bore him imaginatively back to a night voyage through Baghdad's splendours to 'the golden prime Of good Haroun Alraschid'. A true Musselman, he eventually enters the Caliph's illuminated pavilion, and sees his hero, 'Sole star of all that place and time'. The verses teem with pictures: by a canal the damask-work of a sloping moonlit sward is deeply inlaid with 'braided blooms unmown'; diamond rills fall silver-chiming through crystal arches by the side of a lake, seeming to shake the flints that sparkle beneath the shallop's prow; a sudden splendour flushes the slumbering garden grots and bowers with rich gold-green, and, 'flowing rapidly between Their interspaces', counter-changes 'The level lake with diamond-plots Of dark and bright', making the dark-blue round of the sky, 'Distinct with vivid stars inlaid', grow darker as the voyager leaps ashore from his silver-anchored boat, on the last stage towards the penetralia of his quest. The unceasing song of the bulbul in the lemon grove, 'Apart from place, withholding time, But flattering the golden prime Of good Haroun Alraschid', may indeed owe something to Keats's immortal nightingale, but this does not relate it to the eternal world of art or poetry. The attempt to impose such esoteric significance can only blur a poem which is most distinctly seen as a highly artistic evocation of one of the romantic worlds of Tennyson's boyhood.

If any poem surpasses it in *Poems, Chiefly Lyrical*, it is 'Mariana', where the surroundings are contrastingly ordinary. The author had no particular grange in mind, only 'one which rose to the music of Shakespeare's words' in *Measure for Measure* (at the end of III.i): 'there, at the moated grange, resides this dejected Mariana'. The reunion of Shakespeare's heroine with Angelo is totally alien to Tennyson's creation. He supplied a familiar Lincolnshire setting, with glooming flats when 'thickest dark did trance the sky'; a sense of stagnation is emphasized by the sleep of the sluice and its blackened waters, and by the clustered marsh-mosses which creep over it. Just as the garden scene of 'Song' ('A spirit haunts the year's last hours') reflects feelings ('My very heart faints and my whole soul grieves At the moist rich smell of the rotting leaves . . . Heavily hangs the broad sunflower Over its grave i' the earth so chilly; Heavily hangs the hollyhock, Heavily hangs the tiger-lily') so 'The level waste, the rounding gray', the cold winds that wake the grey-eyed morn, and other features of the scene, express Mariana's forlornness. Functioning like the lone cypress in 'Me my own Fate to lasting sorrow doometh', the poplar by the grange, the one tree in the whole of her landscape ('the level waste' with its grey 'rounding' along the horizon) casts its shadow of hopeless melancholy when the moon is low 'Upon her bed, across her brow'. The psychological landscape or *paysage intérieur* created by such outward features played a part in the development of French Symbolist poetry. Other details fall into two categories: those at the opening which, like the garden of Wordsworth's 'The Ruined Cottage' in the first book of *The Excursion*, are the index of hopelessness in a lovelorn woman long abandoned by her lover; and those sharp or distinct sounds, such as the shrieking mouse behind the mouldering wainscot (repeated in *Maud*) or the sparrow's chirrup on the roof, half registered by Mariana in a dazed, distraught state which makes her imagine old faces glimmering through the doors, old footsteps above, and old voices calling her from outside. 'The slow clock ticking' is an incidental reminder of time; a more intuitively reson-ant and artistic one is registered by the poem as a whole, which compasses a complete day, significantly from darkening eve to sunset. Though it concludes with a satisfying finality – the tired-of-life monotony (expressed throughout in the refrain) being broken by an outburst of satiety – this cyclical movement confirms an unbroken recurrence, the tenor of a heart-breaking existence.

Perhaps Tennyson included in 'Mariana' images which had assumed emotional significance for him at times of depression. For this the origin may have been hereditary, or unhappiness at the rectory, or loss of faith engendered by intellectual debate at Cambridge. 'In deep and solemn dreams' shows him waking after visions of golden realms, and again of a happy company on the Somersby lawn one bright morning when 'sweet winds tremble o'er The large leaves of the sycamore' and the barley spears are still heavy with dew. He is friendless in the surrounding darkness and lies 'Hopeless, heartless, and forlorn'. Dramatic disguises in 'Supposed Confessions of a Second-Rate Sensitive Mind' cannot conceal the sincere expression of that 'beauty and repose of faith' which he shared with his mother in boyhood. He has lost his belief in free-will, and his spirit is shaken with doubt and fear. The vacillation which reduces him to a weary state of life and death poses a dilemma to which Tennyson harks back in *In Memoriam*, xxxiii ('Leave thou thy sister when she prays . . .') and xcvi ('There lives more faith in honest doubt . . .').

Three poems on memory disclose interesting developments. The versification of 'Memory! dear enchanter!' hardly communicates conviction; it assumes the disenchantment of experience in a series of images, some borrowed and rather hackneyed, one trite ('In every rose of life, Alas! there lurks a canker'). Remove all the embroidery which obscures 'Ode to Memory' (but which conveys the genuineness of the effort to evoke pictures of the past), and rare evocations of Lincolnshire, the rectory surroundings, and the garden at Somersby, are left:

> Come from the woods that belt the gray hill-side,
> The seven elms, the poplars four
> That stand beside my father's door,
> And chiefly from the brook that loves
> To purl o'er matted cress and ribbèd sand . . . .
> Pour round mine ears the livelong bleat
> Of the thick-fleecèd sheep from wattled folds,
>   Upon the ridgèd wolds . . .
> No matter what the sketch might be;
> Whether the high field on the bushless Pike,
> Or even a sand-built ridge
> Of heapèd hills that mound the sea,
> Overblown with murmurs harsh,
> Or even a lowly cottage whence we see
> Stretched wide and wild the waste enormous marsh,
> Where from the frequent bridge,
> Like emblems of infinity,
> The trenchèd waters run from sky to sky;
> Or a garden bowered close
> With plaited alleys of the trailing rose,
> Long alleys falling down to twilight grots,
> Or opening upon level plots
> Of crownèd lilies, standing near
> Purple-spikèd lavender . . . .

In the third poem, 'Ay me! those childish lispings roll', Memory brings pain as well as happiness, and wears the guise of Life and Death. When he wakens, the hope born of Memory in the poet's dreams (recalling the link between memory and the hope of childhood in the ode) turns to wan despair, as joy does at the end of 'In deep and solemn dreams'. The fragment ends with a long, overladen simile on the 'delirium-causing throes' of anticipation in a famished serpent coiled round a palm tree, as he spots a herd of lordly elephants 'Winding up among the trees'.

'The Deserted House' gives a memorable image for the body at death, but concludes conventionally (taking us back to St Paul, with whom the creative idea originated) and with a feeble expression of regret: Life and Thought have departed to a glorious city, where they have bought an incorruptible mansion; 'Would they could have stayed with us!' 'A Dirge', influenced by the song in *Cymbeline* (IV.ii), has a more sustained excellence. 'The Ballad of Oriana', echoing 'Fair Helen of Kirconnell' in Scott's *Minstrelsy of the Scottish Border*, is much more daring; in narration its heroic story displays balladic virtues which never falter, but the cumulative effect of the 'Oriana' refrain, following four out of five lines in every stanza, is to carry the poem dangerously near the brink of self-parody. Its finest lines, 'When the long dun wolds are ribbed with snow, And loud the Norland whirlwinds blow', occur in a framework of regret to a retrospective narrative, giving the latter a Lincolnshire setting. Equally popular with Tennyson's Cambridge friends, but less declamatory and more exquisitely subtle in its dance-rhythms, 'Anacaona' ends disappointingly, and never excels the opening lines:

> A dark Indian maiden,
>> Warbling in the bloomed liana,
> Stepping lightly flower-laden,
>> By the crimson-eyed anana,
> Wantoning in orange groves
>> Naked, and dark-limbed, and gay,
> Bathing in the slumbrous coves . . .
>> Of sunbright Xaraguay . . . .

'A Fragment', on the Colossus of Rhodes, published in *The Gem*, October 1830, exemplifies Tennyson's more Miltonic style of description, with some grandiloquent phrasing: 'A perfect Idol with profulgent brows Farsheening down the purple seas . . . between whose limbs Of brassy vastness broadblown Argosies Drave into haven', and (of Egypt) 'Awful Memnonian countenances calm Looking athwart the burning flats'.

Several efforts during this period illustrate Tennyson's mediocrity in the sonnet, a form in which, unlike Milton and Keats, Shakespeare and Wordsworth even more, he never excelled. If the subject rouses him, he rarely sustains it; often it is complicated or confused by excessive imagery. The extreme occurs in 'Love' (a series of three, beginning 'Thou, from the first'), where the final 'sonnet' is swollen to sixteen lines, fifteen of which describe a renaissant serpent. Tennyson's obsessional interest leads not only to distracting disproportion (as in the third of the poems on memory) but to anticlimax and inappropriate associations, immortal love being presented in the 'living light' which emerges from the brow of a serpent: the woods which it illumines may symbolize this world, as at the opening of Dante's *Divina Commedia*. Great poems appeal not merely by subject and sound but by the beauty of internal design which unfolds thought and feeling in disciplined artistry, the rhythm of which takes command over the outward form to which it is bound. The best of Tennyson's earlier sonnets are Petrarchan in mould, as in 'She took the dappled partridge fleckt with blood' and the Miltonic 'Hail, Light, another time to mortal eyes'. 'Me my own Fate to lasting sorrow doometh' (addressed possibly to Hallam) is weakened by rhymes in '-y' and '-eth' (the latter an archaism which, like the '-èd' participial ending, was indulged in at this stage for metrical convenience). This kind of effeminacy was also deliberately cultivated for atmosphere, as in 'Sonnet' ('Check every outflash'), rhymes and phrases in which are recollected in 'The Lotos-Eaters'. The sonnet 'Life' anticipates the 'Life piled on life Were all too little' of 'Ulysses'.

Tennyson's vatic conception of poetry, probably first inspired by Milton, persisted, though its presentation in 'The Poet's Mind' is devoid of cogency; its thought is radically second-hand, originating perhaps in Gray's 'Ode for Music' ('Hence away, 'tis holy ground!') but developed mainly from Wordsworth's 'A Poet's Epitaph'. In more confident tones and some ingenious but illogical tropes 'The Poet' offers a more Shelleyan view: the heaven-born poet is 'Dowered with the hate of hate, the scorn of scorn, The love of love'; his mission has been to fling abroad 'the wingèd shafts of truth' until the world showed like a great garden, and Freedom reigned, not by the sword but by wisdom. The pen is mightier than the sword; her right arm whirled 'But one poor poet's scroll, and with *his* word She shook the world'.

How much 'The Mystic' owed to reading, how much to visionary trance-experience, remains conjectural. Tennyson associated poetic genius with the transcendental, and pursued it to the end of his life for the re-assurance of his faith. Life with its 'wayward varycolored circumstance' is essentially formless and extrasensory. Time present, past, and future are 'three but one'; in T. S. Eliot's words, it is 'eternally present'. To the metaphysical Tennyson life is 'One shadow in the midst of a great light, One reflex from eternity on time, One mighty countenance of perfect calm'. The mystic hears 'Time flowing in the middle of the night, And all things creeping to a day of doom'; his perception extends almost to the eternal, infinite world which invests all lives. An effluence from the white flame of this region is referred to in the fragmentary dramatic monologue 'Perdidi Diem', where the speaker, commenting on the loss of a day, says he has lost 'A life, perchance an immortality'. In more thrilling verse than 'The Mystic' he describes how this effluence, God's 'sovran subtil impulse', informs first the Blessed in heaven, descends to the highest spheres ('Prompting the audible growth of great harmonious years'), then reaches the visible universe and the planets. (*In Memoriam* visualizes spiritual ascent in such a cosmogony.) In a sublunary vein of regret the speaker, to whom, as to Shelley, the soul is an eternal mystic lamp in a charnel world of death, is tormented with fruitless discontent, and likens his state to that of young ravens fallen from the nest one dim, dripping, moon-enfolded night, and calling unheard to their mother, who fails to minister 'aerial food', or win them to their wonted rest 'upon the topmost branch in air'.

In finely woven and embroidered blank verse another fragment, 'Sense and Conscience', gives an allegorical presentation of some of the 'unwaning presences' in the world of 'The Mystic'. Conscience, aware that he has not used Time's treasures as he ought, to 'embattail Spirit', recalls how he set the arch-enemy Sense in the highest offices, was drugged by his most stealthy potion, and lulled in deep shades by pleasurable flowers, music, and delicious dreams, until put to shame by Memory, who came from far. Upstarting, he fell from lack of strength, and wept tears of fire which destroyed the flowers' fragrance and golden hue. After hewing them down with his sword, he lived on bitter roots supplied by Memory, and lay sleepless on the bed of thorns which she and Pain had strown for him. Subtly wrought in detail, most of all perhaps in the full portrayal of Memory, the descriptive narrative is necessarily protracted, but its moral implications, not far removed from those of 'The Lotos-Eaters' and 'Ulysses', point the way to key passages in *Idylls of the King*.

(On the question of sense and spirit 'The Vision of Sin' provides an interesting contrast in presentation. Its subject is the expense of spirit in a waste of shame, and it was written after the exhibition of J. M. W. Turner's 'Fountain of Fallacy' in 1839. The poem is most successful in conveying the whirling measure of the sensual dance to which the youth who had proved too heavy for his winged steed succumbs, until cold, heavy mists of satiety close in on the palace of the specious fountain. God's 'awful rose of dawn' remains 'far withdrawn' and unheeded. Then, as if prophetically, another vision shows a lean grey man riding across a withered heath to a ruined inn, where he joins aged inmates in a festive 'hob-and-nob with Death'. Disillusioned and cynical, he scoffs at virtue, freedom, and utopianism, and suggests a *danse macabre*: 'Death is king, and Vivat Rex, Tread a measure on the stones, Madam – if I know your sex, From the fashion of your bones.' No one understands the answer to the cry 'Is there any hope?' as God declares Himself in 'an awful rose of dawn' on the far glimmering horizon.)

'It is not growing like a tree In bulk, doth make man better be', nor is the quality of *The Lover's Tale* to be measured by its length; 'Mariana' and 'Recollections of the Arabian Nights' have greater distinction and far more artistic unity. All in all, however, *The Lover's Tale* is Tennyson's first major work after *The Devil and the Lady*. Hallam thought him 'point-blank mad' when he withdrew it from publication in 1832. The original of 1827–8 had been revised, but a fourth part, 'The Golden Supper', was added much later, and numerous minor revisions and several reductions and omissions were made before the whole was published in 1879. Even so, the blank-verse descriptive narrative of the earlier version had much to recommend it; it was thought to be Shelleyan, but Tennyson claimed that it was written before he had 'seen a Shelley'.[4] 'Allowance must be made for redundance of youth . . . . It is rich and full . . . . The poem is the breath of young love', he said in 1868. It was based on a story (X.iv) in Boccaccio's *Il Decamerone*.

Part I tells how Julian falls in love with his foster-sister Camilla, with whom he has grown up from the cradle. So blind is his devotion that he does not realize her love for Lionel, and faints when she declares it. This narrative takes up more than half the whole work, and may at times seem unduly subtilized in thought and imagery. Tennyson's principal purpose is psychological, to present events as recalled by a lover who is highly sensitive, poetically endowed, and neither cured of his passion nor recovered from the illnesses that prostrated him after the loss of his beloved. Love, this section concludes, seeks out Memory; they tread the 'paths where Love had Walked with Hope'; and Memory feeds the soul of Love with tears. The Goddess of the Past who is summoned to the narrator's aid is the 'great Mistress of the ear and eye'. 'The Present is the vassal of the Past' and, though the lover's senses are weakened through age and sickness, what they gleaned and garnered is stored in the 'granaries of memory', dimmer sight giving memory 'a keener edge'. (Like the pines that *fledged* the hills at the opening of the poem, the 'granaries' metaphor is a borrowing from Keats: 'Ode to Psyche', and 'When I have fears that I may cease to be'.) Though he begins quietly, re-experience of the past awakens all his old feelings; flash upon flash its images come, 'Moved from the cloud of unforgotten things' that lies on the mind's horizon. Sometimes he dwells on lovesick fancies, or expresses thought in finely extended imagery. A notable feature is the sequence of Biblical images which highlight the ecstasy of love and the agony of disillusionment: a land of promise flowing with milk and honey, a Holy Land where the Temple stood; and, not far from 'The Hill of Woe', 'exceeding sorrow unto Death', 'knotted thorns through my unpaining brows', and 'the body of my past delight, Narded and swathed' and laid 'in a sepulchre of rock Never to rise again'.

Part II contains some of Tennyson's most smoothly-flowing and successful blank verse. It tells of the grief which oppresses Julian until, in his fevered dreams, he has visions of Camilla. 'Alway the inaudible invisible thought, Artificer and subject, lord and slave, Shaped by the audible and visible, Moulded the audible and visible': mind, subject to the outward world of experience, creates visions over which the individual has no control. In a vision Julian hears that Camilla is dead, and joins her funeral procession. In another, as they sit together, the light of her eyes makes him feel as if he is in prison darkness; as they gaze at a picture she had painted of a ship in a storm, an earthquake makes the ground under them reel, and they are caught up and whirled together in the storm at sea until he finds he is clutching only her phantom, which he flings away; a calm follows, and he sinks weltering in the dark. Part III, even briefer, describes how the vision of the tolling bell and funeral procession recurs, until all is metamorphosed into wedding festivities; the bride (Camilla) leaps from the hearse, and is claimed by the Lionel of Julian's first funeral vision, while he is left standing by the empty bier.

It is not clear whether Tennyson at one time, assuming that the story was known, and sufficiently conveyed through the sufferer's narrative, deemed the poem complete at this point. Though he had added Part IV by 1868, he did not choose to publish *The Lover's Tale* until a pirated version appeared. The style of the conclusion is more detached. Julian, with the marriage-bells 'echoing in ear and heart', had rushed away, unable to continue his story, which is resumed by one who befriended him in a subsequent illness. Julian stays at home until, eleven months after the marriage of Camilla and Lionel, he hears the bell tolling her death. Three days later he visits her tomb, finds her heart beating, and takes her to his mother's house. Grief had driven Lionel from home, and Julian rode away shortly before Camilla's travail began and a boy was born. After his illness, Julian returned with his friend, sent for Lionel, and prepared a great feast, at a dramatic point in which Camilla and her son were presented as the most beautiful of Julian's treasures to Lionel, whose countenance, 'glowing with the sun of life, And love, and boundless thanks', was more than the giver could bear. Julian and his friend rode away at once, with no farewell. The narrator apologizes for the lengthiness of his description and account, but his style is direct, relatively plain for the most part, and sometimes matter-of-fact. It is as if Tennyson, conscious of the emotional and imaginative excesses in which he had luxuriated during his novitiate, used this contrasting device to emphasize their dramatic validity.

8
Art and Life

Perhaps Tennyson noted what W. J. Fox wrote in his 1831 review of *Poems, Chiefly Lyrical*, 'A genuine poet has deep responsibilities to his country and the world, to the present and future generations, to earth and heaven', and in this spirit wrote his prefatory sonnet 'Mine be the strength of spirit' to *Poems*, published at the end of 1832. The reference to town and tower, and the hope that he will win the wise suggest that he did, but the evidence is blurred and outweighed by the imagery. Several poems in the volume show that he heeded such advice, and its successes indicate considerable poetic advance.

Other poems manifest an interest in a variety of subjects on which he was unable to attain, or maintain, significant heights. From the time it was ridiculed by Croker 'O Darling Room' has amused readers by its sickly exquisiteness; it reads so much like parody that its earnestness has been doubted. The morbid fancy of 'My life is full of weary days', though disburdened of most of its concluding nonsense, still ends with the melancholic's wish to know, when his friend visits his grave, whether the woodbines are in bloom. The *taedium vitae* of the poem may be feigned, but 'Sonnet', with its daring rather than expletory use of 'human' in the first line ('Alas! how weary are my human eyes'), suggests that the poet's depression was frequent and not short-lived.

His libertarian sentiments in 1830 found expression in two sonnets prompted by the Polish uprising against the Russians. 'Sonnet' ('Blow ye the trumpet') is marked by an orotundity of style in keeping with the rousing appeal with which it opens; 'Poland' directs scorn against the oppressor. Neither has the sustaining power to end strongly; the second has a patched-up conclusion. Recourse to fine-sounding names which characterizes the former adds to the Miltonic style of 'Alexander', perhaps a greater achievement in sonnet form, although it fails to reach a satisfying finality in substance. 'Woe to the double-tongued' is more effective; the humbug of political demagogy in England ('the land's disease'), ready to create civil strife for selfish ends, stirs unfailing invective.

'The Sisters' ('We were two daughters of one race') excels in form; its sharp, curt style befits a ballad in which the revenge-seeker has only one intention. The crescendo of the wind in one refrain excites anticipation; the other leads up to a rare, relentless irony. 'Forlorn', a much later ballad, forms an interesting contrast. Its rhythm and repetition help to express its subject, the maddening torment of a woman torn between conflicting temptations to conceal her shame in either suicide or marriage. The heartlessness of the first poem and the psychological realism of the second are in rapport with their art forms. One is traditional in subject; the other, modern.

'The May Queen' is in a different key; at first it succeeds in conveying excitement and piping notes, but its rhythmical see-saw and the long reiteration of its refrain inevitably tend to excite ridicule. The tones of the New Year sequel, with its antithetical frost and flowerlessness, are a little more subdued (not 'You must wake' and 'Effie shall go' but 'If you're waking'), though the dying girl has lost none of her decision ('You'll bury me, my mother, just beneath the hawthorn shade'). Her directing self-possession and unnatural primness are part of the emotional engineering within a situation which anticipates lying lonely in the grave when the flowers and swallows return. So pathetically appealing was the poem that Tennyson added a more Victorian conclusion for publication in 1842. The May Queen blesses the clergyman who has brought her peace, and speaks kindly of Robin, whose love she affected to despise in the days of her pride. Death is far sweeter to her than life, and she looks forward to the home of the blessed where the wicked cease from troubling; there she will be joined by her mother, her sister Effie, and by the clergyman. 'The May Queen' was, it seems, Tennyson's first effort to use poetic talent for the comfort and assurance of the public; never again did he administer so mawkishly to its sentimental piety.

The passionate hypersensitiveness of 'Fatima' (an oriental name with no particular reference) is Sapphic, and the lover's frustration ('I *will* possess him or will die') differs markedly from that of the forlorn heroine in 'Mariana in the South'. The latter poem occurred to Tennyson when he was in the Pyrenees with Arthur Hallam, who described it as a kind of pendant to 'Mariana', and found in Sappho 'much congeniality to Alfred's peculiar powers' of transmitting a mood through external circumstances. In the same stanzaic form as its predecessor, 'Mariana in the South' presents the same human situation. It is more fluent and melodious; its deserted lover is Catholic, and the setting, exotic and more colourful. Instead of the poplar we have 'a sick willow sere and small' that shrinks in the steady glare; the empty river-bed becomes dusty-white; and a blinding wall builds up a furnace of heat. An image seems to pass the door within, raising Mariana's hopes, but a black shadow accompanies the house by day, and rounds to the east as the sun declines. A dry cicala sings. She flings back the lattice-blind, and leans over the balcony as 'large Hesper' glitters on her tears. Night deepens, and she thinks of the night that knows no morn.

Pyrenean scenery supplied imagery for the setting of 'Oenone', where another forlorn one calls repeatedly on Mount Ida, above Troy, to hearken ere she dies. (The recurrence of the refrain throughout is too prolonged to have the effect a similar mode has in 'Mariana'; rather the reverse. Tennyson cited Theocritus in justification, and the poem is steeped in classical expression.) Oenone's fate turns on Paris's choice of Aphrodite as the fairest of the three goddesses; in token thereof he presents her the apple of discord, and she promises him the most beautiful and loving wife in Greece. Left disconsolate after her desertion by Paris, the mountain nymph is filled with fiery thoughts, which are as yet hardly defined. She will discuss them in Troy with the wild Cassandra, who is haunted by a fiery vision and the sound of armed men. (Cassandra is warned of Troy's destruction; Oenone dimly foresees her own self-immolation on the funeral pyre of Paris, as in the Greek tradition which is the subject of Tennyson's late poem 'The Death of Oenone'.) When she begins the narrative of her lost happiness, her *taedium vitae* is reflected in a scene similar to that of 'Mariana in the South': the grasshopper is silent, the lizard rests like a shadow (the inactive cicala of the 1832 text was omitted), the winds are dead . . . 'I alone awake.' How different when she observed the goddesses' arrival, and 'the crocus brake like fire, Violet, amaracus, and asphodel, Lotos and lilies'; and a wind arose, causing the wandering ivy and the vine above to riot premonitorily. Hera offered power, and Paris was tempted; cold, observant, and angry, Pallas declared that self-reverence, self-knowledge, and self-control alone lead life to 'sovereign power', and that her wisdom would help him through shocks, dangers, and deeds, strengthening endurance with action, and making his will in all experience accord with the pure law' which brings 'perfect freedom'; then (in the most pictorial passage of all) Venus moved seductively towards Paris, and whispered her beguiling promise. Devastation in Oenone is imaged in the felling of the pines 'that plumed the craggy ledge High over the blue gorge, and all between The snowy peak and snow-white cataract Fostered the callow eaglet'. Never again will she see them swept through by the morning mist, or overlaid by 'narrow moon-lit slips of silver cloud Between the loud stream and the trembling stars'. The passion she feels for Paris in her jealousy has its Sapphic intensity; it was first awakened when, in apprehension of Aphrodite's wiles, she urged her lover to give the prize to Pallas.

'The Hesperides' emphasizes the strength of Tennyson's vatic belief in poetic inspiration; it is comparable to Coleridge's in 'Kubla Khan': 'Weave a circle round him thrice, And close your eyes with holy dread, For he on honey-dew hath fed, And drunk the milk of Paradise.' The poetic visions of the past which filled the earth with loveliness (in 'Timbuctoo') flung strange music, and odours of Paradise, on the winds. On the western coast of Africa such music was heard by Hanno, coming like voices in a dream from the Hesperides. In varied measures Tennyson's incantatory repetitions weave their spell. The golden apple which is to be guarded is the treasure of intuitive wisdom which has been hoarded through the ages. Sunset-ripened in the west, it is watched over by Hesper, the evening star; he and his three singing daughters and the dragon form the golden chain round the golden tree. Danger comes from the 'cool east light'; 'Hesper hateth Phosphor, evening hateth morn'. The implications are not inconsistent with those of 'The Poet's Mind' and 'The Poet'. The cool light of reason is inimical to the wonder and mystery of life; philosophy will clip an angel's wings, as Keats wrote. The wisdom which is beyond analytical knowledge and invested with 'awful mystery' must be guarded for the benefit of mankind. 'If the golden apple be taken, The world will be overwise'; wise in its conceit, it will suffer from hubris and shallowness.

Images such as those of 'Inscription by a Brook', 'the lady ash' fitfully sweeping 'her yellow keys' with twinkling finger, and 'Full fields of barley shifting tearful lights On growing spears', illustrate Tennyson's quick response to recurring beauty of detail in English landscapes. 'The Ruined Kiln' blends Keatsian impressions – filmy stubbles warm and bare, October sleeping on his sheaf – with gossamers twinkling into green and gold, dappled cloudlets, and sparrows in a jangling throng. 'The Progress of Spring' is more ambitious, rich with rapid evocations ('The groundflame of the crocus breaks the mould', 'The starling claps his tiny castanets'), but less successful when, after whispering of the balm she brings from the South, Spring speaks with prosaic lapses of working old laws of Love to 'fresh results' in flowers, and urges man to wed his soul with hers, that she may mark 'new developments, whatever spark Be struck from out the clash of warring wills'. The poet reflects on the greater sanity of man were he to accept Spring's gradual process, but the verse labours to accommodate dwindling thought to a large stanzaic mould.

'The Miller's Daughter' is alive with details of an English scene (no particular one, though it is near the wolds: 'if I thought at all of any mill it was that of Trumpington near Cambridge', Tennyson wrote). Literary influences have been suggested (that of Mary Mitford's 'The Queen of the Meadow' must have been minimal), but the subject is largely imaginary, and the setting is subsidiary to the thoughts, recollections, and character of one who in serene age has few regrets about his past. The poem reaches its central point of recall when the narrator describes how he, the squire's orphan, was wakened from a day-dream by a leaping trout, as he angled in the higher pool by the mill-house, and caught sight of a beautiful reflection like a warm, wavering sunbeam in the dark, dimpled beck. Looking up, he saw the miller's daughter leaning from the casement, and fell wholly in love with her there and then. Before he dared declare his love, he would come down from the wold and haunt the mill, listening to the groan of the brook beneath it or observing the white hillside chalk-quarry gleam fitfully to the flying moon. The 1842 text contains a more convincing, less poetically fallacious, account of their wooing. The first of two songs presented to Alice by the squire's son is quite traditional but one of Tennyson's best; the second was so empty and rhyme-ridiculous that it was replaced by one hardly in keeping with the youthful donor but more consonant with the setbacks that life was to bring. Despite the loss of their child (on which the poet is fastidiously vague), mutual love was strengthened. The poem is rounded, at the opening, with a memory of the last miller which, expressing the narrator's admiration ('a soul So full of summer warmth, so glad, So healthy') sets the tone of the whole, and, at the end, with a proposal from the squire to his wife that they walk across the wolds to the old mill. This is the first of Tennyson's English idylls; there is nothing mawkish in it, as in 'The May Queen'. It expresses a sensitive, manly genuineness, and it ends, not with regrets, but with forward-looking action, 'Where Past and Present, wound in one, Do make a garland for the heart'.

'The Miller's Daughter' is a remarkable accomplishment, for its author felt less imaginatively at home in contemporary life than in the classical world, the historic past, and the glories of art and literature. 'Tennyson, we cannot live in art', R. C. Trench said when they were at Trinity, and his words struck deep. The poet's dilemma is projected in at least two leading poems of his 1832 volume. He prefaced 'The Palace of Art', the more ambitious of these, with a brief introductory poem to Trench, asserting that every kind of Beauty, including those of Good and Knowledge, is a snare if its love becomes so engrossing that it excludes love of one's fellow-men. (Later he showed in no uncertain manner the same attitude towards religion.) Like other Apostles who ardently supported this view, he was probably influenced by Shelley's *Queen Mab* (ii.59–64): 'But, were it virtue's only meed, to dwell In a celestial palace, all resigned To pleasurable impulses, immured Within the prison of itself, the will Of changeless Nature would be unfulfilled. Learn to make others happy.' In what follows the shortened and revised 1842 version of Tennyson's poem is observed; one omitted passage stressed the moral non-commitment of the aesthete equally devoted to every form of beauty. The palace is a pleasure-house for the soul, who reigns there alone, high up above the world. Its many rooms, 'each a perfect whole From living Nature', supply nurture for every mood. Some are hung with tapestries:

> One seemed all dark and red – a tract of sand,
>   And some one pacing there alone,
> Who paced for ever in a glimmering land,
>   Lit with a low large moon.

The numerous pictures include presentations of St Cecily, Arthur ('mythic Uther's deeply-wounded son'), classical subjects, and 'every legend fair Which the supreme Caucasian mind Carved out of Nature for itself'. Portraits of the wise hang round the royal dais, and all parts of the palace are artistically adorned. The soul rejoices to feel 'Lord over Nature, Lord of the visible earth, Lord of the senses five'; her 'God-like isolation' makes her indifferent whether the world is at peace or war, and superior to the prurient, torpid swine on the plain. At the height of her intellectual pride, God strikes her with despair, 'lest she should fail or perish utterly'. Fear and horror reduce her to a state of helpless stagnation; she is like a star apart, unmoved by the hollow orb of Circumstance which is 'rolled round by one fixed law' (Tennyson's note indicates that Circumstance alludes to both life and the outer sphere of the Ptolemaic universe), or like

A still salt pool, locked in with bars of sand,
  Left on the shore; that hears all night
The plunging seas draw backward from the land
  Their moon-led waters white.

Exiled from God, she hates life and death, time and eternity. After four tomblike years, she flings away her royal robes, and is ready to accept life in a cottage below. Whether by chance or design, this ending is ambiguous: 'with others' *probably* signifies no second divorce from life. The best features of the poem are its stanzaic form and vignettes of the kind illustrated above.

Although the title and some of the story were of Italian origin, the crux of 'The Lady of Shalott' (the web-mirror curse theme) was introduced by Tennyson, who later declared that, had he been aware of the Maid of Astolat story in Malory, his poem would probably not have been shaped as it was. His lady lives apart, enisled and embowered, weaving by night and day a magic web with the colours suggested by the outside world which she sees in a mirror. (The Lady of Shalott image in Lawrence's earlier novels connotes merely the self-seeing, self-conscious one.) Though 'half sick of shadows' when she sees a reflection of two young lovers, she is afraid of a curse if she looks at the outer reality. The flashing appearance of Sir Lancelot in the mirror has such vitalizing effect that she springs to the window, and sees his burning helmet and plume as he rides down to Camelot. The web flies out and floats away, the mirror is cracked from side to side, and she feels the curse of death upon her. Like 'The Palace of Art', the poem contains enough artistry to indicate Tennyson's urge to write poetry entirely for art's sake. The inadequacies of the 'weaving' are aesthetically presented in the correlatives of a story so imaginatively integrated that it confirms the conviction with which it was devised. The 1832 ending lacks the finish and human touch of its revised form, but the

Philistine failure to understand the message which it conveys ('*The web was woven curiously, The charm is broken utterly*') has great relevance. 'Sir Launcelot and Queen Guinevere' (with the song 'Life of my Life within my blood') is all that survives of an intended companion-piece in the same stanza. Guinevere seems part of the joyous spring, and skims the plain on her mule more fleetly than 'she whose elfin prancer springs By night to eery warblings, When all the glimmering moorland rings With jingling bridle-reins'. The words impart crescendo to the sound effects. There is no hint of shadows to come; a man would give everything to 'waste his whole heart in one kiss Upon her perfect lips'.

Great actions of the past, whatever their origin, maintain their appeal because they present life at a higher, more intense pitch than the contemporary world. So Tennyson thought, it seems, when he began 'A Dream of Fair Women'. He imagined himself a balloonist lifted high above the world of the present; detached, but seeing the whole in true perspective. The incongruity of contemporaneities and his higher subject, as well as (one suspects) some problem with his imagery, made him jettison this opening. The verse, almost in the stanzaic mould of 'The Palace of Art', runs more freely, as when the subject, arising from thoughts on Chaucer's *The Legend of Fair Women*, is introduced: 'In every land I saw, wherever light illumineth, Beauty and anguish walking hand in hand The downward slope to death.' The poet hears 'sounds of insult, shame, and wrong, And trumpets blown for wars'. He starts, resolved to do noble things; but sleep bears him down, and he dreams he has wandered far into an old still wood (the world of ancient time), where the fragrance of violets recalls a period when he was innocent and joyful. The heroines whose woe he hears are Helen and Iphigenia, Cleopatra, Jephthah's daughter, then (very briefly) Rosamond, Queen Eleanor's victim. Before he can see others, dawn wakes him, and he observes Venus regnant in the east. His ineffectual struggle to return to his dream-world is the subject of a conclusion which is less felicitously conceived and expressed than the noble strain of 'The balmy moon of blessèd Israel Floods all the deep-blue gloom with beams divine' with its accompanying simile:

> As one that museth where broad sunshine laves
> 　　The lawn by some cathedral, through the door
> Hearing the holy organ rolling waves
> 　　Of sound on roof and floor

Within, and anthem sung, is charmed and tied
   To where he stands, – so stood I, when that flow
Of music left the lips of her that died
   To save her father's vow.

'The Lotos-Eaters' – based on a passage in Homer's *Odyssey* (ix) –
hints at more potent influences through its Spenserian stanza (cf.
The Faerie Queene, I.i.41 and ix.40, and Thomson's *The Castle of
Indolence*, I.v–vi). The languid air of the enchanting land to which
Ulysses' weary sailors come is subtly conveyed; rhythmic sleight
makes it affect the image of the waterfall, which seems to pause in its
descent; 'all things always seemed the same'. The recurrence of
'seem' or 'seemed' emphasizes a land of illusion. As soon as the
opiate affects a sailor,

        to him the gushing of the wave
Far far away did seem to mourn and rave
On alien shores; and if his fellow spake,
His voice was thin, as voices from the grave;
And deep asleep he seemed, yet all awake,
And music in his ears his beating heart did make.

The enhancement of dream-distancing impressions in these lines,
chiefly through a succession of long 'a's and 'e's, illustrates the finer
auditory effects by which, more than by its captivating pictorial
images, the poem makes an appeal in perfect accord with its *dolce far
niente* subject. The alternations of the Choric Song indicate the
dilemma of Ulysses' men, worn out, spiritless, prone to seek
justification for a life of sensual ease with total abandonment of
responsibilities. Improvements were made for the 1842 edition,
principally the addition of the sixth section of the Choric Song,
where the guilt of family recollections leads to further excuse-
mongering, and the revision of the eighth, where the ideal of the
indolent defeatist is to lie on the hills like the Epicurean gods of
Lucretius (whose amenities are part of the gift promised by Hera to
Paris in 'Oenone'), self-indulgent but indifferent to the wars and
suffering of mortals. 'The Lotos-Eaters' presents an attitude to life in
a dual correlative, one part legendary and descriptive, the second
generalized (possibly with an allusion to contemporary England in
section vi) and rhetorically dramatic; by implication but only
incidentally it impugns the 'Eat, drink, and be merry, for tomorrow

we die' philosophy. To associate the poem with the aesthetic lure of an imaginative world which evades reality seems both arbitrary and redundant.

'To J. S.' is the first of those sincere epistles in which Tennyson turned his thoughts and feelings with apparent ease into the medium of verse. It was written to comfort James Spedding after the loss of his brother. The poet alludes to his own father's death, but Spedding's loss is rarer, for 'this star Rose with you through a little arc Of heaven': 'A man more pure and bold and just Was never born into the earth.' Tennyson will not give the usual advice or reflection; when he attempts to console, he admits failure. His best lines are reserved for the dead:

> Sleep sweetly, tender heart, in peace:
>   Sleep, holy spirit, blessèd soul.
> While the stars burn, the moons increase,
>   And the great ages onward roll.
>
> Sleep till the end, true soul and sweet,
>   Nothing comes to thee new or strange.
> Sleep full of rest from head to feet;
>   Lie still, dry dust, secure of change.

9
Darkness and Living Light

Tennyson's disdain for the life to oneself, for oneself, without regard to the outside world, is nowhere more graphically presented than in the dramatic monologue 'St Simeon Stylites'. The satire is not directed against an individual (Charles Simeon of Cambridge has been suggested) but against the exalted egoism of those who, like St John Rivers in *Jane Eyre* or Becket in *Murder in the Cathedral*, act, or are tempted to act, for their own eternal glory. St Simeon is a more extreme type; he has no concern for others. He would like to think he is an example, and that he has been given a power of miraculous healing through which God has reaped a harvest in him, thereby increasing his chance of being crowned a saint in Heaven. His earthly glory is anticipated when the people who believe in his miraculous power flock round his pillar and hail him as a saint. He does not live for them; they are 'foolish'. His steadfast withdrawal from the world for his own ends is imaged in the aerial isolation which he has increased with the years.

The situation is grimly comical, almost grotesque at times, as Tennyson's reading of the poem indicated, according to FitzGerald. St Simeon is a humbug who exaggerates his sins on the assumption that the more he repents the surer his chance of eternal happiness. All is extreme: he is the basest of mankind; he *batters* the gates of heaven with *storms* of prayer; if his afflictions were increased ten-hundredfold they would weigh ten-hundredfold less on him than his sins had done. His mental stocktaking of his self-inflicted sufferings and life-denials is statistical, as if he were building up credit or insurance for the life to come. It is not the asceticism (repulsive at times) that is condemned, but the self-importance and assumed deserts of this miserable sinner. While God and the saints in heaven enjoy themselves, and men on earth, and even the beasts, have their comforts, he virtuously denies himself and bows down twelve hundred times a day to Christ, the Virgin Mary, and the saints. If he is not to be saved, nobody deserves to be; nobody has suffered more (or more ludicrously, the poem suggests). Martyrs died only one death; his life is a protracted dying; if he had known a way of making it more slowly painful, he would have followed it. God knows he is not responsible for being called a saint by silly people, but he has endured more than 'many just and holy men, whose names Are registered and calendared for saints'. He tells the people below that Pontius and Iscariot were seraphs compared with him, and that they should mortify their flesh to escape devilish appetites as he has done. God has made him 'an example to mankind, Which few can reach to'. His senses begin to fail; he has a tantalizing vision of an angel holding out a crown, and implores the saints not to let him be fooled. Precise to the end, he announces (after calling for a priest to administer the sacrament) that he will die at quarter to twelve that night. Finally he asks God to aid 'this foolish people', by letting them take example (undoubtedly from himself). Tennyson's carica-ture indicates a warped, self-distorting fanaticism. 'The man whose eye Is ever on himself doth look on one, The least of Nature's works', Wordsworth wrote.

In spirit and texture 'St Agnes' Eve' provides a splendid contrast: 'Make Thou my spirit pure and clear As are the frosty skies . . . . As these white robes are soiled and dark, To yonder shining ground; As this pale taper's earthly spark, To yonder argent round; So shows my soul before the Lamb.' Humility and fervour harmonize with bright purity of imagery, and the dramatic lyric ends in ecstatic expectation. 'Sir Galahad', intended as 'something of a male counterpart', has less unity, and is marred by didactic self-righteousness: 'My strength is as the strength of ten, Because my soul is pure'; 'I never felt the kiss of love, No maiden's hand in mine. . . . Me mightier transports move and thrill; So keep I fair through faith and prayer A virgin heart in work and will.' It hardly reaches a climactic ending, but soars midway with the vision of the Holy Grail: 'Ah, blessèd vision! blood of God! My spirit beats her mortal bars, As down dark tides the glory slides, And star-like mingles with the stars.'

'The Two Voices' was most probably completed before Hallam's death. It is not another 'Supposed Confessions' on the loss of Christian faith; nor is it a morbid suicidal poem, though it contains persistent arguments against the worthwhileness of life. Some of its thought was familiar from Cambridge debates; some sprang from

Tennyson's own depression; some may have come from Hallam, who thought of suicide. Compared with the dragon-fly, is man a wonderful organism? Does not the whole universe contain a superior species? In the long slow process of the race, would the loss of an individual, however unique, be significant? Could seeking refuge in death be felt as dishonour, since death is the end of awareness, and the dead are soon forgotten? The rhyme-scheme and end-stopped lines strengthen the insistency of the argument. Knowledge gives the devil's advocate ample scope, but after a while the interest develops more deeply on the positive side, which depends less on reasoning than on intuition, experience, and feeling. Youth has hopes of sowing 'some generous seed, Fruitful of further thought and deed', and of living, even dying, not selfishly, but for some good cause. The inner debate anticipates *In Memoriam*, the one who seeks the 'springs of life', 'the law within the law', knowing full well that 'age to age succeeds, Blowing a noise of tongues and deeds, A dust of systems and of creeds'. Death is not the end, for beyond the world of the senses one is aware of the Perfect and Eternal towards which life labours. Mystic gleams of a pre-existence run counter to the idea of mere finiteness, suggesting a spiritual progress from state to state (as in *In Memoriam*). Then comes the absolute of experience:

'Whatever crazy sorrow saith,
No life that breathes with human breath
Has ever truly longed for death.

''Tis life, whereof our nerves are scant,
Oh life, not death, for which we pant;
More life, and fuller, that I want.'

The conclusion of the poem may have been influenced by that of 'The Ancient Mariner'. The speaker's recovery of faith in life is indicated by his instinctive blessing of the happy family among the churchgoers. The grounds for this faith cannot be explained; it comes from a hidden hope (and this essentially is all the second voice can say; it is no more than a little whisper, but it is silver-clear). Spiritual resurgence is expressed not merely in words and vernal flowers, but in the flow of the verse, freed at last from the constrictions of reasoning doubt. If making 'a happy fire-side clime To weans and wife' is 'the true pathos and sublime Of human life', Tennyson's Sabbath scene is not sentimental. The power that breaks from a sullen heart to feel, 'although no tongue can prove', that 'every cloud, that spreads above And veileth love, itself is love' foreshadows the crucial 'I have felt' of *In Memoriam*. 'The Two Voices' presents a resolution of questioning which probably helped Tennyson to accept Hallam's death with a degree of philosophical calm. He could not have dismissed his sorrow as 'crazy' at the end of 1833.

A renewal of spirit through Nature, such as we find at the end of 'The Two Voices', is sought in 'From sorrow sorrow yet is born', which could have been written shortly after Hallam's death, as was 'On a Mourner'. Nature in the latter poem, as in Wordsworth, is seen to live and love everywhere, bringing recovery to the heart until the sorrower inclines to the 'one wide Will'; Hope and Memory are united in love, and Faith comes with Virtue (moral strength) and a promise of empire, such as greeted 'Troy's wandering prince' at dead of night, 'so that he rose With sacrifice, while all the fleet Had rest by stony hills of Crete'. Aeneas's determination is expressed in the elevating emphasis of 'rose' and in the sound of the concluding words, and the question arises how comparable his spirit is with that of the ageing hero in 'Ulysses', which was written, according to Tennyson, soon after his friend's death, and with a greater feeling of his loss than many poems in *In Memoriam*.

How much 'Ulysses' and 'St Simeon Stylites', the latter particularly, stimulated the development of Browning's monologues is a matter for conjecture. 'Ulysses' could have been at an embryonic stage before Hallam's death; its incipience is antithetically evident in 'The Lotos-Eaters'. Several of its principal features originate from Dante's *Inferno* (xxvi.90ff.): the departure by night, the overpowering of domestic affections by the urge for knowledge or discovery of the untravelled world, the scorn (like Hamlet's) for a brute ('bovine' or 'vegetable') existence, and Ulysses' regard for virtue (manly resolve) and intelligence. Some critics take umbrage that zeal for new experience makes him impatient with life at home and the administering of unequal laws to a race whom he describes as 'savage'. He cannot help it: 'that which we are, we are'; old age impels him to travel while he can. His son Telemachus is better qualified by temperament to forward the slow process of civilization. Ulysses does not undervalue his work, or speak condescendingly of it; he prefers a more exciting life, and belongs, like Columbus and Sir John Franklin, to the equally worthy, but more heroic, group of those driven to adventure and exploration, whatever their fate. How much of Tennyson is implicit in this poem? It 'gave my feeling about the need of going forward, and braving the struggle of life perhaps more simply than anything in "In Memoriam" ', he wrote. In this respect it echoes 'The Two Voices'; the resolution not to yield to the blows of chance springs from the thirst for 'More life, and fuller'. The metaphorical significance is higher, like that of 'Merlin and the Gleam': 'all experience is an arch wherethrough Gleams that untravelled world' the non-finite margin of which 'fades For ever and for ever when I move'; like the mystic gleams of 'The Two Voices', the knowledge sought is 'Beyond the utmost bound of human thought'. 'The long day wanes' like the darkening days of 'Morte d'Arthur'; 'the deep Moans round with many voices'. Yet, despite the sorrow, emphasis is on 'work of noble note' that 'may yet be done'. The possibility of reaching the Happy Isles and seeing 'the great Achilles, whom we knew' hints at the poet's dearest hope that he and Hallam would meet in the world to come.

'Life piled on life Were all too little . . . .' 'Tithon', composed about the same time as 'Ulysses', and originally intended as a pendant to it, expresses the plight of one to whom an unnatural immortality was given. Like the Struldbrugs in *Gulliver's Travels* (III.x), Tithonus was not endowed with perpetuity of youth. No longer is he enraptured in the arms of Aurora, the dawn goddess; he lives in everlasting pain, knowing enjoyment only through memory. The persistence of her brightening at dawn, and Tithonus's recollection of their love, his mortal frame molten in her immortal, while her lips that dealt him kisses 'balmier than opening buds' moved 'In wild and airy whisperings more sweet Than that strange song I heard Apollo sing, While Ilion like a mist rose into towers', are a recurrent torment. He wishes the hours, her ministers, would carry him swiftly from the cold light of the east and lap him 'deep within the lonely west'; better still, if he could be restored to earth. 'Why should a man desire in any shape To vary from his kind, or beat the roads Of life, beyond the goal of ordinance Where all should pause, as is most meet for all?' The lament with which the poem opens may have an intended ambivalence; it may express the poet's grief for Hallam, but dominantly it is Tithonus's regret that he has been debarred from the natural cycle of life:

Ay me! ay me! the woods decay and fall,
The vapours weep their substance to the ground,
Man comes and tills the earth and lies beneath,
And after many summers dies the rose.
Me only fatal immortality
Consumes: I wither slowly in thine arms . . . .

The key word is 'fatal': Tennyson looks forward (as 'The Two Voices' and 'Ulysses' suggest in advance of *In Memoriam* and 'Wages') to an immortality that is active and progressive. The poem, in its revised, slightly extended, and more familiar form ('Tithonus', with 'swan' for 'rose'), did not appear until 1860.

Most of 'Tiresias', another dramatic monologue, was written about the same time as 'Ulysses'; the final paragraph, following closely a passage in Pindar, one of his favourite poets, and added much later, was quoted by Tennyson as a 'sample of his blank verse'. The Theban prophet had sought truth and scaled 'the highest of the heights With some strange hope to see the nearer God' until, after following a torrent to a secret olive glade, he saw the nakedness of Pallas Athene, and for his offence was stricken blind and plagued with prophecy that was never heeded. His power of seeing Truth came from the higher Beauty he had perceived. Nobody regarded his warnings:

Who ever turned upon his heel to hear
My warning that the tyranny of one
Was prelude to the tyranny of all?
My counsel that the tyranny of all
Led backward to the tyranny of one?

It is as if the poet who proclaimed that Freedom 'shook the world' through the medium of one poor poet's scroll is disillusioned. An evil generation seeks a sign; and Tiresias persuades Menoeceus to sacrifice his life in atonement for the curse which his ancestor Cadmus brought on Thebes by offending the war-god Ares. In this world 'Virtue must shape itself in deed', and Tiresias, old, incapacitated, and ignored, wishes he were gathered to his rest, mingling with the kings of old, where 'the wise man's word, Here trampled by the populace underfoot', is 'crowned with worship'. There he will find the men he knew (a hint of Hallam), and strive again for glory. The paganism of 'Tiresias' expresses Tennyson's belief in spiritual progress after death, and his will to turn his gifts to the benefit of mankind, despite the realization that higher and fundamental truths are likely to be ignored by the majority of one's countrymen.

Though the reference to twelve books with 'faint Homeric echoes' in its apologetic framework ('The Epic') is fictional, 'Morte d'Arthur' seems to have been designed as a part of a work which might have been continued before the inception of *Idylls of the King* had Tennyson received the encouragement he would have liked. Its wider imaginative implications (the change from Malory's summer to winter, for instance) were such that he was able to incorporate it in the final book of the *Idylls* with no more than the substitution of 'So' for 'And' and the omission of a line made redundant by the new context. The opening line, 'So all day long the noise of battle rolled', suggests an epic continuation at least as heroic as that recalled in 'Ulysses' by 'Far on the ringing plains of windy Troy'. One of Tennyson's most finished works, 'Morte d'Arthur' accommodates classicisms and archaisms with ease; its blank-verse rhythms vary dramatically in speech and in descriptions which are fully accord-ant to action and scene. In wealth of pictorial and sound effects, its splendours range from the sparkling brilliance of Excalibur to the 'long glories' of the winter moon above the level lake, the serenity of this scene giving sudden antithesis to the clash of Bedivere's armour among echoing cliffs, as he makes his way along 'juts of slippery crag' that ring 'Sharp-smitten with the dint of armèd heels'. Much was drawn from Malory in expression as well as in substance, but the finest effects are Tennyson's, the shriek of the queens becoming hauntingly evocative:

A cry that shivered to the tingling stars,
And, as it were one voice, an agony
Of lamentation, like a wind, that shrills
All night in a waste land, where no one comes,
Or hath come, since the making of the world.

'Merlin and the Gleam' shows that Tennyson had Hallam's death in mind when he wrote this epic scene or epyllion: 'Arthur had vanished I knew not whither, The king who loved me, And cannot die.' Bedivere speaks for the poet: 'the days darken round me'. The shock of Hallam's death to the Apostles is alluded to in the dissolution of the Round Table, and the inscrutability of fate, in

'God fulfils himself in many ways'. Arthur's remarks on the efficacy of prayer arise from Ulyssean sentiments: 'For what are men better than sheep or goats That nourish a blind life within the brain, If, knowing God, they lift not hands of prayer . . . ?' 'The Epic' ends with Christmas bells that, like those in *In Memoriam* (cvi), ring out war and ring in peace.

In the delights of creative artistry such as that of 'Morte d'Arthur', as well as in the 'measured language' of those brief elegies with which *In Memoriam* began, Tennyson was able to numb his sorrow and bring relief to 'the unquiet heart and brain'. 'Over the dark world flies the wind' almost certainly expresses his distress at the time, and conforms strikingly to the pattern of *In Memoriam* poems where feelings are externalized in the natural scene. The disguise is faint in 'Oh! that 'twere possible', after its rather unsatisfactory extension for inclusion in *The Tribute*. The poet is haunted by a shadow, and the fact that it is 'Not thou, but like to thee' makes him cry out, 'Ah God! that it were possible For one short hour to see The souls we loved, that they might tell us What and where they be."[5] He sees the shadow in the 'silent woody places' around his birthplace; it haunts him in the great city, and makes him half-dream of meeting and happy laughter on the morrow, only for him to find in the shuddering dawn that the 'abiding phantom' is cold.

Greater detachment and creative artistry are achieved in 'Break, break, break', which was 'made in a Lincolnshire lane at 5 o'clock in the morning between blossoming hedges'. Sorrow has sunk deep, but it can be contemplated with the degree of tranquillity which is necessary for poetic achievement of a high order. The mellifluousness of Tennyson's lyrics is apt to lull critical perception, general impressions being formed without regard for detail. 'Break, break, break' works mainly by parallel and contrasting thoughts. The heartbreak sounded by the sea, at the end as well as at the beginning, remains, but life around goes on unchanged, in childhood, youth, and later years. The fisherman's boy shouts with his sister as they play on the shore; the sailor lad sings in his boat; ships continue their course, but the thought of their disappearance (over the horizon imagined behind the hill) makes the poet think of a vanished hand he would love to touch. The breaking of the sea is comparable in its persistence to the dissolution of all efforts to express his 'deeper anguish' (*In Memoriam*, xix). The 'cold gray stones' at the foot of its crags convey the feelings of nature's indifference towards human deprivation, and 'the tender grace of a day that is dead' remains irrecoverable. Finality is accepted.

Higher resolves are the subject of 'Youth' and 'The Voyage', the first a poem of 1833, the second probably of 1836. The poet recalls youth first as a period when he looked forward; then, of grief at departed joys. He has reached a point of irresolution, uncertain whether to turn his thoughts backward or forward. His maiden thought (in Keats's words) is becoming darkened. Then, as in *In Memoriam* (cxxviii), he is aware of 'An energy, an agony, A labour working to an end', and the urge comes to participate in the heroic struggle of mankind. The ending of 'The Two Voices' is revived; as he climbs in the storm towards the morning sun, a rainbow shines, shadows fly, and the green fields below are seen as 'realms of Love'. Then, as clouds clear, godlike figures are revealed 'Rayed round with beams of living light' on a mountain that gleams with triple peaks.[6] 'The Voyage' expresses his new joy and resolution. The mariners also make their way towards the sun; tackle and sail sing in the breeze. At night the moon and stars shine. At times, in warmer climes, the whole sea burns, or they tear the dark with 'wakes of fire'. A Vision flees beyond the waste waters, and they follow in hope to gain upon her. Sometimes she is lost; sometimes she appears 'Like Virtue firm, like Knowledge fair'; now she crowns the sea like Heavenly Hope, or (and this recalls 'The Poet') bears the blade of Liberty with 'bloodless point reversed'. Only one sailor is daunted; his eyes are dim. 'A ship of fools', he sneers, then weeps, before casting himself overboard one stormy night. Sails are never furled, nor is an anchor dropped; whatever the clime, the ship drives on until its crew are old, physically infirm, yet undefeated in purpose: 'We know the merry world is round, And we may sail for evermore.' The allegory is patent: testifying to Tennyson's recovered faith in life, even beyond death, it recalls 'Ulysses' and anticipates 'Merlin and the Gleam'.

10

English Idylls

Tennyson's bias towards classical and Arthurian subjects was strong. For this reason, and in response to the advice of friends, he made resolute efforts as he matured to direct his poetry towards his contemporary world. Having no great work in hand for long intervals, he was often contented with sketches or with poems of more patent narrative unity. The subject and design of some of the former were suggested by idylls of Theocritus, who had also presented scenes of contemporary life. The term 'idyll' has been used with liberality of convenience by some critics of Tennyson; here it implies a short, finely wrought presentation of life, usually rural in background; it may be predominantly descriptive or narrative. Combining these two elements with reflection and excellence of form, 'The Miller's Daughter' is a much better example of the genre than 'The May Queen', which is tripartite and episodic, like three selected, non-consecutive, chapters from a novel.

'The Lord of Burleigh', 'Lady Clara Vere de Vere', and 'Lady Clare' are usually related but hardly idyllic in form. The last is a contemporary ballad, implicitly extolling the virtues of Lord Roland for marrying his true-love, though she has proved to be of lowly birth. The first, based on a true story,[7] is also a poem of true love, the lord, disguised as a landscape-painter, wooing a village girl and marrying her, then taking her to stately homes on their way to the cottage he has promised. At length they reach a mansion more majestic than any she has seen, and proudly but kindly he tells her 'All of this is mine and thine.' She falters, bears up, and, strengthened by his kindness, becomes a noble lady, much loved by the people, though her elevated social position proves too much for her, and she dies an untimely death. She is buried in her wedding-dress 'That her spirit might have rest'. It is a pretty story, told at the wooing stage with a preciousness that almost invites parody, and barely escaping sentimentality at the end. 'Lady Clara Vere de Vere', as the aristocratic prolongation of the title suggests, is made of sterner stuff. It is a dramatic lyric, more lyrical then dramatic. Yet the speaker's scorn for the lady who has tried to break his heart is witheringly conveyed. He cannot 'stoop to such a mind'; 'The lion on your old stone gates Is not more cold to you than I.' He tells her that 'A simple maiden in her flower Is worth a hundred coats-of-arms', and that 'Kind hearts are more than coronets, And simple faith than Norman blood'. He reminds her of the young man she has succeeded in killing by her remorselessness, and urges her, if time is heavy on her hands, to help the poor and needy, and pray for a human heart. Tennyson's rejection of the class distinctions of his age had obviously a popular appeal.

'The Gardener's Daughter' belongs to a slightly later compositional period than 'The Miller's Daughter', and is less serene and philosophical. Springing from the deep affection which existed between Arthur Hallam and Emily Tennyson (Eustace and Juliet) and the poet, its recollections are youthful, almost as tremulous with love as *The Lover's Tale*, and concentrated mainly on the outing of a single day. Much is imaginary, Eustace and his friend (the speaker) being painters. In 'The Ante-Chamber', which Tennyson intended as an introduction to his dramatic monologue, the speaker invites a guest to look at Eustace's self-portrait; it is not a likeness (though some readers mistook it for Tennyson), but some lines clearly apply to Hallam, who is described as more mature and outward-looking than his painter-friend. Finally the guest is invited to another room to see another countenance. The speaker is Tennysonian; his fancy is more luxurious than Eustace's, and he has an eye for the picturesque in landscape and detail. The prologue, like much else, was omitted from a poem that grew and grew, and is still, as the author acknowledged, 'full enough'. 'The Gardener's Daughter' is a retrospect prompted by the anniversary of the morning when the two painters left their cathedral city, and the speaker saw his 'Rose in roses', and discovered his love was not in vain. The scene he recalls is the focal point of the poem, a picture in itself, perhaps prompted (though transferred to a humble setting) by Tennyson's temporary infatuation with Rosa Baring. Previously the pastoral view from the garden to the city had been invoked:

> A league of grass, washed by a slow broad stream,
> That, stirred with languid pulses of the oar,
> Waves all its lazy lilies, and creeps on,
> Barge-laden, to three arches of a bridge
> Crowned with the minster-towers.

The fields were 'dewy-fresh, browsed by deep-uddered kine', with lime trees feathering low, each 'a summer house of murmurous wings'. 'The mellow ouzel fluted in the elm', and even the nightingale was heard. An English countryside and garden are seen with a painter's eye by a poet who is 'Lord of the senses five'. Love's ambience is in 'one warm gust, full-fed with perfume', as the painters enter the garden. That night, after receiving the rose from his loved one, the speaker could not sleep for joy, and heard the heavy clocks sounding the drowsy hours that stole over the mute city, 'distilling odours' on him 'as they went To greet their fairer sisters of the East'. Happiness follows for both pairs of lovers, but the interim is left to the imagination, as the listener looks anticipatingly towards the picture, the unveiling of which discloses the painter's 'first, last love', the idol of his youth, the darling of his manhood, and now 'the most blessèd memory' of age. The final revelation is surprising, for the poem is richly suffused with youthful love and sensuousness.

From 1833 to 1842 Tennyson felt it expedient, as a means of interesting readers in his renderings of ancient stories, to give them a contemporary framework. To the modern reader 'The Epic', as a presentation of 'Morte d'Arthur', is dated and rather fatuous. After playing forfeits and kissing the girls, the poet Everard Hall, his host Francis Allen, and the narrator (half-awake, after cutting eights and falling three times on the ice) sit round the wassail-bowl while the parson holds forth on the Ecclesiastical Commissioners, geology, and the decay of faith. Francis puts his trust in the poet, and he (Everard), in the wassail-bowl. It transpires that Everard burned his epic of twelve books on King Arthur, only the eleventh being saved. He thought that a truth looks freshest 'in the fashion of the day', and asks 'Why take the style of those heroic times? For nature brings not back the Mastodon, Nor we those times.' After referring disparagingly to his work as 'faint Homeric echoes, nothing-worth', he consents to read his fragment, and is soon heard 'mouthing out his hollow oes and aes, Deep-chested music'. The pretence is kept up at the end of his recital, the parson waking to grunt his praise.

'Perhaps some modern touches here and there Redeemed it from the charge of nothingness', the narrator comments. Yet his dream on the return of Arthur 'like a modern gentleman Of stateliest port', with hints of his immortality and the coming of the day when war shall be no more, reflects the true bias of Tennyson's ambivalence.

'The Day-Dream' is fanciful, but its framework has greater congruity with its subject. Lady Flora's dreamy eyes remind her lover of the Sleeping Beauty, and he narrates the legend hopefully while she continues her embroidery. Whether there is virtue in the three-times-three design of the work is not apparent. The story moves inward from the present to the past until the Sleeping Beauty is awakened by the Prince's kiss, and from this, outward with their departure to the conclusion ('Moral', 'L'Envoi', and 'Epilogue'), in which the lover asks his unresponsive lady whether it would be pleasant to sleep a hundred years through wars and scientific achievements. He wishes he could waken her with a kiss, 'The prelude to some brighter world'. The poem grew from 'The Sleeping Beauty' (published in 1830), and is most effective in circumstances external to the story, when the long-pent stream of life and activity in the palace is suddenly released. Love brings life to 'A perfect form in perfect rest', and the princess follows the prince 'Through all the world'. The lady of the corollary remains unmoved, and her lover courteously tells her that, such is her beauty, he could not but tell her the tale in earnest and in sport, however unwisely.

To the exquisite refinement of this artificial world the stern story of 'Dora' (from 'Dora Creswell' in *Our Village*) affords a startling contrast. Miss Mitford's rural scene has more life and colour, and her heroine's mission with the child when his grandfather is harvesting is successful. The happy ending in Tennyson is delayed: Dora returns to the child's mother; when they reach her uncle's home, in the hope of persuading the old man to relent, they find him fondling his grandson. No miracle is wrought by the child; it is only when he hears of his son's dying repentance that farmer Allan's guilt-ridden conscience finds relief in tears and remorse. Wordsworth flattered Tennyson when he told him that he had endeavoured all his life to write a pastoral like 'Dora'. The poem is bare in its Biblical or Tolstoyan simplicity, but rather monotonous in movement and texture; whether the French term *simplesse* conveys its quality, as Matthew Arnold thought, is questionable. Dora's two visits to the harvest-field end effectively with the reiteration of 'and the reapers reaped, And the sun fell, and all the land was dark'. In conjunction with her repeated bowing in sorrow, the second incidence of this passage (ll.99–107) suggests the influence of Wordsworth's note, and even more of his Biblical illustrations, in defence of repetition as a device for communicating deep feeling.[8]

Two poems, 'The Talking Oak' and 'Amphion', belong to the period of 'Will Waterproof's Lyrical Monologue', and have the same light, free assurance of manner. Their fancies probably came to Tennyson in the Epping Forest region, the dialogue of the first suggested by the oak of classical mythology at Dodona and the 'Run, run, Orlando; carve on every tree, The fair, the chaste, and unexpressive she' of *As You Like It*. The oak had seen none more beautiful in his five hundred years than Olivia; she moved so fleetly that 'The flower, she touched on, dipt and rose, And turned to look at her.' He wished he were the slender young neighbouring beech, that she might clasp him. His sap was stirred despite his age; as she kissed the name carved on his bark, his 'vapid vegetable loves' (originating from Andrew Marvell) responded 'With anthers and with dust'. Charming but leisurely, the verse is punctuated by the lover's blessing as the aged tree gives him the assurance he seeks. The mock solemnity of the ending contrasts with the gaiety of 'Amphion', where trees trip to the movement of the verse. The bard wishes he lived in those classical times when the legendary musician had the skill to make trees move to his music. Given such power, he would soon clear a space for his garden; the only response he gets is the heehaw of a jackass and the gaping of oxen. The modern Muses have become withered Misses who write books on exotics for conservatories in gardens of artificial design. He prefers nature, even the meanest weed that blooms or runs to seed.

The duologue 'Walking to the Mail' bears a slight resemblance to the fourth idyll of Theocritus. The blank verse accommodates itself to the styles of the two countrymen as they converse on their way to the turnpike road, giving, with every appearance of casualness, interesting sidelights on an age of rich and poor. A schoolboy prank (based on an Eton story) illustrates the cruelty of rich sons towards animals. A titled landlord leaves his home, his wife, and country, taking his 'morbid devil' with him (as did his tenant farmer, who returned to the house he had vacated on finding that its ghost was flitting with him). The landlord had married a cottager's daughter; she was 'out of her sphere' and 'What betwixt shame and pride,

New things and old, himself and her, she soured To what she is: a nature never kind!' The last drop in his cup of gall was Chartism; his bailiff finding a Chartist pike, he was afraid he would be murdered in his sleep. Such are the reports of one whose rather insensitive character is expressed in energetic and economical speech; his interlocutor, gentler in tone, suggests that the absentee landlord's 'nerves were wrong', and asks why sound people like themselves should go the way of the world, which 'charts us all in its coarse blacks and whites, As ruthless as a baby with a worm, As cruel as a schoolboy ere he grows To Pity – more from ignorance than will'. Appropriately the first glimpse of the world they see with the approaching mail is three piebalds and a roan. Thus, obliquely and by obvious contrivance, the idyll indicts the discrimination and injustice of an unnaturally class-ridden age.

Combining dialogue with narrative description and songs, 'Audley Court' bears a resemblance to the seventh idyll of Theocritus, and gives poetic status to a meat pie 'with golden yolks Imbedded and injellied'. This is part of the picnic repast enjoyed by Francis and the narrator in the orchard at Audley Court, which they have chosen in preference to the crowded town and its noisy quayside feast. Francis is a farmer's son, and their talk ranges from friends and acquaintances, deaths, marriages, and races, to farming, the four-field system, and the price of corn. They fall out on the Corn Law question, but agree wholeheartedly in their concern for the King's health. Francis, who had wooed a woman 'sharper than an eastern wind', and turned from her as a thorn turns from the sea, sings a carefree song, lauding independence over the lot of the soldier, the clerk, the public servant, and the lover. His friend, who does as he pleases, sings a yearning love-song. Very happily they return in the evening moonlight, descending to the quiet town and gloomy quay, where they see the harbour-buoy like a phosphorescent star dipping with 'one green sparkle ever and anon', just as Tennyson saw it when he descended the hill above Torquay.

The speaker in 'Edwin Morris' (written in North Wales, near the Llanberis lakes) recalls, with reference to his sketches, pleasant rambles near the lake. His contrast between the ruins of a castle in harmony with its rocky base and 'a Tudor-chimnied bulk Of mellow brickwork on an isle of bowers', one of the homes of invading Mersey millionaires, is significant. The poet Edwin Morris, a finical Admirable Crichton who 'seemed All-perfect, finished to the finger nail', had talked glowingly of love (his expression occasionally drawn from passages once intended for 'The Gardener's Daughter'. Tennyson could now look with some critical detachment on his own excesses; had he not been 'A full-celled honeycomb of eloquence Stored from all flowers'?). The traditional man-made views of the curate, 'God made the woman for the man, And for the good and increase of the world', anticipate *The Princess*. The narrator could not agree with him, nor was his experience to square with the over-smooth ideality of Morris. For by the time the bracken had rusted on the crags his love-suit had withered, 'nipt to death by . . . The rentroll Cupid of our rainy isles'. In response to Letty's note, he crossed the lake, and saw her 'Like Proserpine in Enna, gathering flowers'. They kissed and swore faith, while a silent cousin stole upon them and departed. With pugs and poodles yelling, out came trustees, aunts, and uncles, a cotton-spinning chorus, shrieking 'What, with him!' Compelled to go in, she went; 'and in one month They wedded her to sixty thousand pounds, To lands in Kent and messuages in York, And slight Sir Robert with his watery smile And educated whisker'. Yet the speaker in this monologue remembers her with affection, for she moves among his visions of the lake, recalling a period which is the one oasis in 'the dust and drouth' of his city life. With 'Locksley Hall', 'Edwin Morris' is a precursor of *Maud* and 'Aylmer's Field'.

Another Llanberis poem, 'The Golden Year', suggests that belief in the millennium is to be expected from an unworldly poet. Utopians, however, should not ask *how much* but how. Like Shelley in the final chorus of *Hellas*, the poet Leonard believes in the cycle that brings back the golden year, with equal division of wealth; people will be different – eagles, wrens, or falcons – but much can be done through the press and Christianity to create prosperity for all. Age overtakes us, however; and he wonders when each will live for all, and peace be universal. Pragmatic old James dismisses his vision; the millennium will not come in our time, or in our children's time; it is like 'the second world to us that live'. To the ancients it was in the past; to us it is in the future. To achieve it, we must toil; to have ideals and not work for them is as if the sower, his mind on the harvest, failed to sow. How Tennysonian is this belief was to be shown in 'The Holy Grail'. In Carlylean accents James concludes that 'unto him who works, and feels that he works, This same grand year is ever at his doors'. As if to confirm his statement, the slate-quarry blast is heard, its great echo buffeting round the hills from bluff to bluff.

More positively than 'Tiresias', the legend of 'Godiva', which Tennyson remembered as he stood gazing at Coventry's three tall spires from the railway bridge while waiting for the train, is concerned with virtue that shapes itself in deeds. It is not only the modern prattlers of rights and wrongs, he begins, who have loved the people and loathed to see them overtaxed; Godiva acted on their behalf. Another feature of the city was, one suspects, imprinted on the poet's memory and transferred to the imaginary past in the echoic passage which signals the conclusion of her triumphant ordeal: 'and all at once, With twelve great shocks of sound, the shameless noon Was clashed and hammered from a hundred towers, One after one.'

The use of a contemporary setting for this old story recalls the framework for 'Morte d'Arthur' and the more extensive one for *The Princess*, based on the festivities organized by a Mechanics' Institute which Tennyson observed in the Lushingtons' grounds near Maidstone. The Prologue presents a varied scene, from Sir Walter Vivian's house in Grecian style to Gothic ruins, from museum items of every age and clime to the Institute's instructive and entertaining display of the latest scientific wonders. Games, including cricket, are played, and men and women join in a country-dance beneath the 'broad ambrosial aisles of lofty lime' which resound 'with bees and breeze from end to end'. University friends discuss their escapades; one speaks of his tutor, 'rough to common men' but 'honeying at the whisper of a lord'; another, of the Master, 'as a rogue in grain Veneered with sanctimonious theory'. The Conclusion describes the view at the end of the day:

> The happy valleys, half in light, and half
> Far-shadowing from the west, a land of peace;
> Gray halls alone among their massive groves;
> Trim hamlets; here and there a rustic tower
> Half-lost in belts of hop and breadths of wheat;
> The shimmering glimpses of a stream; the seas;
> A red sail, or a white; and far beyond,
> Imagined more than seen, the skirts of France.

Gratitude for the Channel which has preserved England from French hysteria is expressed by a Tory college friend of the narrator, who reminds him that 'ourselves are full Of social wrong', and that wildest dreams are 'but the needful preludes of the truth' (a thought related to 'The Golden Year'). The genial day, the happy crowd, and 'the sport half-science' have filled him with faith. 'This fine old world of ours is but a child . . . Give it time To learn its limbs; there is a hand that guides.' His euphoria continues as he observes Sir Walter addressing the parting throng:

> A great broad-shouldered genial Englishman,
> A lord of fat prize-oxen and of sheep,
> A raiser of huge melons and of pine,
> A patron of some thirty charities,
> A pamphleteer on guano and on grain,
> A quarter-sessions chairman, abler none . . . .

When Sir Walter tells the crowd they will be welcome the following year, the applause makes the long line of rooks swerve from the elms, and the deer antlers shake among the ferns on the slopes. The question arises why the 'great Sirs' of the realm should not open their parks 'some dozen times a year To let the people breathe'. Unlike his complacent youthful narrator, the author is ambivalent, safeguarding his optimism with ironic caution.

Central in every way to 'The Brook' is the well-known eponymous lyric, the subject of which, Tennyson noted, is imaginary and not the rivulet at Somersby. Mainly a monologue of recollections, the poem evokes life in an English rural scene, rather in Miss Mitford's manner, and (though written much later) qualifies for association with some of the author's earlier idylls. It is the brook which starts Lawrence Aylmer's reminiscences; it seems to prattle the 'primrose fancies' of his young brother. They had parted, Lawrence for the East, and Edmund – too late – for Italy, where he died. Middle-aged now and bald, Lawrence quotes his brother's lyric at intervals. The sight of the farm at the junction of brook and river recalls how he walked miles with farmer Philip, listening to his interminable self-congratulatory talk, in order to give his daughter Katie Willows time for reconciliation with the cousin to whom she was betrothed. He had succeeded; but, like Edmund, Philip had died, and sweet Katie was in Australia. 'For men may come and men may go, But I go on for ever', the lyric ends. The theme of the poem may derive from Wordsworth's *The River Duddon*: 'Still glides the Stream, and shall for ever glide; The Form remains, the Function never dies; While we, the brave, the mighty, and the wise . . . must vanish.' Tennyson's happy ending suggests the continuity of life, for suddenly, as Aylmer sits musing, a girl appears, her eyes 'a bashful azure', her hair 'In gloss and hue the chestnut', exactly like Katie Willows'. She is her daughter; her family have returned and bought the farm; she is sure her mother will welcome Lawrence. The form is involved; the art with which it is managed is unobtrusive, its mastery concealed in conversational ease and unpretentiousness, the conciseness of which gives innumerable immediate effects of scene and character, from which emerge the humour and the pathos of life.

The idylls are a miscellany. Some have an abiding charm; several present living pictures of rural England. Some of their historical interest has faded, and social criticism does not run as deeply in most as in 'Edwin Morris' or in 'Dora', which illustrate the baneful effect of parentally arranged marriages. Though resentment of class superiority and *apartheid* is recurrent, in none of them is Tennyson roused as deeply as in 'Locksley Hall'. Where they take the form of dramatic monologue or duologue, they are true to character, and almost inevitably present partial truths. In his review of the 1842 poems John Sterling paid tribute to the imagery of 'Morte d'Arthur' and the epic style of 'Ulysses', but felt that the subjects were too remote from the reader; similarly with 'Godiva'. He found the 'most valuable part of Mr Tennyson's writings' in the idylls, which he thought 'a real addition to our literature'. 'The heartfelt tenderness, the glow, the gracefulness, the strong sense, the lively painting, in many of these compositions, drawn from the heart of our actual English life, set them far above the glittering marvels and musical phantasms of Mr Tennyson's mythological romances, at first sight the most striking portion of his works.' Tennyson undoubtedly enjoyed the presentation of aspects of a familiar world in idyllic writing, especially in the style of Theocritus, but his true thoughts on reflecting the contemporary scene are to be found in 'An Idle Rhyme'. 'Oh, what care I how many a fluke Sticks in the liver of the time?' he begins. 'What's near is large to modern eyes', and the age that mistakes its geese for swans is spurned by the next. Stretched by the river (that goes on for ever), he prefers to cool his face in flowers, 'and hear The deep pulsations of the world'. In this brief lyric, itself an idyll, he hints at the greater power of universal subjects. An even shorter dramatic lyric, 'The Little Maid', like Wordsworth's 'A slumber did my spirit seal' (which it resembles in metre and subject, but not in treatment) has this universality of interest and appeal:

> Along this glimmering gallery
>   A child, she loved to play;
> This chamber she was born in. See
>   The cradle where she lay.
>
> This was her study, these her books.
>   Here lived she all her life.
> She touched this mute guitar, and here
>   I wooed her for my wife.
>
> That little garden was her pride,
>   With yellow groundsel grown.
> Those holly-thickets only hide
>   Her grave – a simple stone.

I I

The Princess

'Upon what love is, depends what woman is, and upon what woman is, depends what the world is . . . . There is not a greater moral necessity in England than that of a reformation in female education.' If, as is probable, Tennyson noticed this observation on 'The Burial of Love' in W. J. Fox's review of his *Poems, Chiefly Lyrical*, he must have responded with full approval; one of the deeper pulsations of the world to which he gave ear was the question of women's rights in marriage and society. It needs no historical exposition to demonstrate that from Mary Wollstonecraft's *Vindication of the Rights of Women* (1792) to J. S. Mill's *The Subjection of Women* (1869) woman was subservient to man. Almost another century was to pass before much significant change was noticeable, and the equality of men and women is still a principle recognised more in theory than in practice even at the highest levels. Education is only a means to that end, and Tennyson discussed the poem he projected on this issue with Emily Sellwood in 1839, when a college for women was 'in the air'.

No doubt he had thought of this question at home. There was little scope for his highly gifted sisters; and his admired mother, 'The laws of marriage charactered in gold Upon the blanchèd tablets of her heart', was doomed to endure privations and worse from a self-indulgent husband. To Tennyson she was a finer creature than his father, and he had her in mind when describing the prince's mother in *The Princess* (vii. 298–312): through her he learned to love woman; she was

Not learnèd, save in gracious household ways,
Not perfect, nay, but full of tender wants,
No Angel, but a dearer being, all dipt
In Angel instincts, breathing Paradise,

Interpreter between the Gods and men,
Who looked all native to her place, and yet
On tiptoe seemed to touch upon a sphere
Too gross to tread . . . . Happy he
With such a mother! faith in womankind
Beats with his blood, and trust in all things high
Comes easy to him . . . .

Tennyson's marriage ideal was the partnership he first presented at the end of 'The Two Voices': 'The prudent partner of his blood Leaned on him, faithful, gentle, good, Wearing the rose of womanhood'; in company with their child, they form a trinity as whole and sacred as that of Tom Brangwen, Lydia, and Anna in Lawrence's *The Rainbow*. In attributing the traditional view, 'God made the woman for the use of man, And for the good and increase of the world', to 'the fat-faced curate, Edward Bull', Tennyson not only ascribes its continuation to Church doctrine but demonstrably evinces his disapproval; the artist–narrator of 'Edwin Morris' tells the parson that in regarding woman as a convenience for man he pitches the pipe too low.

Tennyson believed that the story of *The Princess* was original, and owed little, if anything, to earlier writers, including Johnson, whose princess (at the end of *Rasselas*) proposed a college of women, over which she would preside, to raise 'models of prudence, and patterns of piety' for the succeeding age. Whether indebted or not to the oriental story of Princess Turandot, Tennyson acknowledged that he might have been influenced obversely by Shakespeare's *Love's Labour's Lost*, where the king turns his court into a 'little Academe' for men, its students abjuring the company of women for three years; the plan inevitably fails when a French princess and her ladies have to be received for state reasons. Shakespeare's treatment of the subject is sprightly, since it has no serious ulterior theme like Tennyson's, which lies deeper than academic education for women, and is unfolded gradually through 'a parable' intended to interest an age not yet ready in the main to take it seriously. Its mock-heroic is limited to academic pretensions that prove to be unnatural.

The ridiculousness of Tennyson's over-elaborate story (see Appendix C) springs not only from its mock-heroics, and the attempt of its academic maidens to withstand nature, but also from the incongruity of a 'medley' in which the resolution of a modern issue depends on the combat of enemy representatives in medieval panoply. Without the lighter element of fantasy which qualifies it admirably for Gilbert's comic opera *Princess Ida*, it would be more tedious than it is. Tennyson tries to justify his entertaining presentation of a subject which readers could take as lightly or as seriously as they pleased with the pretence that it had been 'drest up poetically' by one of seven college students who told the story,[9] each in turn taking the hero's part (a game played by Tennyson with other students at Trinity College), in response to Lilia's espousal at Vivian Place of women's cause, and her wish that she were a princess and could build 'Far off from men a college like a man's' where she would teach them 'all that men are taught'. The ladies were to give the narrators relief at intervals by singing songs. At the end the men had demanded a 'mock-heroic gigantesque' manner throughout, but the women, who hated banter, had insisted on a solemn close, and then suggested that the whole should be 'true-heroic'. The poet–narrator, forced to compromise between mockers and realists, had decided to move 'as in a strange diagonal' from one style to another.

The placing of the original songs in this ingenious and seemingly improvised piece of indirection does not suggest that they were sung to give the narrators 'breathing-space'. The first, 'Tears, idle tears', occurs after only twenty lines of the fourth part. It expresses 'the passion of the past, the abiding in the transient', Tennyson said, observing that few knew it to be 'a blank verse lyric'. Deepened by the loss of Hallam, its passion is universal, regret for the irrecoverable awakening thoughts of friendship, death, and love.[10] Memory of 'the days that are no more' creates feelings as fresh as 'the first beam glittering on a sail, That brings our friends up from the underworld', and as sad as the last beam 'which reddens over one That sinks with all we love below the verge'; it is as sad and strange as the earliest pipe of half-awakened birds in dark summer dawns 'To dying ears, when unto dying eyes The casement slowly grows a glimmering square';[11] it is as dear as 'remembered kisses after death', and as sweet as those 'by hopeless fancy feigned On lips that are for others'; it is as 'Deep as first love, and wild with all regret'. Perhaps the range of moving experience is too wide and visualized for a single lyric; only through regular linking with the refrain is it kept in disciplined form. The 'Death in Life' crescendo moves the maid who sings it to tears which earn the reproach of the princess, who thinks the song consists of fancies hatched in silken-folded idleness, and trivial compared with progress towards the 'great year of equal mights and rights'. Invited to sing a forward-looking song, 'not a death's head at the wine', the disguised prince apes a treble voice as he extends an old song on the swallow winging south from his own land and fits it to his own love-suit, conjuring the bird bound for a fickle clime to be his wooer. His overt amorousness is dismissed as the knavery of men 'who lute and flute fantastic tenderness' while they prepare the victim for sacrifice, 'paint the gates of Hell with Paradise, And play the slave to gain the tyranny'.

The opening of the sixth section presents Ida (with Lady Psyche's babe) symbolically high on the palace, where she sings in triumph over her fallen enemies. The seed has grown into a huge tree they would have felled; it will now contribute to the happiness and welfare of mankind. Its iron nature having shattered weapons of destruction, it will continue to grow and bear fruit of power until, 'rolled With music in the growing breeze of Time, The tops shall strike from star to star, the fangs Shall move the stony bases of the world'. Almost as wholly as 'Tears, idle tears' this proud claim moves in blank verse, the exception recurring regularly in the first four stanzas, where the quickening repetition of exultation intro- duces two anapaestic feet at the end of each introductory refrain.

In the last section, after being kissed by the princess when he is on the brink of death, the prince wakes in the depth of night and hears her read 'Now sleeps the crimson petal', then the idyll 'Come down, O maid, from yonder mountain height'. Persian in form and character, the first is in complete accord with the time and human situation, its images (the most memorable being 'Now lies the Earth all Danaë to the stars') reflecting Ida's heartfelt thoughts. The second poeticizes the dilemma which has to be resolved as she is swayed by love. The cold Alpine heights are associated with death, and represent the Death in Life which has kept her aloof from mankind in accordance with rigid principles. Love belongs not to the distant heights but to the fertile valleys, with their myriads of rivulets, the 'moan of doves in immemorial elms', and the 'murmuring of innumerable bees'. The first lyric may have supplied D. H. Lawrence with the title of his first novel; the idyll suggested imagery which he developed antithetically and symbolically in the last chapters of *Women in Love*.

The femininity of the princess is first shown towards Aglaïa, who represents the 'glory' of motherhood. Believing that this was not too apparent, Tennyson added six intercalary songs in the 1850 edition: (i–ii) 'As through the land at eve we went', (ii–iii) 'Sweet and low', (iii–iv) 'The splendour falls on castle walls', (iv–v) 'Thy voice is heard through rolling drums', (v–vi) 'Home they brought her warrior dead', (vi–vii) 'Ask me no more'.[12] All of these fit their narrative contexts; four serve to reinforce the thematic role of the child. The songs (eleven in all) are 'the best interpreters of the poem', Tennyson wrote.

For the 1851 edition, in order to emphasize the unreality of his story (not his subject), Tennyson added passages on the prince's trances or 'seizures'. Metaphysically, it seems (though he had no high regard for her university curriculum), he agreed with the princess that creation is the birth of eternal light, but that human beings see only in part, and live therefore from thought to thought, making 'one act a phantom of succession', and creating, from weakness, 'the shadow, Time'. Such Platonism is expressed in Shelley's 'The Sensitive Plant', where love and beauty are eternal, but 'in this life Of error, ignorance, and strife' the eternal light is invisible, 'and all things seem, And we the shadows of the dream'. Tennyson's narrators are 'seven and yet one, like shadows in a dream'; the prince belongs to a family which does not know shadow from substance, and is subject to waking dreams. His trances make him feel as if he moves in a world of ghosts and is the shadow of a dream. So he feels when excited by the sight of Ida, after being summoned to join the geological expedition; and again, when he is angrily dismissed by her and thrust out of the university with his friends. After reading Ida's letter to her brother Arac, leader of the Southern army, he remembers her plea that his life should be spared, and other hopeful intimations, until the thought comes of the curse whereby one of his family is doomed to fight and fall; thereupon the king (his father, whose views on women are opposed to his), the armed camp, and the college turn to hollow shows, and he dreams that he is the shadow of a dream, until he wakes and finds the lists ready for the tournament. It seems a dream as he fights and falls. Lying unconscious in his room, he is beyond the world of 'weird doubts'; when he recovers, the mural paintings and the princess herself appear unreal, until she kisses him, and her falser self slips from her like a robe. The change in her kills his doubts and haunting sense of hollow shows. Tennyson seems to imply that the supreme world is spiritual; compared with this, the accidents of time, place, and outward forms are specious and insignificant. In true love the union of spiritual and temporal creates a new reality. Whatever the thought, he does not present it effectively but stutteringly. Many readers might imagine the prince's weird doubts are an excuse for a fantastic tale, which makes him seem a weakling compared with the more solid Sir Walter in the recognisable contemporaneity of the Conclusion.

There is 'scarcely anything in the story which is not prophetically glanced at in the prologue', Tennyson claimed. The cosmopolitanism of Sir Walter's collections, the 'tilt and tourney' of old Sir Ralph, and 'the tale of her That drove her foes with slaughter from her walls', foreshadow the medley inconsequence of the narrative, with hints of the prince's father, and of Ida and Lilia's feminist militancy. Lilia had attached her colours to the broken statue of Ralph; it was her wish to be a princess and found a college where women would be taught 'all that men are taught'; the penalty for a male intruder would be death. Walter junior light-heartedly expressed a sincere wish for female company at his college, and insisted that Lilia should be the princess – 'Grand, epic, homicidal' – of the proposed story, which was to suit the time and place: 'A Gothic ruin and a Grecian house, A talk of college and of ladies' rights, A feudal knight in silken masquerade', and the strange experiments organized by the Mechanics' Institute for public entertainment. Princess Ida's students have classical exemplars set before them in lectures, sculpture, and painting; they believe in evolution, and geologize; the narrative quarrel between two kingdoms which arises ultimately from the breaking of the princess's betrothal pact is fought in medieval fashion and (at Lilia's insistence) with no quarter. The medley of story and lyric turns from mock-heroic to medieval heroic, and thence to forward-looking Victorian earnestness. It reflects the growing eclecticism of nineteenth-century culture, its imitative styles and scientific progress, its traditional prejudices, its minority views on women, and its evolutionary faith.

An artful rather than artistic work, *The Princess* is a medley of styles, their heterogeneity varying from spirited absurdities to the highly poetic, through a range of heroic effects, often incongruously placed but deceptively poker-faced at times. Each of the princess's blowzy bodyguard is like a spire of land 'Cleft from the main, and wailed about with mews'; Lady Blanche boasts that she has led her to all the Castalies, and fed her with the milk of every Muse; Gama appeals for reconciliation between his daughter and Lady Psyche on the strength of the nights they had spent discussing 'sine and cosine . . . and right ascension'. Mock-heroic incongruities are based occasionally on anticlimax (v. 211–14, 318–19), sometimes

(*above*) Mary Turner's home, Caistor (from the market-place); (*below*) Langton
Hall (home of Bennet Langton) near Somersby

The rectory and brook at Somersby

The church at Somersby

(*left*) portrait of Tennyson's grandfather George, by Sir Thomas Lawrence
(*right*) his father George Clayton Tennyson (from an oil painting)

4

Louth Grammar School

The poet's mother

(*above*) the Great Gate, Trinity College, Cambridge; and Arthur Hallam; (*below*) the chapel and Great Court, Trinity College

(*above*) Tennyson, in profile, with the Harden family and Arthur Hallam (reading
Scott aloud) on the *Leeds* from Bordeaux to Dublin, 9 September 1830; (*below*)
Clevedon Church, by the Bristol Channel

(*above*) the Sellwoods' house, Horncastle, facing the market-place, with the churchyard just apparent across the road on the left; (*below*) Shiplake Church, where Tennyson and Emily Sellwood were married

8

(*above*) Chapel House, Twickenham; Edmund Lushington
(*below*) Park House, home of the Lushingtons, near Maidstone

(*above*) Farringford from the lawn
(*below*) Tennyson's study at Farringford

Tennyson and his family at Farringford
(photograph by Oscar Gustav Rejlander)

Thomas Woolner, R.A.

Charles (Tennyson) Turner

Edward FitzGerald

F. D. Maurice

13

(*above*) an artist's impression of Bayons Manor for Charles Tennyson d'Eyncourt's
Eustace, 1851
(*below*) Aldworth

Alfred (Lord) Tennyson, 1888, by Barraud

Punch on Tennyson's peerage (22 December 1883); Lord and Lady Tennyson with Hallam Tennyson

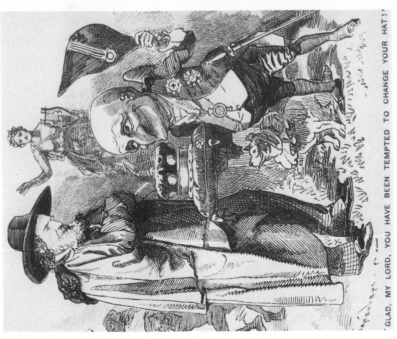

'GLAD, MY LORD, YOU HAVE BEEN TEMPTED TO CHANGE YOUR HAT!'

on epic formalities such as the placing of 'He said' after a long speech, on the use of heroic similes in situations unequal to them (i. 223-4; v. 332-40; vi. 311-13), and, more often, on hyperbole (iii. 96-100; iv. 409-21; vi. 142-51, 318-20). Fine descriptive effects are common: thoughts in the eye of Melissa, Lady Blanche's daughter, are as fair as bottom agates which appear to wave and float in crystal currents of clear morning seas, and it is no more strange that she and Florian whom she tends fall in love than 'when two dewdrops on the petal shake To the same sweet air, and tremble deeper down, And slip at once all-fragrant into one'; with epic splendour, in the white wake of Venus, the morn furrows the orient with gold; the geologizers descend from lean and wrinkled precipices, by coppice-feathered chasms and clefts, until they see their lamp-lit tent shine like a glow-worm in the gloom; the virgin marble shrieks under iron heels when the wounded are carried through the Vestal entrance; the lark shoots up and shrills morn after morn in flickering gyres while the prince lies 'silent in the muffled cage of life'; and the princess's tenderness turns to love 'like an Alpine harebell hung with tears By some cold morning glacier', frail at first but gathering colour day by day.

It is unfortunate that so many of the best images garnered by Tennyson during the early years of his poetic prime were assimilated to a work which is immaturely bizarre in its structural conception, and too ambivalent, complicated, and prolonged to sustain the interest of most readers.

Like the prince's seizures, the high-spirited 'false sublime' disappears from the verse when Ida casts off pretence and accepts reality. Her 'falser self' is reflected in the choice of a curriculum designed for men, based mainly on factual knowledge, and neither preparatory for life nor necessarily conducive to wisdom. Like the maiden aunt of the framework, Princess Ida's students are 'crammed with theories out of books'; she had sought 'far less for truth than power In knowledge'. 'A kindlier influence' (one with their kind or nature) reigns when her maidens minister to the wounded; they move like 'creatures native unto gracious act, And in their own clear element'. Tennyson believed that, 'if women ever were to play such freaks' as extreme feminists demanded, 'the burlesque and the tragic might go hand in hand'. The diagonal which he steers from burlesque to the positive may imply a progressive resultant from the impact of forces favouring women's enlightened emancipation in the course of time. In contrast to the male chauvinism of the prince's father (v. 147–50, 434–45), this includes Lady Psyche's equality of opportunity at all levels (ii. 153–64), but its main emphasis is on the role of women in marriage and society. In insisting that women are whole in themselves and 'owed to none', and that 'they must lose the child' (an intentional ambivalence), the princess, as the sequel proves, acts against nature. The prince is women's champion; men, with their 'Bursts of great heart and slips in sensual mire' are far less 'magnetic to sweet influences Of earth and heaven'. Both must rise or sink together; progress depends not on likeness, which would destroy love, but on woman's readiness 'to live and learn and be All that not harms distinctive womanhood'. Man will be 'more of woman, in sweetness and in moral height'; from him she will gain in mental breadth, nor 'lose the childlike in the larger mind'.

> And so these twain, upon the skirts of Time,
> Sit side by side, full-summed in all their powers,
> Dispensing harvest, sowing the To-be,
> Self-reverent each and reverencing each,
> Distinct in individualities,
> But like each other even as those who love.
> Then comes the statelier Eden back to men:
> Then reign the world's great bridals, chaste and calm:
> Then springs the crowning race of humankind.

This passage echoes 'the Christ that is to be' and the crowning race' of *In Memoriam* (cvi, Epilogue), showing that Tennyson's ideal of 'manhood fused with female grace' (cix) sprang largely from Arthur Hallam. Late in life he defined Christ, the 'human and divine' of *In Memoriam* which he tried to project in *Idylls of the King*, as 'that union of man and woman, strength and weakness'. Lest he should be thought to undervalue manliness, he wrote 'On One Who Affected an Effeminate Manner':

> While man and woman still are incomplete,
> I prize that soul where man and woman meet,
> Which types all Nature's male and female plan,
> But, friend, man-woman is not woman-man.

Here again Tennyson's evolutionary confidence is asserted.

Never a Britomart, Ida eventually recognises the unnaturalness of feminist militancy. So too does Lilia, her tacit admission of error being part of the last comment on the subject, as she rises and removes her colours from the broken statue of one who, in association with a female warrior (Prologue, 118–38) had symbolized her cause. An emblem of stone which is antiquated and headless is significant, the dramatic culmination of the story having, it seems, made Lilia think on 'the future man'. Her last act, Tennyson shows, takes place in the light of a faith that transcends the visible present. The thought is conveyed in words transferred from a rejected passage of *The Lover's Tale*:

> gradually the powers of the night,
> That range above the region of the wind,
> Deepening the courts of twilight broke them up
> Through all the silent spaces of the worlds,
> Beyond all thought into the Heaven of Heavens.

In Memoriam gives this faith a long-term expression; two lines in the poem Tennyson wrote on his own marriage, 'To the Vicar of Shiplake' ('I shall come through her, I trust, Into fuller-orbed completeness'), are more immediately relevant.

12

In Memoriam A. H. H.

This is a composite work, represented best perhaps by the title of the trial edition, 'Fragments of an Elegy'. It consists of a series of poems, written at various periods, mainly in the earlier years, from 1833 to 1849, with reference to Arthur Hallam's sudden death in Vienna at the age of twenty-two. Many are composed singly, others sequentially; ultimately they were arranged in relatively homogeneous groups, irrespective of the order of composition, to present a whole range of feelings, with philosophical and religious reflections, on the way to recovery from the doubts and fears which assailed Tennyson's faith in consequence of the loss of one who had been the mainspring of his hope. The shock revived familiar forms of scepticism (the resolution of which had been the subject of 'The Two Voices') with numbing and sometimes agonizing persistence.

The poignancy of Tennyson's grief in the wintry days of late 1833 after hearing news of Hallam's death is most explicit in his scrapbook lines 'Hark! the dogs howl!' Church clocks knoll in the sleeting wind, and time bears the poet's soul into the waste, as he climbs the frozen wold, seeking the voice, the dear hand, and the honoured brows he would kiss. The cold starry heavens are unaware of his distress, but through a dividing cloud he imagines the daisied grave of a drooping, pale-browed youth. Uncertain forms move darkly, and a 'larger than human' shadow of the man he loved passes by. He extends his arms to embrace him, the cry expires in his constricted throat, and the shadowy form looks down reproachfully, and clasps hands as if in prayer. The wish to embrace and kiss suggests not a habit in life but the yearning of an emotional stress which found another outlet in 'Oh! that 'twere possible'. In less extreme forms it strikes a note of effeminacy in *In Memoriam*; speaking of 'Oh, wast thou with me, dearest, then' (cxxii), Tennyson told James Knowles that anyone who thought he ever addressed Hallam that way would be much mistaken, for he 'never even called him "dear" '. His grief was not easily overcome, and the questioning of God's way continued, but philosophy and religion prevailed. Hallam's enthusiasm for Dante strengthened Tennyson's faith in a God of love throughout the universe, and power broke from him once more 'To feel, although no tongue can prove, That every cloud, that spreads above And veileth love, itself is love'.

In Memoriam reveals a slow passage towards assurance. Grief dies, but love increases with the years, making the earlier poems in the series seem 'The sport of random sun and shade'. Tennyson called it 'The Way of the Soul', signifying the hope that his work would be a comfort to many. He meant his poem to be another *Divine Comedy*, moving from death to marriage, and from grief to faith in human evolution on earth and after death. Whatever its validity, it is no facile theodicy but poetic testimony to personal doubts and their resolution, as honest as the author's conclusion that he had made it too hopeful. He added a section (xcvi) to emphasize the value of doubt in testing faith.

Tennyson wrote these poems with no intention of 'weaving them into a whole, or of publication', until he found he had written so many. Dates are known, or deducible with certainty, for only a minority. Among the earliest are ix, xxviii, xxx, xxxi; poems relative to leaving Somersby for High Beech in 1837 occur late (c–cv); lix (cf. iii) was added in 1851, and xxxix (not included in all editions) in 1869. The earliest part of the Epilogue seems to have been written at the time of Cecilia's marriage in 1842; the Prologue, which is the conclusion of the whole matter, belongs to 1849. Religious orthodoxy, or a close approximation to it, being a criterion of social respectability, it did more than the proclamation of the ideal marriage relationship in *The Princess* finally to convince Mr Sellwood of Tennyson's eligibility for his daughter Emily.

Some analysts of the work find divisions marked by the Christmas poems (xxviii–xxx, lxxviii, civ–vi); others, in the poems commemorating the anniversary of Hallam's death (lxxii, xcix). (These create the impression that *In Memoriam* reflects the poet's spiritual recovery within a period of approximately three years. 'It must be remembered', Tennyson wrote, 'that this is a poem, *not* an actual biography.') The turning-point has been located around lvii, but (although there are broadly only four phases: grief, hope, uncertainty and doubt, recovery and assurance) it is more practical to keep to the poet's nine groupings, the first of which (i–viii) is devoted entirely to grief. In the Goethe allusion with which the sequence opens, there is an oblique reference to the evolutionary thought on which the long-term faith of *In Memoriam* is based: the poet cannot yet rise on the stepping-stones of his dead self to higher things, for if Love does not clasp Grief both may be drowned. He envies the stubborn hardihood of the graveyard yew, and wonders whether he should reject the view that the universe is blind and dying, before it gains a hold on his mind. 'Such clouds of nameless trouble cross All night below the darkened eyes' as he sleeps that he thinks he is like a vase of chilling tears turned to ice by a sudden shock, and hopes for relief when morning wakes his will. The 'sad mechanic exercise' of writing verse exerts a narcotic effect, and he therefore wraps himself in words like 'coarsest clothes against the cold'. The commonplace condolence that death is common breeds no consolation, only thoughts of suffering in store for others from unexpected deaths. Unable to sleep in the early morning, he imagines that he approaches the house in Wimpole Street where Hallam welcomed him; such is his desolation that it appears dark, and the street unlovely; he creeps towards the door like a guilty thing, hears the noise of city life starting up, and sees through the drizzling rain the day dawn blank on the deserted street. To him, as to the lover who has lost his beloved, everywhere is darkened, and his feelings towards his poetry are like the lover's when he finds, beaten in wind and rain, a flower she once cherished. It had 'pleased a vanished eye'; now (and unfavourable reviews are hinted at) it is little cared for but yet unfading, and he trusts it will bloom in Hallam's memory.

The next section (ix–xx) shows more composure and imaginative freedom. (The body of Hallam was landed at Dover, and taken by train to Clevedon, where it was buried in the family vault below the manor aisle of the church.) In spirit Tennyson accompanies the ship carrying 'Arthur's loved remains' to the Severn, and stands by his churchyard grave. He had held him 'half-divine', more highly than his own brothers, and 'Dear as the mother to the son'. He wishes the ship a favourable voyage, imagines himself over it at night, and, though he knows his dreams may be illusory, sees it in a calm like that of his despair and that of the autumnal morning scene around him. Next, like a dove, he leaves his 'mortal ark' and, as the distant sails appear, circles moaning 'Is this the end? Is this the end?', the *abba* formation of the stanza reinforcing the sense of a completed wheeling movement. His sufferings seem to belong to a dream world, and he would not find it strange if, at the port of arrival, he found Arthur greeting him by the hand and 'all in all the same'. Only the thought that his ship still moves gently across the waters makes the storm on land bearable; conversely, the 'fear it is not so' makes it impossible for him to enjoy the sight of the fiery storm-cloud in the evening sky. His fluctuation of feeling from calm despair to wild unrest makes him wonder whether his emotions are superficial, belying his deep unchanged self, or whether they are due to a shock which has made him delirious. As 'Break, break, break' intimates, his deepest sorrow is beyond words; he can express himself only when his 'deeper anguish' falls.

The third group (xxi–vii) introduces a pastoral note. The poet's answer to those who think his private sorrow is disproportionate is that the need for self-expression makes him 'pipe but as the linnets sing'. He recalls walks and talks with Hallam at Somersby through 'four sweet years' before the shadow of death darkened their favourite path, wonders whether the period was as perfect as it seems in retrospect, but knows that life was easier when he could share its burdens with the friend he loved. He would rather die than forget him; it is 'better to have loved and lost' than to live a life of complacency or self-indulgence.

A period of hopeful speculation (xxviii–xlix) begins with the Christmastide bells which bring joy to the sorrowing poet. Despite grief, Christmas Eve is observed for custom's sake; it suggests that, though the same to us, the dead change as they proceed 'From orb to orb, from veil to veil'. Christmas morning therefore is associated once again with dawning hope. Though nothing is known of Lazarus's experience after death, only of the rejoicing when he returned to life, his sister Mary was pleased in her simple faith, and intellectuals are more likely to fail than such worshippers of Christ. If there were no immortality, life would not be worth living, nor would love have risen from sensual to spiritual heights. Such views are consistent with belief in the life and resurrection of Christ, a story of revealed truth more potent than all poetic thought. Spring affords the poet no joy, but he derives solace from the songs he sings, and thinks that, if the spirits of the dead ever turn their attention earthward, Hallam will not be wholly displeased with them. The thought that the graveyard yew will return to its gloom after spring pollination is dismissed as a subjective grief-sprung fallacy; he knows that the departed, like the bride leaving her old home for a new, fulfils high functions in another world. He could share his spiritual ascent in life, but fears they will not meet in 'the secular-to-be', and that he will be 'evermore a life behind'. Hope returns, however, that he will learn from Hallam as he did on earth; that, if death is a kind of sleep, the love of friends will survive when souls reawaken; that, since individuality emerges in this life, it seems unlikely that man will have to 'learn himself anew' after death: and that, though the past may be shadowed by time on earth, it will be wholly clear in the life to come, when the years of Hallam's friendship will be the richest field in an eternal landscape warmed by God's love. Continuing his speculations, Tennyson is convinced that individuality will be preserved after death until all are merged in the 'general Soul'. Then he realizes that his hopes cannot pretend to certainty: thoughts drawn from life and learning merely touch the surface; his poems are 'Short swallow-flights of song, that dip Their wings in tears, and skim away'; and sorrow deepens beneath 'all fancied hopes and fears'.

A period of uncertainty and questioning follows (l–lviii). Yearning for the comfort of Hallam's spirit, he concludes that the higher wisdom of the dead will make allowance for human failings. The expression of his love is inadequate, his words moving only upon 'the topmost froth of thought'. Whatever the frailty of human nature, he believes in holding fast to the good, trusting that good will finally triumph and that no form of life will be utterly destroyed. Speculation is halted, and he feels he is no more than 'An infant crying for the light'. Nature (judging by Lyell's *Principles of Geology*) runs counter to his hopes, for she is indifferent to both individual life ('of fifty seeds She often brings but one to bear') and to whole species. Will man, who trusted that God is love, despite the evidence that nature is red in tooth and claw, and who 'battled for the True, the Just', end 'blown about the desert dust, Or sealed within the iron hills'? If so, he would be more out of tune with nature than the prehistoric monsters which tore each other in the slime. Life would be futile, and the poet would have lost 'the sweetest soul That ever looked with human eyes'. He is convinced that his grief will toll like a 'set slow bell' as long as he lives, but the high Muse counsels patience, and suggests he will 'take a nobler leave'.

Though his grief for Hallam remains unchanged, Tennyson presents him hopefully in a series of poems (lix–lxxi) which suggest that communication with him is possible. As he can pity or love a horse or dog, so Hallam, in his 'second state sublime', will watch him; perhaps he will look back on his earthly life like 'some divinely gifted man' of peasant origin who, after reaching one of the realm's highest offices, looks back affectionately on the early haunts where his old friend wonders whether he remembers him. Moonlight falling on the poet's bed makes him think of a mystic glory brightening the inscription on Hallam's memorial. Sleep is death's kinsman, and Hallam appears in a series of dreams. Waking after the first, Tennyson knows that the troubled eye of his lost friend reflects his own sorrow; another dream tells him that the grief he expresses is not unmanly; then, after chaotic visions, he sees the peaceful countenance of Hallam; another time he dreams of their journey to the Pyrenees.

A section on the greatness of Hallam (lxxii–xcviii) begins with the anniversary of his death, which dawns grey and wild; whatever the weather, it would have been wan to the poet, who thinks of what Hallam would have achieved, and how weak and ephemeral his praise is in comparison. The second Christmas is calmly observed, but regret remains as deep as ever. Addressing his brother Charles, Tennyson explains why his love for Hallam exceeds fraternal love; he and his brothers had the same upbringing, but his friend's endowment was richer, and he owed him more. Had he himself died, Hallam's grief would have turned to gain; he takes heart from this thought, and believes that death suddenly developed his love of Hallam to the full; his quarrel with death is that they 'cannot hear each other speak'. The lateness of spring delays his expression of sorrow that 'longs to burst a frozen bud'. He recalls what Hallam might have been, especially if he had become his brother-in-law, thinks of the praise he would have won, and indulges the fancy that they could have died together and been received as a single soul by Christ. Believing that Hallam triumphs in 'conclusive bliss' and would urge him to do what he proposes, he extends the hand of friendship to Edmund Lushington, telling him he cannot feel for him as for his predecessor. Spiritual calm comes to him at Barmouth (1839), and he can now return to Cambridge and think of Hallam's mastery in debate there. He wishes he had the nightingale's power to turn grief into joy, and communicate 'the glory of the sum of things' which he feels. Then follow recollection of happiness shared with Hallam at Somersby, and a passage reminiscent of 'The Lotos-Eaters' (Choric Song, vi), followed by the assertion that time has not changed his affection, and an appeal for Hallam's return. After some scepticism, he concludes that those who are spiritually at peace may commune with the dead. The turning-point comes in the course of reading Hallam's letters late one night, when the 'living soul' is flashed on his, and the two are entwined and whirled about 'empyreal heights of thought' to 'that which is', the spiritual presence of God. The section concludes, first with a defence of the kind of honest doubt which Hallam had overcome, then with the poet's sense of spiritual oneness with him (in earthly terms like that of a wife for a husband above her understanding), finally (in a poem addressed to Charles Tennyson, on his honeymoon departure for Vienna in 1836) with a refusal to visit 'That City', which despite all its splendours, of which he had heard from Hallam, he now regards as the haunt of Evil.

The brief group which follows (xcix–ciii) begins with the anniversary of Hallam's death before the departure of the Tennysons from Somersby in early spring. Landscapes dear from their association with Hallam, and the garden and brook dear to the poet, give rise to feelings which become 'one pure image of regret' as Tennyson leaves. The previous night an Arthurian vision (seemingly factitious, though partly suggested by memories of harp and carol) had come to him, the body of Hallam being conveyed in a shallop to the sea, accompanied by three maidens who grew more majestic as each in turn sang prophetically of stages in human progress towards the 'one far-off divine event' with which *In Memoriam* concludes.

Christmas falls strangely in the new home at High Beech; the bells on New Year's Eve are urged to ring out evil and ring in reform; the poet looks forward to a more Christian world and 'The closing cycle rich in good'. Hallam's birthday (1 February) is celebrated cheerfully. So opens the final section (civ–cxxxi) of *In Memoriam*, in which death is swallowed up in victory. Tennyson has decided not to brood over sorrow, but turn to his kind; he thinks of the wisdom he might have learned from Hallam, and makes light of the accomplishments of lesser mortals. To think of what Hallam might have become makes him realize that knowledge is inferior to wisdom. With spring his regret blossoms, making him yearn for 'some strong bond which is to be', and which will be all the richer for being delayed; the maturing of the individual through time and experience is part of the long-term process of evolution. He can now revisit Wimpole Street happily; the planet, seen as sad Hesper, the evening star, ready to die with the buried sun, is now Phosphor, the morning star. He wishes to 'slip the thoughts of life and death', and commune again with Hallam. The evidences of geology, and his failure to find God in nature, do not weaken his faith that God is love and 'all is well'. Despite 'vast eddies in the flood Of onward time' the human race will continue to make progress; all is 'toil cöoperant to an end'. Hallam's spirit is part of the universe, and Tennyson associates him with evolving good; a noble type, ahead of his age, he is now with God, the spirit that lives and loves, working in the human race until all ends in Him. The relationship of the marriage-epilogue is rather contrived and anticlimactic, especially in comparison with the Prologue, which remains one of the most considered and enduring expressions of religious wisdom.

It would have been miraculous had Tennyson's aggregations worked out artistically from first to last, but it is to his credit that he let his 'elegies' speak for themselves without any artificial linking or applied design. Despite their chronological pretence, the general effect is diary-like, as T. S. Eliot noted; yet the arrangement is not always felicitous. There are awkward discontinuities as well as repetition; one or two poems (noticeable especially in the sixth section) contribute little; occasionally commonplaces are given dignified dress. Pendants such as xxxix (cf. ii) and cxix (cf. vii) are hardly in context, the former being inserted mainly to ensure that botanical accuracy has not been overlooked. Nor would it be easy to justify the slotting-in of xcvi after xcv. Two poems addressed to Charles Tennyson (lxxix, xcviii) and two to Edmund Lushington (lxxxv and the Epilogue) occasion some surprise; they differ in mode from the inner communing which pervades the work, and lxxxv reduces Hallam to a background third while the poet and Lushington occupy the front of the 'stage'.

Dependent on the latter's marriage, the Epilogue provides a particularity which is bold with reference to Tennyson's evolutionary faith and contractile *vis-à-vis* his general elegiac purpose: 'rather the cry of the whole human race than mine', he told Knowles; ' "I" is not always the author speaking of himself, but the voice of the human race speaking through him', he wrote. This is evident in the New Year's Eve poem (cvi), but the universality of the subject has further widening resonances in the imaginative appeal of passages which link the death of Hallam with typical family losses and suffering. Every day is one of heartbreak: the father has yet to hear of the loss of his gallant son in battle; the mother, of the burial of her sailor boy at sea; the girl, of her fiancé's accidental death. Tennyson's loss is associated with the departure of the bride from one home for greater responsibility in her new; his continued

love from a lower sphere, with that of a poor girl whose heart is set
on one of higher rank. The anniversary of Hallam's death brings
memories of bridal or birth to myriads, and of death to myriads
more:

> O wheresoever those may be,
>   Betwixt the slumber of the poles,
>   Today they count as kindred souls;
> They know me not, but mourn with me.

Other common domestic situations strengthen the link between
author and reader (cf. xiii and xx in relation to xix and xcvii), while
'Do we indeed desire the dead' (li) associates the thoughts of others
with his own prayer in the previous poem, and ends with the
assurance that the dead, 'With larger other eyes than ours', 'make
allowance for us all'. Professor Henry Sidgwick thought the
importance of the poem lay principally in 'the unparalled combination of intensity of feeling with comprehensiveness of view and
balance of judgment, shown in presenting the *deepest* needs and
perplexities of humanity'. With reference to the Victorian age, the
validity of this assessment can hardly be exaggerated; Tennyson
combines reflections on its new teleological uncertainties with
feeling and personal conviction in ways to which 'the common
reader' could readily respond. Quoting Johnson on Gray's 'Elegy'
further, one could say that *In Memoriam* 'abounds with images'
which found 'a mirrour in every mind', and with sentiments to
which 'every bosom' returned an echo. With thoughtful readers this
is undoubtedly true of much of the poem today.

Many who had been disturbed by tragic losses, or by religious
questioning nurtured by evolutionary anticipations of Darwinism,
found assurances in the faith of a poet who had clearly confronted
the evidence of nature and, like Hallam, fought his spectral doubts.
Such faith was based on the belief that God is a spiritual presence
which works in man through love. Religion beyond this is a matter
of 'Believing where we cannot prove'. Tennyson's belief in immortality (and he was apt to declare it with an overwrought emphasis
more indicative of gnawing doubt than of irrationality) was
nurtured by the conviction that life without it is not worth living
(xxxiv, lvi). Even if nature is 'red in tooth and claw With ravine',
such a conclusion is untrue to life, as Hardy, a writer more
imaginatively horrified by a Darwinian universe, did not hesitate to

declare: 'Thought of the determination to enjoy. We see it in all nature, from the leaf on the tree to the titled lady at the ball. . . . Even the most oppressed of men and animals find it, so that out of a thousand there is hardly one who has not a sun of some sort for his soul.' Tennyson's conviction of immortality derives from visionary rather than from mystical experience (xcv), even more from intuition deeper than any ratiocination (cxxiv):

> I found Him not in world or sun,
>   Or eagle's wing, or insect's eye;
>   Nor through the questions men may try,
> The petty cobwebs we have spun:
>
> If e'er when faith had fallen asleep,
>   I heard a voice 'believe no more'
>   And heard an ever-breaking shore
> That tumbled in the Godless deep;
>
> A warmth within the breast would melt
>   The freezing reason's colder part,
>   And like a man in wrath the heart
> Stood up and answered 'I have felt.'

The lavish profusion of nature was apt to appal him, 'from the growths of the tropical forest to the capacity of man to multiply, the torrent of babies'. It was as if 'some lesser god had made the world, But had not force to shape it as he would'. After such Hardyan thoughts he exclaimed in 1892,

> Yet God *is* love, transcendent, all-pervading! We do not get *this* faith from Nature or the world. If we look at Nature alone, full of perfection and imperfection, she tells us that God is disease, murder and rapine. We get this faith from ourselves, from what is highest within us, which recognizes that there is not one fruitless pang, just as there is not one lost good.

Tennyson abandons the rarer question whether immortality is the lot of all living things; he can only trust that 'not a worm is cloven in vain'. His evolutionary theory owes much to Robert Chambers' *Vestiges of Creation*, which was published anonymously in 1844. On man's spiritual ascent, in the individual and in the race, in this life and after death, he has little doubt. 'I am ready to fight for *mein liebes Ich*, and hold that it will last for aeons of aeons', he said late in life. Just as man evolved from the ape, so he moves upward, working out the beast; whatever setbacks in the course of time there are, all is 'toil cöoperant to an end'. Hallam's spirit had risen 'from high to higher' before his death: 'Rapt from the fickle and the frail', the keen seraphic flame pierces with gathered power 'From orb to orb, from veil to veil', the circuits of its orbit rounding higher heights and deeper deeps as it progresses. The poet fears that he will always be 'a life behind' in 'the secular-to-be', until finally in the course of 'tenfold-complicated change' individual souls are merged in the 'general Soul'. It is from this 'vast' that the soul is drawn when it becomes one with the child in the womb. Tennyson trusts that the child born to the Lushingtons will be 'a closer link Betwixt us and the crowning race' of those who, 'No longer half akin to brute', understand Nature's purpose. God is not only love and law but the 'one far-off divine event, To which the whole creation moves'.

Perhaps it needs to be said that the orbs and their ever-increasing circuits should not be taken literally; Hallam makes a spiritual progress from 'state to state', not an interplanetary one. An embodiment of God and Nature on earth (cxi), he is mixed with God and Nature after death (cxxx). Like Shelley's Adonais

> he doth bear
> His part, while the one Spirit's plastic stress
> Sweeps through the dull dense world, compelling there,
> All new successions to the forms they wear;
> Torturing th' unwilling dross that checks its flight
> To its own likeness, as each mass may bear.

Tennyson uses 'matter-moulded forms of speech' or metaphor to express the spiritual, its evolution as well as its presence or effects. In this respect the orb resembles the hand and touch metaphors. God's finger touched Hallam in Vienna's fatal walls; the poet yearns for the spirit of the deceased to descend and 'touch and enter'; during his trance the dead man touches him from the past; he believes that God ('What is, and no man understands') is an evolutionary force: 'And out of darkness came the hands That reach through nature, moulding men'.

Critical as was the question of immortality for Tennyson, the significance of his emphasis on the struggle towards righteousness on earth in *In Memoriam*, even more in *Idylls of the King* (as 'The Holy

Grail' attests), should not be underestimated. 'Ring out the old, ring in the new . . . the valiant man and free, The larger heart, the kindlier hand . . . Ring in the Christ that is to be' is related to the 'closing cycle rich in good', the summer that sleeps long in the seed of this world. The son of God addressed in the exordium represents the 'highest, holiest manhood'. 'For God is glorified in man', Browning had written in *Paracelsus*, the ending of which bears such a distinct resemblance to Tennyson's thinking that indebtedness seems more than probable: God 'dwells in all, From life's minute beginnings, up at last To man – the consummation of this scheme of being, the completion of this sphere Of life'; 'hints and previsions' of power, knowledge, and love in lower natures 'all lead up higher, All shape out dimly the superior race' when man appears; with the perfection of all mankind, and not till then, 'man's general infancy' begins, with a new 'tendency to God'. 'Such men are even now upon the earth', Paracelsus declares, and it is in this kind of context and spirit, not from the idolatry of idealization, that Tennyson considers Hallam 'half divine'.

Tennyson and Hallam both read Italian literature, and Dante was undoubtedly one of the Tuscan poets they read and discussed at Somersby (lxxxix). It was from Dante that the idea of the orbs and 'tenfold-complicated change' came, the stages of spiritual ascent in the *Paradiso* being indicated by ten heavens. The first nine exercise an influence on the inhabitants of the earth. Six are planetary, beginning with the moon; they include the sun, the fixed stars, and the *Primum Mobile*, which imparts motion to the heavens it surrounds. There is no motion in the tenth, the Empyrean, the abode of God and the Blessed, where place and time are transcended. It may be no accident that white moonlight preludes the movement towards the crowning race at the end of *In Memoriam*, and that, after the trance in which the united spirits of the poet and Hallam are whirled 'About empyreal heights of thought' to 'that which is', a breeze fluctuates 'all the still perfume', rocks the heavy-folded rose, and flings the lilies to and fro. Its annunciation of the dawn, as East and West 'without a breath' mix their dim lights and 'broaden into endless day', indicates a spiritual significance which recalls the twenty-third canto of the *Paradiso*, where Beatrice invites Dante to behold the host of Christ's triumph, and all the fruit harvested by the circlings of the spheres. His sight is overmastered by the wisdom and power which opened the roads between earth and heaven. She then asks why he is so enamoured of her face that he does not turn towards the fair garden which blossoms beneath

Christ's rays. There is the rose wherein the divine word was made flesh (cf. xxxvi), and there are the lilies by whose odour men were led to pursue the right road. The thought and the imagery of the two poets are close, as are the endings of their works, Tennyson's God of love and law being comparable to 'the love that moves the sun and stars'.

Unlike the 'awful rose of dawn' which is God's hopeful but distant answer to the guilty in 'The Vision of Sin', the rose in *In Memoriam*, sometimes in conjunction with warmth or fragrance, connotes spiritual joy or peace; a similar significance is conveyed by the crimson cloud towards which the ship bearing Arthur is steered in Tennyson's dream (ciii). Love, a star which broods over the eternal landscape of the spiritual world, creates 'A rosy warmth from marge to marge' (xlvi), an association spiritually comparable to that of the orient star and crimson seas observed from Barmouth when odorous breezes have dispelled doubt and death, and brought serenity to the poet (lxxxvi). The spring is the time for Hallam to return in his mortal form, with the hope of unaccomplished years on his brow, but only the mellowing summer, when 'the sunbeam broodeth warm', and the scent of roses is blown over rippling waves of corn, is appropriate for his appearance in his finer state of increasing fulfilment after death (xci). When Tennyson 'slips the thoughts of life and death' in his imagined pentecostal communion with Hallam, 'every dew-drop paints a bow' and 'every thought breaks out a rose' (cxxii).

The last poem is a reminder that *In Memoriam* records a growing assurance, not an absolute faith. It refers to Tennyson's 'former flash of joy', but expresses uncertainty whether Hallam's spirit had visited him during the trance which brought the visionary experience of being rapt 'About empyreal heights of thought'. He fears he will evermore be a life behind in spiritual evolution after death, but holds, after insisting that individuality will be preserved, that he will know Hallam when they meet (xlvii). In the next poem, after statements in the Prologue and elsewhere (xxx for example) which comprehend or imply the main articles of his religious belief, he presents his general caveat:

> If these brief lays, of Sorrow born,
>   Were taken to be such as closed
>   Grave doubts and answers here proposed,
> Then these were such as men might scorn:

Her care is not to part and prove;
  She takes, when harsher moods remit,
  What slender shade of doubt may flit,
And makes it vassal unto love.

True to himself, he rejects the conventional route of pastoral elegy, and, after keeping pace with the thought and questioning of his age, essays a work which will be intellectually and spiritually satisfying. Random influences from art cannot express his deepest sorrow, but they may help him to be vocal, and he does not disdain a few pastoral touches. They are most evident in xxi–iii, where the poet takes grasses from Hallam's grave to make pipes whereon to blow, thinks of the path they followed, cheering the way with song, and laments the change following the period when the 'lavish hills' murmured happily of Pan,

And many an old philosophy
  On Argive heights divinely sang,
  And round us all the thicket rang
To many a flute of Arcady.

Urania (Heavenly Wisdom) reprehends his daring to speak on religious matters, and urges him to descend to his native Parnassian stream, where he may hear his laurel 'whisper sweet About the ledges of the hill' (xxxvii). His Hesper–Phosphor poem reverses a Greek epigram, which may have caught his notice in Shelley's translation:

Thou wert the morning star among the living,
  Ere thy fair light had fled; –
Now, having died, thou art as Hesperus, giving
  New splendour to the dead.

Tennyson thought his stanza original, having 'no notion till 1880 that Lord Herbert of Cherbury had written his occasional verses in the same metre'. It forms the second quatrain of his Mariana poems, and mediates some of his early political ones, notably two written before Hallam's death, 'Hail Briton!' and 'You ask me, why, though ill at ease'. Not surprisingly its exercise in the long series of poems that helped to break this initial shock, and presented 'the imaginative woe, That loved to handle spiritual strife', is considerably varied; in the hands of a less masterly writer, it could soon have become monotonous. This charge has been levelled against Tennyson; FitzGerald thought *In Memoriam* had 'that air of being evolved by a Poetical Machine of the highest order'. (Thoroughly conservative in his tastes, he had little time for anything written by Tennyson after 1842; 'I do not forget however to sweeten my imagination with Tennyson's *old* poems', he wrote in May 1851. 'Had I Alfred's voice, I would not have mumbled for years over In Memoriam', he informed Frederick Tennyson the following December, asking what could it do but make us all sentimental.) Sometimes compression of thought leads to stiffness, but usually Tennyson's economy is notable for a simplicity reached after the shedding of all dross. Here and there a succession of end-stopped lines imparts a metronomical effect, but this is usually avoided in variations which are markedly dependent on the incidence of natural pause and emphasis. There is nothing exceptional in lx ('He past; a soul of nobler tone') as an example of this kind of composition; every line except one is end-stopped, but the position of intralinear pause and stress changes continually, and the poem reads easily. More striking are the introductory emphases in xcv (ll.25–32), where the repetition of 'and strange' at regular stress intervals sets up a rhythm that carries one forward with a sense of the continuity of Tennyson's impressions. Nothing is more technically remarkable than the supreme command with which the poet repeatedly, in brief and lengthy passages, takes the verse in his stride, making it subservient to thought, until it is lost in movements so rhythmically true to subject and feeling that attention is sustained and absorbed in a process of total recognition. More than any other factor, such expressiveness makes the art of poetry in metrical form, and its pursuit by readers, worth while. If it aspires to music, it is precisely because, as Pater said, it is impossible in music to distinguish form from substance, or subject from expression.

With this in mind, the indictment of Hallam's death anniversary, at the end of lxxii, may be contrasted with the celebration of his birthday in cvii. The weather in both is characterized by stormy blasts; in the climax of the first it becomes one in imagery and rhythm with the poet's feeling; its sharpness in the second contrasts with the cheerfulness within, and all in sound and movement is antithetically consonant with its subject. The full new life that seems to flow from nature, and bring peace to the poet at Barmouth, becomes the shaping spirit of a poem that rises and dies away within the well-adjusted mutations of a single sentence. A 'fuller wave' of inspiration has a similar influence, though the tempo is quickened and more climactic, in the poem that begins with the unTennysonian sibilance of 'Oh, wast thou with me dearest, then'. This kind of disciplined flow could be illustrated from three endings, the first expressing Hallam's eloquence in Apostolic debate:

> Who, but hung to hear
> The rapt oration flowing free
>
> From point to point, with power and grace
>   And music in the bounds of law,
>   To those conclusions when we saw
> The God within him light his face . . . .

More varied and subtle, the second evokes the breeze and its effects on tree and flower after the night of trance at Somersby, creating simultaneously a sense of the spiritual within the natural which ends with strong confirmation of faith:

> And sucked from out the distant gloom
>   A breeze began to tremble o'er
>   The large leaves of the sycamore,
> And fluctuate all the still perfume,
>
> And gathering freshlier overhead,
>   Rocked the full-foliaged elms, and swung
>   The heavy-folded rose, and flung
> The lilies to and fro, and said
>
> 'The dawn, the dawn', and died away;
>   And East and West, without a breath,
>   Mixt their dim lights, like life and death,
> To broaden into boundless day.

The final example is the most sweeping, in full accord with the vast range of its thought; it occurs at the end of *In Memoriam*, where moonlight suggests a mystical blessing on the marriage of the Epilogue, and the vision moves forward uninterruptedly through thirty-six lines to the 'one far-off divine event'.

In Memoriam contains a number of succinct expressions which heighten or concentrate thought, the quiet metaphor in 'O wheresoever those may be, Betwixt the slumber of the poles' being one to ponder over; another is the 'broken lights' representing the little systems which have their day and cease to be. Higher in its reference and positive in its import, this image is ancestral to the spiritual descent which ends in Eliot's 'broken images, where the sun beats' in the kind of waste land dreaded by Tennyson at the end of *Idylls of the King*. More vividly memorable, however, are some of the more sensuous evocations. So many are drawn from nature that others, such as the storm of high-built organs in Cambridge colleges, as their rolling thunder-music shakes 'The prophet blazoned on the panes', are easily overlooked. Characteristic features of the Lincolnshire scene are quickly sketched (c). Elsewhere the sea-blue bird of March flits by when rosy plumelets tuft the larch; countless waves of ripening wheat ripple round the lonely grange; nearer Somersby, the brook babbles by many a sandy bar, floods the haunts of hern and crake, and fragments into silver arrows the sailing moon in creek and cove; or one hears 'behind the woodbine veil The milk that bubbled in the pail, And buzzings of the honied hours'. By the rectory the sycamore towers in full foliage while wych-elms chequer the lawn 'with dusk and bright', or the beech gathers brown and the maple burns itself away. The sweep of the scythe in morning dew is heard; in the summer the landscape may be observed 'winking through the heat', or, in the dusk of eve and early morn, the white kine glimmering in upland fields. There are recollections of rose-carnations that feed the humming air with spice, of the sunflower raying round with flame her disk of seed, and of the gust 'that round the garden flew, And tumbled half the mellowing pears'.

More imaginatively satisfying are scenes which stir deeper chords, when external elements give vivid expression to the poet's feeling. Two poems written during the period when Tennyson imagined the ship bringing Hallam's body to England exemplify this by force of contrast. One is of even tenor, the morning calm, interrupted only by the chestnuts pattering to the ground, extending from the high wold, where the dewy furze and gossamers twinkling into green and gold catch the poet's attention, over 'yon great plain That sweeps with all its autumn bowers, And crowded farms and lessening towers, To mingle with the bounding main'. Any calm he possesses is a calm despair, suggesting calm on the seas, waves that sway themselves to sleep, and 'dead calm in that noble breast Which heaves but with the heaving deep'. Later, as rising winds whirl away the last red leaf, and the sunbeam seems dashed on tower and tree, only the thought that Hallam's remains are unaffected at sea enables him to bear the loud strain and stir of the barren branches; anxiety, however, makes it impossible to pore over, and enjoy, the spectacle of the rising cloud that 'onward drags a labouring breast, And topples round the dreary west, A looming bastion fringed with fire'. Tennyson's complex emotions are expressed primarily by the changing scene; incidentally also, but with subtle continuity, by aural and rhythmic features, such as the steady insistence of 'That rises upward always higher', the painful heavy drag of the next line, and the sudden incidence of depression brought by 'topples', before growing fear of the unknown, a 'looming bastion', turns into besetting alarm.

Some poems in which the natural scene embodies the thought stand out as independent units, among them 'The Danube to the Severn gave The darkened heart that beat no more', where the hush brought by the rising tide and the sound it makes as it falls convey more completely and simply than any abstract statement the poet's inability to communicate his deepest, abiding sorrow; (words, as he says elsewhere, 'half reveal And half conceal the Soul within'). The antithetical imagery of the Hesper–Phosphor poem (cxxi), to which reference has been made, falls into this category. Attention has also been drawn to the Barmouth lyric 'Sweet after showers, ambrosial air', one of the poems most subtly true to Tennyson's experience, in which imagery and movement are fused in one sustained thought. The most compact example of this type needs no comment beyond a reminder that its closing regret preludes the yearning for trust 'In that which made the world so fair':

Now fades the last long streak of snow,
   Now burgeons every maze of quick
   About the flowering squares, and thick
By ashen roots the violets blow.

Now rings the woodland loud and long,
   The distance takes a lovelier hue,
   And drowned in yonder living blue
The lark becomes a sightless song.

Now dance the lights on lawn and lea,
   The flocks are whiter down the vale,
   And milkier every milky sail
On winding stream or distant sea;

Where now the seamew pipes, or dives
  In yonder greening gleam, and fly
  The happy birds, that change their sky
To build and brood; that live their lives

From land to land; and in my breast
  Spring wakens too; and my regret
  Becomes an April violet,
And buds and blossoms like the rest.

13

The 'Locksley Hall' Poems and *Maud*

Tennyson's evolutionary faith supplied no comforting reassurances on worldly issues; he was no facile optimist. Progress was an exceedingly long-term process; it could be observed in this or that direction; tendencies in others were even retrogressive. Human corruptibility might gradually be reduced, but he had no doubt, as he tells us in *In Memoriam*, that 'vast eddies' would continue in 'the flood of onward time'. When, in 'Ring out, wild bells', he prayed for an end to 'the feud of rich and poor', 'the want, the care, the sin, The faithless coldness of the times', 'foul disease', and 'the narrowing lust of gold', he had in mind the appalling socio-economic conditions of a class-ridden, wealth-producing England which by and large was guilty of *laissez-faire* and mammonish exploitation, and which was quite content to leave altruistic enterprise and education to churches and other voluntary organizations. He knew Carlyle by 1839, and must have become familiar with his *Past and Present* indictment of man's oppression by 'his Mock-Superiors', and of 'plethoric plenty' in which 'the people perish'; from Charles Kingsley and others he learnt about abject poverty and working-class conditions before he read *Alton Locke* (1851).

Such wrongs stirred Tennyson so deeply at times that he was compelled to vent them in verse. His artistic problem was to publicize them without incurring ostracism; he resolved it by recourse to the mask of fiction, first in 'Locksley Hall', which may have been written as early as 1837–8. Locksley is the name of Robin Hood, a militant champion of the poor against wealthy oppressors in Scott's *Ivanhoe*;[13] Tennyson's hero curses 'social wants', 'social lies', and 'gold that gilds the straitened forehead of the fool'. The fact that his comrades sound the bugle-horn to call him is a

diversion, for his thoughts and feelings clearly belong to the
nineteenth century; he is Tennyson's mouthpiece, and the fictional
background is contemporary. He and his heiress cousin Amy had
been in love but, in obedience to her acquistive parents, she had
married someone no better, in his estimation, than a clown, who,
when his passion fades, will consider her 'Something better than his
dog, a little dearer than his horse'.

The hero of this monologue is a prey to strong feeling, and he later
admits that his words are wild. What can he do when 'Every door is
barred with gold, and opens but to golden keys'? The long swinging
eight-stressed trochaic lines consort with the excitement which
continually gets the better of his judgment. Like Dante, he believes
that 'a sorrow's crown of sorrow is remembering happier things',
but it pleases him to recall the 'wild pulsation' of his youth when he
'dipt into the future' and saw 'all the wonder that would be'.
Characteristically his vision of airborne commerce spelling prosperity is crossed by the thought of aerial war until the battle-flags
are furled 'In the Parliament of man, the Federation of the world'.
Now everything is out of joint; he knows that the menace of 'a
hungry people' exists. 'Knowledge comes, but wisdom lingers', he
repeats with Tennysonian irony, for he next inveighs against the
weakness that springs from woman's inferiority to man, and takes
comfort in a dream of marriage with some savage woman in one of
the tropical isles of Eden. Admitting that once again he is the fool of
fancy, he recovers his sense of racial superiority and his belief in
progress: 'Forward, forward let us range, Let the great world spin
for ever down the ringing grooves of change.' (Why Tennyson did
not correct this is puzzling. 'When I went by the first train from
Liverpool to Manchester (1830), I thought that the wheels ran in a
groove. It was a black night and there was such a vast crowd
. . . that we could not see the wheels', he wrote.) The social criticism is less noticeable than the optimism; it reflects a somewhat
unbalanced mind. Only interpreters who succumb to biographical
fancies can suggest that the exaggerated attack on gold as the key to
success sprang consciously from private authorial resentment. The
poem ends with a characteristic outburst: as the youthful hero
indulges self-congratulatory thoughts on his 'founts of inspiration',
he sees a blackening storm-cloud, and trusts it contains a thunder-
bolt that will wreck Locksley Hall. (The storm and other ideas for
the poem came from Sir William Jones's prose translation of the
seven Arabic poems entitled *The Moallakāt*.)

Partly to ensure that he had not been misunderstood, but more to use the same mouthpiece for expressing some of his worst fears, Tennyson wrote the complementary poem 'Locksley Hall Sixty Years After' in 1886. All is changed: the speaker is eighty and a wiser man; the fires that shook him in youth, the follies, furies, curses, and passionate tears have gone; 'Cold upon the dead volcano sleeps the gleam of dying day.' He tells us that Amy died in childbirth, and her husband, the Squire who has just died, has proved sound and honest, a better man than he; 'youthful jealousy is a liar', he admits. His son (the speaker's; Tennyson had his dead son Lionel in mind), who believed in ideals and 'looked beyond the grave', had died heroically; his grandson, the new heir of Locksley Hall, to whom he addresses his commentary on the times, thinks death the end of life's over-tragic drama. The old man is egoistically overweening, even cynical at times. The grandson will not suffer, after being jilted by the 'worldling born of worldlings', the 'would-be-widow wife'; the accident that almost derailed the train bringing him to Locksley Hall must have been caused by 'a vicious boy'. We have reached the age of disillusionment. The old cry of 'Forward, forward' has gone, and the speaker wonders what progress has been made since 'Christian love among the Churches looked the twin of heathen hate', or revolutionary France turned to bloodshed after preaching 'all men's good'. He has learned (like George Eliot) that the present is the fatal daughter of the past, and denounces demagogues who, preaching egalitarianism, threaten to overwhelm the state with the supremacy of the lowest common factor. 'Tumble Nature heel o'er head', he says, 'and, yelling with the yelling street, Set the feet above the brain and swear the brain is in the feet.' There is no time for reticence or reverence when 'maiden fancies' are set 'wallowing in the troughs of Zolaism', nor can one expect war to end as long as the world population continues its Malthusian increase. He then turns to the social ills that stain an era of scientific advance:

Is it well that while we range with Science, glorying in the Time,
City children soak and blacken soul and sense in city slime?

There among the glooming alleys Progress halts on palsied feet,
Crime and hunger cast our maidens by the thousand on the street.

There the Master scrimps his haggard sempstress of her daily bread,
There a single sordid attic holds the living and the dead.

There the smouldering fire of fever creeps across the rotted floor,
And the crowded couch of incest in the warrens of the poor.

He sees 'Reversion ever dragging Evolution in the mud', but has not
surrendered his belief in progress: 'Forward then, but still remember how the course of Time will swerve, Crook and turn upon itself
in many a backward streaming curve.' He urges the heir of Locksley
Hall to follow the example of his predecessor, who for sixty widowed
years had helped 'his homelier brother men, Served the poor, and
built the cottage, raised the school, and drained the fen'. His
grandson must follow Light, and do the Right, until he sees that 'the
highest Human Nature is divine'. Whatever his subjective idiosyncrasies, the speaker undoubtedly voices Tennyson's criticisms and
his ideals. The two monologues may be unsubtle, both in the hero's
character and the presentation of his views, compared with
Browning's best, but their impact is immense.

The itch to associate Rosa Baring with the fiction of 'Locksley
Hall' suggests the need to be wary of exaggerating autobiographical
influences in *Maud*. In 'The Roses on the Terrace', which is clearly
not devoid of fiction, Tennyson recalls her blush fifty years earlier
(probably at Harrington Hall), when he took the liberty of
addressing her as his rose. There is no evidence that they were in
love; in her later years she remembered mainly his conversation at
balls, and the pride she felt in the verses he addressed to her. He
could declare his whole heart was vassal at her feet in a fanciful
poem, but nothing written with her in mind has the authentic
feeling of the contemporary sonnet he sent to Sophy Rawnsley, nor
can one believe Rosa was quite the dancing partner of 'Three
Sonnets to a Coquette'. No doubt she took pleasure in his high-
flown flattery, notably in 'Early Verses of Compliment to Miss Rose
Baring', where the thought 'East and West and North and South'
bear not a rose like 'the rose of roses' is an obvious precursor of the
lyric 'Go not, happy day' in *Maud* (I.xvii), which had been intended
for *The Princess*. It is misleading to assume that there is much more
than a poetical link between *Maud* and the younger Tennyson; if the
love it expresses came more from experience than from imagination,
it overflowed from the author's love for his wife in their first years at
Farringford. The Isle of Wight supplied the setting for the poem.
Farringford, Sir Charles Tennyson tells us, is 'the dark, solitary
house "half-hid in the gleaming wood"', from which the roar of the
sea and scream of the down-dragged shingle could be heard on

stormy nights'; contributions to the Hall garden and its surroundings came also from Swainston with its cedars, home of Sir John
Simeon, who played an important role in the development of Maud
from 'Oh! that 'twere possible', the lyric disguising Tennyson's grief
for the loss of Hallam; subsequently another early lyric, 'See what a
lovely shell', was involved. During the composition of the poem, as
Tennyson testified, 'cannon was heard booming from the battle-
ships in the Solent before the Crimean War'.

Maud is pre-eminently a lyrical poem; equally it is dramatic, its
central character (the one speaker) so abnormal and psychotic that,
until he is sympathetically realized, the work cannot be appreciated
as a whole. Its titles are revealing: first it was 'Maud or the
Madness', later 'Maud: A Monodrama'. Tennyson described it as

> the history of a morbid poetic soul, under the blighting influence
> of a recklessly speculative age. He is the heir of madness, an
> egotist with the makings of a cynic, raised to sanity by a pure and
> holy love which elevates his whole nature, passing from the height
> of triumph to the lowest depth of misery, driven into madness by
> the loss of her whom he has loved, and, when he has at length
> passed through the fiery furnace, and has recovered his reason,
> giving himself up to work for the good of mankind through the
> unselfishness born of his great passion.

'Giving himself up to work for the good of mankind' seems too free a
comment, but the passage supplies a valuable key to the poem. Its
peculiarity, Tennyson added, 'is that different phases of passion in
one person take the place of different characters'. In the Locksley
Hall poems the speaker looks at the past and the world around him
from a relatively fixed point, the one brief period in which he speaks.
The hero of *Maud* lives repeatedly in the present, expressing a
succession of inner experiences, which sometimes recall the distant
past but more often reflect immediate surroundings and those near
events, happenings or expectations, which excite his feelings. There
are many chronological intervals, brief and more frequent as the
drama approaches its climax, few and more protracted in the sequel
of breakdown and recovery.

'This poem is a little *Hamlet*', Tennyson said. For his hero and
Shakespeare's, the time is out of joint, as it is for the speaker in
'Locksley Hall'; each is morbid and suicidal; each suspects that his
father's death was caused by a person dear to one he loves (to

Hamlet's mother in the one, to Maud in the other); each acts with revengeful impulse, killing a relative dear to his beloved, who dies in consequence. Finally each, as a result of his own weakness, admires the man of action; *Hamlet* ends with Fortinbras's return from a successful war, and *Maud* with the hero's expectation of fulfilment in military action. The circumstances for each work are so different that some of these common features must be accidental; the family background of the story undoubtedly owes much to *The Bride of Lammermoor*.

The principal difference between Shakespeare's drama and *Maud* is that the major events of the former take place visibly on the stage, whereas the whole of Tennyson's drama is interior, fully exemplifying the truth of Wordsworth's early realization:

> Action is transitory – a step, a blow,
> The motion of a muscle – this way or that –
> 'Tis done, and in the after-vacancy
> We wonder at ourselves like men betrayed:
> Suffering is permanent, obscure and dark,
> And shares the nature of infinity.

In fact, the subjective presentation of *Maud*, where the perceiver is the prey of his own excitable–depressive mind, will tend to make the reader suspicious; justifiably so, because life is for all, to some degree or other, a process of subjective impressionism. For this reason (and perhaps a slight failure in authorial communication is indicated) one wonders how uncertain the catastrophe would have remained – whether Maud really had died – but for the notes Tennyson left to eliminate misconception.

The poem begins with a sudden explosion of feeling, which expresses more than the hero's revulsion from the hollow where his father was killed. To his fevered imagination the fringing heather above it looks like blood, and blood drips from its red-ribbed ledges. The silent horror which echoes 'Death' suggests the suicidal fear which attracts him to the place: 'Must *I* too creep to the hollow and dash myself down and die?' he asks, and 'Were it not wise if I fled from the place and the pit and the fear?' Even at the height of his love he can think of easeful death: 'for sullen-seeming Death may give More life to Love than is or even was In our low world, where yet 'tis sweet to live'. The 'yet' has the force of an admission, and the 'doom assigned' in war, to which he commits himself finally, indicates a readiness to relinquish life. The curse which he fears the returning Maud will bring him emphasizes her attraction; 'some dark undercurrent woe' seems to draw him to the Hall before the catastrophe.

In him also the present is fatal daughter to the past. Maud, he had come to feel, was his 'by a right, from birth to death' ('Mine, mine', he avidly insists, as if Maud were his lifeline), for their fathers had betrothed them when she was born, as Maud's mother, regretful of the feud between the two houses, had told her. 'Houses' has *Romeo and Juliet* overtones, but the household Fury which sprinkled the feud with blood in the hero's eyes associates him with the helpless victim of some Greek tragedy. 'We are puppets, Man in his pride, and Beauty fair in her flower', he contends. He is sorry for himself; his father's death, caused by the failure of a speculation which had brought immense wealth to Maud's father, had caused his and his mother's decline, and he had lost his freshness in caring for her. How much of his suicidal temperament was hereditary? If only he could be dear to someone, he keeps saying to himself, he would recover self-esteem; if Maud's smile were all that he dreamed, 'the world were not so bitter But a smile could make it sweet'. Her chivalrous battle-song stirs a wish for manliness in him, that the man he is may cease to be.

Knowing his weakness and fearing the worst, he affects indifference at Maud's return, and indulges in the cynicism which is his safeguard: her beauty may be perfect, but it is 'Faultily faultless, icily regular, splendidly null'. Yet, 'Luminous, gemlike, ghostlike, deathlike', growing and fading and growing, it haunts his sleep until he can bear it no longer but seeks the solitude of his 'dark garden ground', where his torment is imaged in the sea's 'broad-flung shipwrecking roar' which he hears, followed by 'the scream of a maddened beach dragged down by the wave'. He yearns for quiet woodland ways where he can philosophize and escape the cruel madness of love. Maud, like Marvell's ill-fated fawn, has 'but fed on the roses and lain in the lilies of life'; she is ill prepared for wifehood in the world of 'plunder and prey' which he, its victim, sees in nature, and which 'no preacher can heal'.

Fear engendered by his psychosis makes him see deception and conspiracy afoot. Maud's smile which had warmed his heart the livelong night appears like a coquettish snare the next morning; perhaps her brother (that jewelled mass of millinery, oiled and curled like an Assyrian bull, and smelling of musk and insolence) had suggested she should employ it to win a vote for him at the election. The croaking raven of suspicion warns the hero not to be their tool; contrariwise, when the storm of his contempt has abated, he tells himself not to be the fool of angry pride. He knows that he is swayed by feelings too powerful to be restrained, and fears that, as a result of living in solitude, a prey to imagination, morbid hatred, and horror, he is humanly half petrified.

Further recognition from Maud gives him new life, but he is sickened by jealous dread when he sees her riding with two at her side, one of whom had inherited wealth, 'the power that all men adore' and 'the grace all women desire'. The thought of gold maddens him; he had imagined it flying from the ruined autumnal woodlands when his father, in a wind that wailed like a broken worldling, walked for the last time from home. Now (the thought – not the feeling – prompted by the d'Eyncourt pretensions of Tennyson's uncle Charles, and by the mining inheritance of his favourite aunt's husband in County Durham) he scorns the suitor, a young new-made lord, as proud of his 'gewgaw castle' as of his title, and heir to the gold which his grandfather had made by exploiting miners until he was 'Master of half a servile shire'. He realizes that this contempt for his rival is 'splenetic, personal, base', that it comes from 'A wounded thing with a rancorous cry', at war with himself and society. Soon his feelings are roused again, in condemnation of one who recently preached against the maintenance of a small English army. As he sobers, he wishes he could hear Maud's chivalrous battle-song again; it would encourage him to think she could not mistake his rival, a 'wanton dissolute boy', for 'a man and a leader of men'.

Despite their mutual scorn, the hero longs to give Maud's brother 'the grasp of fellowship', but he is met by a curving contumelious lip and a gorgonizing British stare. His reflection makes him realize that she will have much to fear if, as he fondly believes, she is in love with him; for her sake therefore he curbs his anger against this 'lump of earth' who has inherited all his father's evil. He takes the opportunity of his absence to seek her out, knowing that she is 'the one bright thing' to save him from madness, crime, or suicide. She accepts him, and they spend a golden day together. After taking her home, he feels his blood coursing fully, more warmly and sweetly than ever before; when she closes her door, it is as if the Gates of Heaven are shut against him. Supreme happiness makes his poetic spirit obsessionally hyperaesthetic: he has seen the rose of passion in

her cheeks, on her lips, in the South, and the West, and beyond its
horizon; he has seen daisies turn rosy when brushed by her delicate
tread, and heard rooks calling 'Maud, Maud, Maud, Maud'; he
now hears her light steps in the pattering fall of the 'dry-tongued
laurels'. The cedar sighing for Lebanon in the long breeze expresses
his feelings; it reminds him of the starry head of her who has made
his life a perfumed altar-flame, and of Eve in the thornless garden of
Eden (before the Fall). He rests beneath it, and sees a livelier
emerald twinkling in the grass, and a purer sapphire melting into
the sea. The stars that crown his happy day remind him of the time
when he wished to be a peasant rather than nurtured to understand

> A sad astrology, the boundless plan
> That makes you tyrants in your iron skies,
> Innumerable, pitiless, passionless eyes,
> Cold fires, yet with power to burn and brand
> His nothingness into man.

Now, having risen 'out of lonely Hell', he wonders if it is because the
earth has moved nearer the stars that they look so bright in their soft
splendours. His whole world is changed.

Recalling his boyhood delight in *The Arabian Nights*, the hero
thinks the Hall garden with its perfume and roses is a Persian garden
from which he is excluded by the Sultan, Maud's brother, who has
returned. He waits outside the gate at night, listening to the dance
music which succeeds a 'grand political dinner'. His emotions beat
to the polka rhythm, and he notices the planet of Love beginning to
fade in the daffodil sky of dawn. (In conjunction with Orion, the
daffodil is associated with death at the beginning and end of the
poem.) The soul of the rose enters this hypersensitive lover as
the music clashes; he imagines it awake all night in expectation of
Maud's coming, and holds colloquies with it and the lily (the
symbol of her purity and fidelity) as he waits for his queen to appear.
Certain of her approach, he believes his beating heart would hear
her if it had been buried a century; it would 'start and tremble under
her feet, And blossom in purple and red'. With this double prolepsis,
the final image suggesting bloodshed, Part I suddenly ends. The
division first appeared in 1859; a further division, in the sequel, was
made in 1865, with the careless retention of the section number 'VI'
from Part II at the opening of Part III.

The lover recalls how, after he was struck by Maud's brother in front of her babe-faced suitor, a mad impulse to avenge his father seized him; the pistol shots in the duel which followed seemed to reverberate with 'a million horrible bellowing echoes' from 'the red-ribbed hollow behind the wood', thundering up into heaven 'the Christless code, That must have life for a blow'. When his opponent fell, he heard a cry for a brother's blood which will ring in his heart and ears as long as he lives. Such a climax underlines the melodramatic quality of *Maud*; it is based on a sensational story, and orchestrated with subtle variations to present a psychological monodrama ranging emotionally from heaven to hell.

The lover has fled, and grief makes him (like the mourner in Rossetti's 'The Woodspurge') fix his gaze on a small object, a sea-shell which, though frail, has withstood the shock of 'cataract seas that snap The three-decker's oaken spine Athwart the ledges of rock, Here on the Breton strand'. Although he buoys his fancy with the thought that neither Maud nor her brother is dead, he is haunted by a Maud-like ghost that flits along land and main. He then hears that his beloved is dead (the section which makes this clearer was added for the 1856 edition), and his yearning for her is expressed in 'O that 'twere possible'; 'Ah Christ,' he cries, 'For one short hour to see The souls we loved, that they might tell us What and where they be.' In a dream he hears her singing as of old, then wakes up in the city. The phantom-shadow crosses wherever he steals, until

> the broad light glares and beats,
> And the shadow flits and fleets
> And will not let me be;
> And I loathe the squares and streets,
> And the faces that one meets,
> Hearts with no love for me:
> Always I long to creep
> Into some cavern deep,
> There to weep, and weep, and weep
> My whole soul out to thee.

He is confined to a madhouse, where he imagines that he is buried and his heart-beats are the hoofs of horses overhead. The inmates and their babble revive his critical spleen a little; the dead who haunt him confuse his mind. He had one certain thought: that it is lawful to fight in a public cause, but not to spill life for a private blow. He thinks he may be only half dead, and wishes some kind heart would bury him deeper, only slightly deeper, that he may have peace. Like the shell, he is 'Frail, but a work divine'; and one wonders just how Tennyson's pity was roused for such a character. He had more in mind, one suspects, than any depressing symptoms which ever made him apprehensive about himself; possibly, some patient he knew at one of Allen's homes; possibly, one of his brothers.

The lunatic, the lover, and the poet are of imagination all compact; in varying degrees at different stages of the poem they unite in the hero. His recovery, which brings release from confinement, does not make him normal; a heavenly vision in which Maud appears, and tells him that he will find rest for his soul in the coming war, suggests how his mind works. It lightens his despair to think that England can rise above mammonism against tyranny; that its men need not be an unkind, divided 'little breed', but can unite for a noble cause. He is no longer the man who wished to bury himself in self, or retire in philosophic seclusion; at last he can be one with his kind. The passionate ballad sung by Maud inspires him; his rose has become 'The blood-red blossom of war with a heart of fire'.

An outcry against Tennyson's 'glorification of war' (as it was described by Goldwin Smith) was inevitable; nor could the hero's cutting remarks against clergy pacifists and young Tory representatives be forgiven. Few readers fully realized the artistic validity of extreme thought in a dramatic poem true to its central character; with reference to it, the poet added courageously, 'I do not mean to say my madman does not speak truth too.' There are times when nations rise from sloth and ignominious peace to fight against evil, though in retrospect the Crimean War does not appear to be a shining example. War is no panacea in the poem; it is the lesser of two evils; the new heroic spirit has reduced England's lust for gold only 'for a little'. Tennyson uses the psychotic mask of his story to stress the ills of a country that is radically unchanged. 'O, let me not be mad, not mad, sweet heaven!' cries Lear, whose sufferings bring home to him the abuses of his age. The denunciations of *Maud* come from one on the brink of madness ('O let the solid ground Not fail . . . What matter if I go mad . . . '). All's wrong with his world until he is loved. Peace, when the spirit of Cain prevails in mercenary lust, is a curse, he declares; it has produced civil war which is viler for not 'openly bearing the sword'. Only the ledger lives, and the poor are hovelled like swine; 'Timour-Mammon grins on a pile of children's bones'. Better 'War with a thousand battles, and shaking a hundred thrones'! The speaker knows that he has been 'raging', but the feeling that flares in his wounded psyche is fuelled by facts, noticeably from *Past and Present*; not surprisingly, he comes to a Carlylean conclusion:

> Ah God, for a man with heart, head, hand,
> Like some of the simple great ones gone
> For ever and ever by,
> One still strong man in a blatant land,
> Whatever they call him, what care I,
> Aristocrat, democrat, autocrat – one
> Who can rule and dare not lie.

Yet, however extreme the hero's views, 'Ode on the Death of the Duke of Wellington' shows that they are undoubtedly rooted in Tennyson's more sober belief:

> Not once or twice in our rough island-story,
> The path of duty was the way to glory:
> He that walks it, only thirsting
> For the right, and learns to deaden
> Love of self, before his journey closes,
> He shall find the stubborn thistle bursting
> Into glossy purples, which outredden
> All voluptuous garden-roses.

14

Patriotism and Politics

Tennyson grew up in a period when, as a result of the horrors produced by the French Revolution, and by the long struggle against Napoleonic imperialism, anti-Gallic sentiments in England were almost endemic. Nevertheless the jingoism of 'English Warsong' and 'National Song' against 'the ancient enemy', even though they appeared in 1830, and however rousing their choric metres, is as astonishing as the triteness of their clichés: hearts of oak, Merry England, the only land of the free. The sonnet 'Buonaparte' (1832) boasts of the lessons 'the island queen who sways the floods and lands From Ind to Ind' taught the French. Revolutionary and imperialist alarms from France brought Tennyson more than once to boiling-point. He damns the 'blind hysterics of the Celt' and the 'red fool-fury of the Seine' in *In Memoriam* (cix, cxxvii) and, in 'Beautiful City' (1889), observes how often Paris, 'the crater of European confusion', with its 'passionate shriek for the rights of an equal humanity', had proved its revolution to be only evolution 'Rolled again back on itself in the tides of a civic insanity'.

The admiration which Tennyson could not help voicing late in life at the end of *Harold* for heroism in defence of England appears early in 'Hail Briton!', where he contrasts the 'haughtier aims' of the Saxons who 'gave their bodies to the death' with contemporary politicians who aim at nothing higher than popular applause. A nobler testimony to the influence of such patriots on their countrymen appears in 'Tiresias':

No sound is breathed so potent to coerce,
And to conciliate, as their names who dare
For that sweet mother land which gave them birth
Nobly to do, nobly to die.

Though elated by the passing of the electoral Reform Bill in 1832, Tennyson reveals a rooted distrust of demagogues during this period. In 'Woe to the double-tongued' he optimistically forecasts the doom of these 'Lords of the hustings, whose mob-rhetoric rends The ears of Truth', these 'blind leaders of the blind' who wish to foment riots and 'civil blood'. 'Hail Briton!' betrays the fear that 'the neighbourhood of . . . unstable Celtic blood' will rouse passion and destroy judgment. Traditional law and order are threatened by loud-mouthed ranters against all forms of power, each (unlike freedom-fighters of the past) less interested in the general good than in becoming 'the light ephemeris That flutters in the popular breath'. Extreme political parties leave 'The middle road of sober thought', and the bonds of fellowship are snapped; wisdom lags behind knowledge, and temporary expedients are preferred to 'seasonable changes'. The fable of 'The Goose' suggests that a revolution will destroy what is of most value.

For Tennyson this is freedom of speech. If it were lost, he declares in 'You ask me, why, though ill at ease', he would leave Britain, however great and wealthy it might be, for a warmer clime; he stays because it is a land 'Where Freedom slowly broadens down From precedent to precedent', and where 'diffusive thought' is given time to work. The subject is continued in 'Love thou thy land', which begins with emphasis first on reverence for traditional values, then on the need for knowledge. Progress will not come if people give priority to personal gain; it needs to be based on discussion and experience; it comes from growth or gradation, not from conservative or innovatory extremism. He believes that, even if the clash between old and new continues to create civil strife, the wise will learn from error, and the future will benefit. 'Of old sat Freedom on the heights' expresses the wish that her age-old wisdom will retain its perennial youth and save England from extremes. More despondently 'I loving Freedom for herself' declares that 'change by just degrees With reason and with law' may bring unprecedented progress, but offers cold comfort in the thought that, if the worst should happen, Confusion and War like Order and Peace are ministers of Truth. We learn from our mistakes; there is a divinity that shapes our ends, rough-hew them how we will. Beyond the altruistic dream of love that will 'leaven all the mass, Till every soul be free', the poem 'Freedom' (Tennyson's first political utterance as a peer') is contrived entirely from old ideas, and even from some of his early verse. Hallam Tennyson comments, 'It carried on the feeling of his old political poems, the same feeling which Bacon had expressed, that "Men in their innovations should follow the example of time itself, which indeed innovateth greatly, but quietly, and by degrees scarce to be perceived." '

A French invasion scare after Louis Napoleon's *coup d'état* roused Tennyson in January 1852 to write a number of verses, all but one of which were published anonymously or pseudonymously in the press. 'Rifle Clubs!!!', directed principally against Napoleon the slaughterer, is notable for its condemnation of peace born of sloth or avarice. 'Britons, Guard Your Own' stresses friendship for the French people, but works on anti-Catholic feeling against their dictator, who has won the support of Rome. 'For the Penny-Wise' emphasizes the folly of British military unpreparedness, as 'The Penny-Wise', with its reference to 'Four hundred thousand slaves in arms' in France, had done. Two poems signed 'Merlin' in *The Examiner* continue the campaign. 'The Third of February, 1852' takes the House of Lords to task for appearing to condone the *coup d'état*: England is the one voice in Europe, and must speak out against 'this French God, the child of Hell' synonymous with war; descendants of barons who spoke in manly strain at Runnymede may 'dodge and palter with a public crime' but, despite the bawling of Manchester Liberal peacemongers, the tyrant will not be spared one hard word, and England's honour will be maintained. The second, 'Hands All Round!', is in popular form, its choric appeal for freedom against tyranny being climaxed with 'the great name of England'. It states that 'the best cosmopolite' is the true patriot, and the true Conservative is he who 'lops the mouldered branch away'; it admits that 'Too much we make our Ledgers, Gods'; toasts the wiser French, and America, 'Gigantic daughter of the West', urging her not to stand by while the mother country resists tyrant powers unaided. Another poem, appearing a week later, praises the manly style of these two poems, and trusts that the freedom of the press will not be abused; anonymity assists it in the furtherance of public ends, and 'Taliessin' urges it not to 'work with faction's tools To charm a lower sphere of fulminating fools'. He then turns to cankers of the state, attacking mammonism ('hogs' in 'commercial mire' that discount higher values), the worship of Respectability, with church observances to atone for weekly worldliness (as in Samuel Butler's Musical Banks), and the feebleness of a Church more interested in forms than in truth. After lamenting the revival of Romanism (free subjects plunging their doubts among Carlylean 'old rags and bones') and the reduction, by young intellectual students of the universe, of the One in all to 'An essence less concentred than a man', he asserts the need for 'a manlike God', Godlike men, and readiness for war. Early 1852, in short, saw a critical ferment in Tennyson which broke out later in *Maud*. Another French invasion scare in 1859 led to the publication of 'Riflemen Form!' (adapted from a poem written in January 1852) and to the writing of 'Jack Tar', in which the nation's dependence on the common sailor, rather than on quarrelling party politicians, is underlined.

The greater harmonies of 'Ode on the Death of the Duke of Wellington' befit the burial of a national hero. Tennyson was not commissioned as Poet Laureate to compose it, but felt that it was expected of him. Most of it was written with changing forms of appropriate music in mind: solemn at first in processional pageant, then lighter in thanksgiving through which the tolling bell is heard. Variation continues, from the sound of the sorrowing anthem within St Paul's, and the booming of the cannon, to the happier note of the warrior's victories, which make him worthy to be laid by the side of Nelson; the solemn tone returns with serious hopes for national protection, followed by thoughts of duty and honour as the heroic leader is slowly borne to glorious burial. More peaceful notes, with reflections on the distress caused by his loss, countered by the hope that his soul will have nobler work to do, preface the lowering of the coffin, where lengthened lines consort with the accompaniment of the Dead March and emotional stress, after which the ode concludes calmly, with a glance at the Duke's renown, then at his committal to Christ and God. The ending may not have satisfied its author, but the whole work is to be commended for avoidance of conformity to those traditional artificialities that tend to ossify most English odes written for grand occasions. There are many admirable details of phraseology in this carefully executed poem; it reveals qualities which Tennyson expected in great statesmen; and his hint at the 'slothful overtrust' of politicians could not have been lost in its juxtaposition with reflections on the greatness of one who 'never sold the truth to serve the hour, Nor paltered with Eternal God for power'. Possibly first composed with Wellington in mind, 'Will' contrasts the strong and the weak in images derived from the Scriptural parable of the wise man who built his house on a rock and the foolish man who built his house on the sand. The first of Tennyson's images resembles Wordsworth's on fortitude in 'Elegiac Stanzas suggested by a Picture of Peele Castle'; the second is idiosyncratic and unforgettably evocative:

> as one whose footsteps halt,
> Toiling in immeasurable sand,
> And o'er a weary sultry land,
> Far beneath a blazing vault,
> Sown in a wrinkle of the monstrous hill,
> The city sparkles like a grain of salt.

The Crimean War inspired the ending of *Maud* and 'The Charge of the Light Brigade', which was written in a few minutes after Tennyson had read an account in *The Times* of a gallant but suicidal action at Balaclava. A phrase, which he remembered as 'someone had blundered', recalled the movement of Chatterton's 'Song to Aella', and he adopted this metre for a similar subject. Tennyson's verses were much appreciated by soldiers in hospital at Scutari, and proved so popular that he was induced many years later by A. W. Kinglake, historian of the war, who sent him a memorandum on the subject, to commemorate an even greater action in 'The Charge of the Heavy Brigade at Balaclava'. Its exciting rhythms are varied in accordance with the changing movements of an astonishingly bold uphill cavalry charge which proved successful against tremendous odds. Recollections of strictures against *Maud*, and a discussion with Laura Tennant on the *Pembroke Castle*, made the poet realize that he could wrongly be branded a militarist. In 'Epilogue', which is based on this conversation, he states his views on war and war poetry very plainly: he looked forward to the end of war, and to the time when imperialism for commercial ends would cease; 'who loves War for War's own sake Is fool, or crazed, or worse'. Nevertheless he believed that heroic patriotism should be praised, even if it were for a country in the wrong; in justification of his own verse he wrote, 'The song that nerves a nation's heart, Is in itself a deed.'

The theme of 'Ode Sung at the Opening of the International Exhibition' turns significantly to hopes for world peace and prosperity; (three lines were added to the first draft when Prince Albert died in December 1861, the whole being set to music by Sterndale Bennett for four thousand singers):

O ye, the wise who think, the wise who reign,
From growing commerce loose her latest chain,
And let the fair white-winged peacemaker fly
To happy havens under all the sky,
And mix the seasons and the golden hours;
Till each man find his own in all men's good,
And all men work in noble brotherhood,
Breaking their mailèd fleets and armèd towers,
And ruling by obeying Nature's powers,
And gathering all the fruits of earth and crowned with all her
flowers.

British imperialism persisted, and so did Tennyson's admiration of gallantry. In 1879, more than twenty years after the event, having learned many details from survivors and official records, he wrote 'The Defence of Lucknow', a dramatic account of long resistance by a 'handful' of English during the Indian Mutiny. In 1885 he wrote 'The Fleet', which was published in *The Times* as a warning against neglect of naval defences. Pride in 'old England' which Nelson 'left so great' assumes an imperial dimension: it is lord of every sea and, its small army being scattered, the fleet is her all-in-all. Should those who have the ordering of it bring about England's disgrace, 'the wild mob's million feet' will kick them from office, 'But then too late, too late'. More equable and neat are two short poems on the wisdom of avoiding political extremes at home: 'Compromise' urges the way of caution when the steersman is confronted with 'two channels, moving to one end', one straight to the cataract, the other a detour; 'Politics', addressed to Gladstone, ends with 'while the hills remain, Up hill "Too-slow" will need the whip, Down hill "Too-quick", the chain'.

'The Queen of the Isles', written on Queen Victoria's accession to the throne in 1837, purveys not only some stock Tennysonian responses but the poet's reinforcement of Victorian attitudes on Britain's role in international affairs. A lengthy toast is proposed in vigorous, facile, regular rhythm, wishing her, among other things, a lengthy reign, hearts of oak in council who are no slaves of party, supremacy on the seas to ensure prosperity and balance of power, and readiness to respond with cannon roar like the judgment of God against despots and fools. 'To the Queen', the Poet Laureate's dedication of a new edition of *Poems* in 1851, is very different, typical of many epistolary poems he wrote in directness, sincerity, and seemingly conversational ease. His wish is that she may reign long, that 'children of our children' may say she 'wrought her people lasting good', her land had peace, and her statesmen knew when to increase freedom by passing decrees which maintained the throne 'Broad-based upon her people's will, And compassed by the inviolate sea'. The 'Dedication' to *Idylls of the King*, written soon after Prince Albert's death, pays respect to qualities in the Prince Consort that approached the Arthurian ideal. Unswayed by factions, using his high position neither as 'the lawless perch Of winged ambitions' nor as 'a vantage-ground For pleasure', laborious for the people of England 'and her poor', a promoter of international trade, and genuinely interested in science and art, he was 'a Prince indeed'. 'To the Queen', composed at the end of 1872 as an epilogue–dedication of the enlarged *Idylls of the King*, proudly rejects the suggestion of a London journal that Canada, too costly an imperial burden, should be relinquished:

Is this the tone of empire? here the faith
That made us rulers? this, indeed, her voice
And meaning, whom the roar of Hougoumont
Left mightiest of all peoples under heaven?
What shock has fooled her since, that she should speak
So feebly?

Some detect 'signs of storm', but Tennyson sees those loyal to the Queen 'loyal to their own far sons, who love Our ocean-empire with her boundless homes For ever-broadening England, and her throne In our vast Orient'.

In the early 1830s Tennyson had believed there was no land as great as Britain, and the world would not forget who 'taught the peoples right'. Preservation of the Empire is the central thought in 'Hands All Round', which he adapted from the 1852 version for the Queen's 1882 birthday. The same thought runs through 'Opening of the Indian and Colonial Exhibition by the Queen' (1886), and brings his ode 'On the Jubilee of Queen Victoria' to a climax, after an appeal to the affluent to improve the lot of the lowly and destitute. According to C. V. Stanford, who set this to music, the final lines were added at the Queen's suggestion: 'Are there thunders moaning in the distance? Are there spectres moving in the darkness?' the poet asks, trusting that her people will be led by 'the Hand of Light'. Neither the Queen nor the Poet Laureate could have had an inkling of the worldwide disasters that would accrue in the next sixty years as a result of imperial aggression and colonial rivalries.

Tennyson knew that the present was fatal daughter to the past at home, but he was not disposed to 'play Tiresias to the times' openly. In 1870 he thought England 'the most beastly self-satisfied nation in the world'. At a time of agitation for a further extension of the franchise in 1884, reassurance came with the thought that commonsense had usually 'carried the day without great upheavals', and would continue to be England's salvation provided 'our statesmen be not idiotic'. The viciousness of society, with the poor starving in great cities, convinced him in 1887 that 'a mighty wave of evil' was passing over the world, the outcome of which he would not live to see. Suppression of his fears led to a violent poetic eruption, but only through a mask, in 'Locksley Hall Sixty Years After', where he despondently asks whether 'the Federation of the world' which he predicted in 'Locksley Hall' will ever be attained:

Earth at last a warless world, a single race, a single tongue –
I have seen her far away – for is not Earth as yet so young? –

Every tiger madness muzzled, every serpent passion killed,
Every grim ravine a garden, every blazing desert tilled,

Robed in universal harvest up to either pole she smiles,
Universal ocean softly washing all her warless Isles.

From depression Tennyson swings to euphoria in his Jubilee ode, where he notes 'prosperous auguries' for the Queen and Empress of India. Although the two were inextricably linked, he remained far more assured about the rightness of British imperialism than he did about the state of England and western Europe. There he saw the working of evil forces which would inevitably result, sooner than later, in some kind of 'Armageddon'.

Apart from references to the growing anxieties of his later years, Tennyson's most damning indictments and hometruths reflect fitful alarms rather than undying convictions. On the question of full democracy he was as conservative as Wordsworth in his later years, believing with Goethe that 'The worst thing in the world is ignorance in motion'; he wished demagogues would remember that 'Liberty forgetful of others is licence, and nothing better than treason.' Unlike Wordsworth, whose beliefs were reinforced through years of agonizing over contemporary struggles for political freedom and independence, Tennyson was never roused to great poetic heights by passionately held political principles which made him unwaveringly single-minded in the condemnation of his country's glaring defects.

15
Three Tales

Tennyson was at a loss for suitable poetic subjects after completing his first group of Arthurian idylls, and friends were invited to offer recommendations. Two outlines of true stories from the sculptor Thomas Woolner resulted in 'Enoch Arden' and 'Aylmer's Field'. These poems and 'Sea Dreams' were included in a volume of poetry published in 1864 which Tennyson first thought of entitling 'Idylls of the Hearth'. The tendency in Tennyson criticism to use the term 'idyll' in senses beyond its usual modern connotation, largely in consequence of its wide, miscellaneous classical applications, is as unnecessary as it is confusing. The Poet Laureate had already resorted to story-telling in 'Dora', and he turned increasingly to this practice, partly from the difficulty of finding a significant major subject for poetry, partly because the vogue of fiction convinced him that verse narrative would be popular; nor was the old boyhood wish to be a popular poet inoperative. 'Sea Dreams', 'Enoch Arden', and 'Aylmer's Field' (all in blank verse) are considered here as 'tales' because each forms a more ample or complicated whole than any of the short stories Tennyson presented in monologue form; 'Aylmer's Field' comprises almost a subject for a novel.

'Sea Dreams', written in 1857, suggests contrivance rather than imaginative unity. It is based on a dream of Tennyson (according to the testimony of his grandson Charles) and two of the poet's recollections: his anxieties when the proceeds of his inheritance were in jeopardy, after being invested in Dr Allen's speculative enterprise; and his mother's belief (at Cheltenham) in the doctrines of Dr Cumming. An article by Mary Anne Evans (later famous as the novelist 'George Eliot') in the October 1855 issue of *The Westminister Review* had reminded him of the latter. Dr Cumming was 'the Boanerges' of Crown Court, Covent Garden, a popular preacher of the Scottish National Church whose Apocalyptic zeal made him antagonistic towards every form of heterodoxy, including the scientific, and especially virulent in his denunciation of Roman Catholicism. The poem, when it was first published in 1860, was subtitled 'An Idyll', almost certainly because, like the twenty-first idyll of Theocritus, it embodies a seaside discussion of poetry and dreams.

Thinking that the 'clear germander eye' of their three-year daughter Margaret drooped in 'the giant-factoried city-gloom', a poorly paid clerk and his wife decided to spend a month by the sea. He lost his wages of course, and was worried lest he should lose what savings he had made, all of which he had exchanged for 'strange shares in some Peruvian mine'. On Sunday, the day after reaching the seaside, they attend chapel, and hear a hot gospeller announce the coming doom, fulminate against the Scarlet Woman, and prophesy the casting of Babylon into the sea. Only the previous day the clerk had asked to see his investment entry, and been referred to 'the great Books' (explained in Daniel vii. 10) and told to have faith. (There may be a private allusion here to Dr Allen's religious writings, but the major link is with the preacher of doom.) Afterwards the family enter 'long sea-framing caves', and walk on the cliffs and sands. Before retiring, the wife urges her husband to forgive the man who had lured him into speculation. During the night a violent sea-swell throws up sheets of foam which fall in cataracts down the rocks, creating intermittent thunder-like sounds as if from within the cliffs. Margaret wails and wakes, and her father cries out, 'A wreck, a wreck!' He is certain that the mine does not exist, only a gulf of ruin, swallowing gold; the sea roars ruin.

He has dreamt of being carried by a deep-swelling tide from the sea to the dark depth of a cave, and seeing a lovely star shine larger and larger, before he reaches the landward exit, beyond which a stream and a giant woman covered with earth, sitting near the sunshine, pickaxe in hand, are visible. Then he slips into a land all sun and blossom, with trees as high as heaven, and every bird that sings. As he is borne upstream the woman walks by the edge, and tells him that her strength comes from working in the mines. When, in answer to his inquiry, she tells him that she knows nothing of the shares, the current ceases, thunder is heard, and a mountain confronts them like a wall of burs and thorns. They climb it, and from the summit she points towards the sea, where a fleet of jewels sails before a thundering cloud towards a reef of gold, on which it clashes brittly and vanishes. At this point the dreamer wakes, and finds he has knocked down and broken 'The glass with little Margaret's medicine in it' (surely one of the most inept lines Tennyson ever wrote). His wife urges him to forgive one who, if he is guilty, is for ever his own judge and jury, but the clerk cannot pardon a man who has made God his catspaw, the Cross his tool, and Christ the bait to dupe him.

The wife then tells her dream, of the same coast, with a belt of luminous vapour to the north, in which low music was heard. As it swelled, a ridge of breaker issued from the belt, approaching with thunderous sound, and lighting up the cliffs until they seemed 'huge cathedral fronts of every age'. As the ridge retired with lessening music, statues of kings, saints, and founders fell from these fronts, and dark clusters of men emerged from gaps and chasms of ruin, debating whether the statuary should be restored, until the returning wave with its awful light showed their glaring eyes and impassioned looks, and swept them all, men and statues, out to sea. As the dream continues, the wife fixes her wistful eyes on two images crowned with stars, the Virgin Mother and her child high up on one of the dark cathedral fronts. The Mother begins to totter, and the clinging child cries out. Here the dream had been cut short by Margaret's wail, as the husband's was by the breaking glass.

The husband insists that the roar of the tide and that of 'Boanerges with his threat of doom, And loud-lung'd Antibabylonianisms' contributed to her dream, if not to its music. The juxtaposition of the preacher and the discord over religious antiquities gives the direction of Tennyson's main thought. In her dream the wife finds it strange that the 'wildest wailings' of sectarians are never out of tune with the sweet music that swells and dies in the far-off luminous cloud. The clerk cannot understand how such divisive human passions can be dear to the great Musician; their shrieking is that of true devils with no ear, howling in time with the Devil. His wife tells him how she had yearned for him to forgive the man against whom he had railed, before she disclosed the news that he had died suddenly of heart-disease shortly after her husband left him; if he had done wrong, his angel broke his heart. Margaret has been roused by her father's rough voice; rocking her cradle, and holding his hand, mother sings the 'little birdie' song until the child is asleep. The father forgives, and both parents sleep soundly in consequence. This closing note of love and forgiveness is too cosily Victorian to exhilarate, but the poem is not quite sentimental. The husband realistically maintains that the wrongdoer's 'deeds yet live, the worst is yet to come'.

The poem has larger, Carlylean themes: one, expressed by the impecunious clerk's dream, is on 'honest work' and the false lure of gold; the other relates to the central inspiration of *Idylls of the King*. There are great dawns of spiritual truth in the course of time but, in less enlightened periods, sectarian differences lead to violent disputes until disputants and their outworn creeds have perished. Speaking through narrative imagery, Tennyson conveys the thought expressed in the Prologue of *In Memoriam*: 'Our little systems have their day; They have their day and cease to be: They are but broken lights of thee, And thou, O Lord, art more than they.' He does more, especially in the contention of 'dark' clusters of men on whether or not the dead forms of religion are to be restored; in sweeping them and the forms out to sea to the waste deeps, Tennyson shows kinship with Carlyle.

Sixty thousand copies of 'Sea Dreams', 'Enoch Arden', and 'Aylmer's Field' were soon sold when the first volume containing them and shorter poems appeared in 1864. 'Enoch Arden' was enormously popular, and Tennyson became known as 'The Poet of the People'. In this development A. H. Clough's poetical bias in narrative towards common life with which readers could easily identify (not remote from the contemporary as were the Poet Laureate's medieval and classical subjects) may have been an important factor, for, soon after Tennyson returned from his Pyrenean tour, when Clough read 'In Mari Magno' and cried like a child over it, a request was sent from Farringford to Thomas Woolner for the story which he had told in 1859. The poem which resulted was not written in 'only about a fortnight' (as Hallam Tennyson reported) but over a much longer period, from the end of November 1861 to the following March.

'The Fisherman's Story', as it was first called, is a simple, three-part tale (basically a common one) of a sailor who, after shipwreck, survived about ten years on a tropical island before being able to return home, where he found his wife married to his friend. Some of the nautical minutiae were checked with FitzGerald. Tennyson may have absorbed details from similar stories, such as Crabbe's 'The Parting Hour', and Mrs Gaskell's 'The Manchester Marriage' in the 1858 Christmas number of Dickens' *Household Words*,[14] but 'Enoch Arden' derived principally from Woolner's outline and the poet's imagination, activated by memories of sea-fishing he had witnessed and of scenes in travel books. Interestingly, the crucial situation had been generalized in the Choric Song (vi) of 'The Lotos-Eaters', and even more pointedly in *In Memoriam* (xc).

'Enoch Arden' has three chronological phases, the second including two accounts, of Enoch's wife Annie and of himself during their long separation. The first phase leads from childhood to marriage, with Philip's disappointment at losing Annie. The second, beginning with Enoch's misfortune and his departure as boatswain on a China-bound merchant-ship, in the hope of returning rich enough to give his children a good education, is briefly recapitulated to stress all that is significant to him when he hears so much about local history and affairs from garrulous Miriam Lane, the publican widow with whom he stays on his return:

> His baby's death, her growing poverty,
> How Philip put her little ones to school,
> And kept them in it, his long wooing her,
> Her slow consent, and marriage, and the birth
> Of Philip's child.

The account of Enoch's misfortunes away from home during this long interim period is notable for the brilliant evocations of the tropical island he is fated to endure, as he waits for rescue and return to his family. Finally, when he discovers Annie's married happiness, he sacrifices himself rather than destroy it; given inner strength through prayer, he finds work and lives not unhappily, though without hope; when sickness comes he looks forward to death, revealing his secret just before the end, but making Miriam swear not to divulge it to Annie and Philip until he is dead.

Knowing the story, one can appreciate the artistry with which proleptic touches reinforce a sense of the whole. As the three children whose fates become interlocked play on the shore, Enoch is associated with dissolving sandcastles and shipwreck. When, just before their marriage, Philip sees Enoch and Annie together by the edge of the hazel wood, and creeps down into the wooded hollow 'like a wounded life', we are reminded of the dark evening of a dull November day when Enoch is drawn by the warm light streaming from the rear of Philip's house, and observes from behind a yew, symbolizing death to his waning hope, the happiness within of Annie and his children as members of his old friend's family. Each is an outsider: one leaves with 'lifelong hunger in his heart'; the other comes, after knowing it for years, and steals away, realizing he is cut off from those he loves. For the orphan, first seen as a rough sailor's lad, there is no father's kiss at the end, though he prays to his Father for strength. We recall too how, when they had parted, he had assured Annie he would look on hers when she had said disconsolately that she would never see his face again.

The nine lines of background description at the opening are particularly significant, emphasis on the chasm left by breaking cliffs providing a visual key to the story. The tall-towered mill towards which the long street climbs past a 'mouldered church' hints at an age which attaches higher value to industrial efficiency and profit than to the vitalization of religious thought; no Providence protects Enoch, and Annie, after superstitiously seeking a sign in the Bible, has a dream which she misinterprets as Heaven's sign that she is free to marry Philip. Above the street is a grey down with Danish barrows and the hazel wood hollow, speaking of life through the ages and happiness mixed with sorrow. The reference to heaven may suggest a final Truth which is nearer the natural world than it is to the mouldered church below; unfortunately it cannot be dissociated, in Tennyson's Victorian vision, from the concluding sentimentality of the story, when Enoch draws comfort from the thought of joining his youngest child in heaven. As the law of 1603, exempting from offence a wife who remarried after her husband's unexplained absence for more than seven years overseas, was renewed in 1861,[15] it seems strange that there was much debate over the bigamy of the story. In defence of the ending, 'So past the strong heroic soul away. And when they buried him the little port Had seldom seen a costlier funeral', Tennyson said it bore testimony to Annie's desire to do all she could in honour of her lost husband. The weakness is not in the ritual testimony, but in the writer's expression: love, sympathy, and respect are not financially measurable; 'costlier' has the wrong connotations, and is the most signal stylistic weakness in the poem.

In general, the diction and the varied movement of the verse leave little to be desired. The style, plain and unpretentious for the most part, is strikingly economical at times. Tennyson's attention to detail is illustrated by the restriction of his similes to 'such as might have been used by simple fisher-folk', as may be seen in that describing Enoch's cheerful recognition of approaching death (ll. 824–8); the example given by the author, indicating the confused state of Annie's perturbed mind as her departing husband puts his trust in Providence, is as appropriate as it is simple:

>   she heard,
> Heard and not heard him; as the village girl,
> Who sets her pitcher underneath the spring,
> Musing on him that used to fill it for her,
> Hears and not hears, and lets it overflow.

Contrasting with the general character of the composition are those vivid lines which evoke Enoch's tropical island, with 'the lightning flash of insect and of bird', the 'lustre of the long convulvuses', the 'myriad shriek of wheeling ocean-fowl', and the 'league-long roller thundering on the reef'. Enoch hears and sees these things; he does not admire them. His thoughts are elsewhere: 'what he fain had seen He could not see, the kindly human face, Nor ever hear a kindly voice'. The repetition of 'the blaze' over the island and over the waters to east and west, and the conclusion of the passage with 'and again The scarlet shafts of sunrise – but no sail', convey the torturing unrelief of his existence.

All this makes Walter Bagehot's comments on the ornateness of the poem very puzzling.[16] He claims that if the story were told in 'the pure and simple, the unadorned and classical style', it would not take three pages. Ornate art creates 'a mist of beauty', and he finds an 'absolute model' of it in Tennyson's description of the island, which is definite and precise in all its colour and sound effects. He is more justified in the selection of a second illustrative passage (ll. 91–100), though much of its ornateness is in the actual rather than in the verbal, except for the euphemistic 'ocean spoil In ocean-smelling osier' and the 'Friday fare' which was Enoch's 'ministering'. Bagehot's explanation of an ornateness which is almost non-existent is as misguided as his stylistic assessment: Enoch is coarse and must be idealized; instead of admiring the splendours of the island – and he 'feels nothing else' – he would have been concerned, like Robinson Crusoe, with 'his own petty contrivances and small ailments'. 'A dirty sailor who did *not* go home to his wife is not an agreeable being: a varnish must be put on him to make him shine.' He is made to act rightly but, Bagehot continues, 'Nothing is more unpleasant than a virtuous person with a mean mind', and 'The dismal act of a squalid man needed many condiments . . . .' Hence

Tennyson's need for ornateness in 'Enoch Arden'. Seldom has a critic reasoned himself so self-condemningly outside the poem he is trying to assess; his standards are external and unimaginative; it is as if he had not read Wordsworth's *Lyrical Ballads*, and could not believe in the spiritual nobility of any common man.

When Mrs Tennyson read 'The Sermon', the original of 'Aylmer's Field' which she received from Woolner in July 1862, she was impressed by its form, and thought the story 'very grand and very finely told'. How far such a commendation can be applied to Tennyson's poem is a pertinent question; it contains powerful and moving passages, and bears witness throughout to careful thought and execution. Unlike 'Enoch Arden', it fails to sustain general lucidity, and tends to be laboured. Tennyson found the story 'incalculably difficult to tell', the facts being 'so prosaic', but liked the landscape and cottage-garden scenes (a reversion to idyllic vignettes). It comes most to life in dramatic scenes, more of which seem to be required to make the most of the subject. The vanity of pride in lineage and wealth with which the poem opens and concludes was a form of selfishness against which the poet felt 'a prophet's righteous wrath'; when it trampled on 'holy human love', as in *Maud* (here, between Edith Aylmer and Leolin Averill), his indignation was the greater. He elaborated the basic narrative material provided by Woolner, particularly in the melodramatic or novelistic Indian dagger story, related it to the period of the French Revolution (was this a time for the Aylmers to 'flaunt their pride'?), prepared most of the sermon, and created the ending to which it is the key. The influence of Crabbe is felt in the satire and some of the narrative presentation.

The satire against Sir Aylmer Aylmer, the 'almighty man' who is the 'county God', and his lady, 'a faded beauty of the Baths, Insipid as the Queen upon a card', is trenchant; he loves his only child Elizabeth 'As heiress and not heir regretfully'. When her love is banned, they try unsuccessfully to 'sell her . . . for her good', hoping to catch by 'the baits Of gold and Beauty' any 'eldest-born of rank or wealth' within their compass. The poet's feelings are evident in Leolin's outburst after his rejection by these proud 'worldly-wise begetters' of an heiress: their 'filthy marriage-hindering Mammon made The harlot of the cities', for 'nature crost Was mother of the foul adulteries That saturate soul with body'; let them rest and rot in their name (their Aylmerism, it is elsewhere described) like other 'old pheasant-lords', 'partridge-breeders of a thousand years, Who had mildewed in their thousands'. Nevertheless, when slow un-relieved retribution follows prolonged, inhuman thwarting of their daughter's love, Tennyson is not without pity for these unnatural tyrants; nor does he fail to stir admiration for their unavailing fortitude. The ending has the force of Greek tragedy, and its significance is enlarged by a natural or scientific vision which places man, and his earthly grandeur, in the true perspective of time.

Some of the incidental expression calls for attention. Neat uncordial phraseology is bestowed on 'My lady'; she listens with fingers interlocked and rotatory thumbs on silken knees, and makes a 'downward crescent of her minion mouth' when she hears further proof of Edith's dishonourable conduct. The dagger-sheath is ornamented with jewels set in 'gold that branched itself Fine as ice-ferns on January panes Made by a breath'; one of the bright gardens associated with Edith's kindliness and the love she generates among the poor of the estate is 'almost to the martin-haunted eaves A summer burial deep in hollyhocks'. Another passage contrasting with the general grimness (on Leolin's entertainment of Edith in childhood) contains a most felicitous simile: in the early develop-ment of their 'immemorial intimacy' (a phrase twice borrowed from Woolner) a passion yet unborn may have lain hidden 'as the music of the moon Sleeps in the plain eggs of the nightingale'. Two close-up visual observations in the same passage raise the question whether Tennyson was sufficiently careful to flash a clear image immediately on the inward eye. Just how sanguine is a hue which is 'but less vivid' than 'that islet in the chestnut-bloom' to a reader who has not observed the 'islet'? The poet assumes the reader's familiarity; the description could be more imaginative. Even more enigmatical for some readers will be the fanciful description of a seeding dandelion's head (for which he thought it necessary to provide a clue in a note to 'The Poet'): 'Or from the tiny pitted target blew What looked a flight of fairy arrows aimed All at one mark, all hitting'. The poem contains other expressions which suggest that Tennyson's familiarity with detail made him oblivious of the reader. So cryptic is he at times that he had to supply notes, on 'the gardens of that rival rose' or 'the brand of John', for example; and how many can be expected to recognise stacks of hop-poles in the 'tented winter-field' that becomes a phalanx of summer spears about to wear the garland?

The last view of Edith is memorable. After the thunders of the house have fallen on her, she is 'Pale as the Jephtha's daughter, a rough piece Of early rigid colour' (prophetic of death) over the door by which she withdraws, as she casts a piteous look on Leolin who enters on the opposite side of the room. He is confronted by 'the Powers of the House', and a dramatic scene ensues. The climax is unexpected; it comes during the service Leolin's brother Averill is invited to give in honour of Edith. After seeing the body of Leolin in London, he is emotionally impelled to preach on the worship of the false God found in gold and stately homes, contrasting him with the Lord of love who stilled the Galilean waves, and in whose steps Edith had walked. His denunciation of those who stone to death is directed against the Aylmers until the lady falls shrieking and is carried out. He, 'the Lord of all the landscape round Even to its last horizon, and of all Who peered at him so keenly', follows and reels, unpitied, as he gropes his way out. The text of the sermon is Jesus's lament over the Jerusalem that stoned its prophets, 'Behold, your house is left unto you desolate' (Luke xiii. 34–5). The conclusion follows from it: the mother soon dies, and Sir Aylmer Aylmer becomes imbecile; his one word is 'desolate'. When he dies, his hearse is followed by a 'dark retinue reverencing death At golden thresholds' (the expression for Heaven's entrance in *The Lover's Tale*, used here with obvious satirical ambivalence, as bitter as in the related irony of 'contrived their daughter's good'). The Aylmer family perishes; the Hall is demolished, and the vast estate divided up;

> And where the two contrived their daughter's good,
> Lies the hawk's cast, the mole has made his run,
> The hedgehog underneath the plantain bores,
> The rabbit fondles his own harmless face,
> The slow-worm creeps, and the thin weasel there
> Follows the mouse, and all is open field.

Tennyson remembered the desolation of Babylon which he had versified in his youth (cf. Isaiah xiii. 19–22: 'It shall never be inhabited . . . the wild beasts of the islands shall cry in their desolate houses'). All is open field; nature outlives proud man, but the cruelty of life continues insidiously and viciously (as it had done for Edith and Leolin); the slow-worm creeps, and hawk and weasel pounce on their prey.

16
Idylls of the King

'At twenty-four I meant to write an epic or a drama of King Arthur', Tennyson told his son Hallam; he alludes to the former in 'The Epic', and the seasonal cycle of the whole is implicit in 'Morte d'Arthur', to which it supplies the narrational setting. On the other hand, to say as he did, that the Arthur he drew came to him when he read Malory in his late boyhood is an oversimplification. The hero's union of manliness and gentleness is a quality he admired in Arthur Hallam, and an earnest of the higher race foreshadowed in *The Princess*. That Hallam contributed more than anyone to Tennyson's conception of ideal manhood is clear from *In Memoriam*; his association with the King in 'Morte d'Arthur' is acknowledged in 'Merlin and the Gleam': 'Clouds and darkness Closed on Camelot; Arthur had vanished I knew not whither, The King who loved me, And cannot die . . . .' Discouraged by reviews of 'Morte d'Arthur', especially that of John Sterling, who thought the subject too remote from contemporary life, Tennyson laid aside the work which he had expected to occupy him for twenty years.[17] Epic or drama, it remained largely notional in design, without the full significance of the *Idylls*, the development of which undoubtedly attests a gradual, cumulative planning, not a work designed, or satisfactorily concluded, as a whole.

The *Idylls* have no real centre. A unit of four, composed mainly from 1856 to 1859, was published in 1859; the remainder belongs almost wholly to 1868–72, though 'Balin and Balan' was not concluded until 1874. 'The Coming of Arthur' and 'The Passing of Arthur', which round off the collection, were completed in 1869. Some very significant additions were made in 1873, and the most important passage on the destructive role of Vivien, in 1875. Although the 1859 unit (which had grown from two stories to four) has an antithetical relationship, composition from 'Morte d'Arthur' to 'Balin and Balan' indicates the predominance of an episodic interest. A truer idea of the structuring and quality of this composite whole comes therefore from considering it, not in the order of its arrangement, but as far as is reasonably possible in accordance with the stages of its evolution. 'Enid', it should be noted, was not divided into two parts until 1873, and 'Balin and Balan' was not published until 1885. In this way a semblance of epic entity, a work in twelve books, was reached, the concluding touch being given in 1886, when the two Geraint and Enid stories received their final titles.

The question of origins and differentials is an irrelevance. Tennyson's Arthur is exclusively his; his function is to show 'Sense at war with Soul', or human ideals betrayed by mankind. The damsel whom Merlin tries to seduce, an incidental figure in Malory, has become a creature who wills Arthur's destruction, and uses her feminine wiles to overcome the aged magician who has given him power; the Merlin and Vivien story, like that of Balin and Balan, is mainly Tennyson's own. His Tristram is a degraded knight, not the romantic hero of tradition. Malory's Gwenyver did not proceed to Almesbury until after Arthur's death. Tennyson makes changes as he thinks fit, for both artistic and spiritual reasons. Gerard Manley Hopkins understandably thought the *Idylls* deserved the title of 'Charades from the Middle Ages', but Swinburne (delighted, in view of the 1862 dedication to Prince Albert, to call them 'the Morte d'Albert, or Idylls of the Prince Consort') was guilty of snarling round the wrong tree when he denounced Tennyson for not treating his subject as if it were a Greek tragedy, with the King's ruin a nemesis for his youthful, incestuous fathering of Modred.

With the aim of giving his medieval stories as much human reality as possible, Tennyson avoided the pervasive allegorical treatment that characterizes *The Faerie Queene*; he felt that allegory could be pressed too far, but admitted 'an allegorical or perhaps rather a parabolic drift'. The work bears some resemblance to Tasso's *Gerusalemme Liberata*, where the significance of the besieging army, representing body and soul in unison, is offset by ignoble soldiery who reflect the grosser human appetites. Led by Godfrey, the disciplined army sees God in Christ, the Word made flesh. Arthur is 'Ideal manhood closed in real man'; the Round Table, representing 'the passions and capacities of a man', succeeds for a time in keeping its vows to 'follow the Christ, the King'. It is 'the tableland of life, and its struggles and performances' between the two mysteries of birth and death. At the end Arthur laments that the house[18] which vowed loyalty to him has been his doom; Merlin had known that the vows were such 'as is a shame A man should not be bound by, yet the which No man can keep'. Tancred fails Godfrey as Lancelot fails Arthur, because concupiscence prevails over principle. The struggle which the *Idylls* presents in varying facets is 'not the history of one man or of one generation but of a whole cycle of generations'; it is unending and 'world-wide', 'typified in individuals, with the subtle interaction of character upon character'. Tennyson goes on to say that 'the central dominant figure' is 'the pure, generous, tender, brave, human-hearted Arthur'. It would be more true to say 'the key figure', for Arthur is an undominating background figure in much of the *Idylls*, and this reflects life; the ideal, though acknowledged, is often remote and ignored. The struggle is within: 'The King who fights his people fights himself.'

The form the work was to assume was not decided until after the completion of *Maud* in 1855; Tennyson had already considered the epic and a musical masque.[19] After the publication of the first *Idylls of the King* ('Enid', 'Vivien', 'Elaine', and 'Guinevere'), he 'carried a more or less perfected scheme' in mind of the idylls he would write when 'the time was ripe'. The implications of his son's vague phrasing are made more conjectural by the relatively non-parabolic nature of the first unit, as well as by the self-sufficiency of its design. It began with *Enid and Nimuë: the True and the False*, a trial edition of which was set up in 1857, the antithetical theme being duplicated in the two stories which followed, when the name 'Vivien' (from an influential passage of the vulgate *Merlin* in Southey's edition of Malory) was substituted for Malory's 'Nimue'. Uncertainty about the completion of the *Idylls* explains the comparative lack of symbolism in the descriptive narrative of the 1859 stories. Their most important link is the infidelity of Guinevere. (The first version of the Merlin story was finished before 'Enid' was begun, and 'Guinevere' was completed before 'Elaine'.)

The Enid story (which became 'The Marriage of Geraint' and 'Geraint and Enid') was drawn principally from Lady Charlotte Guest's *Mabinogion*. Geraint dotes on his wife Enid, the Queen's favourite, but when he hears a rumour of Guinevere's guilty love for Lancelot he urges the need to protect his marches as a pretext for taking his wife from a court which might taint her morals. At home, forgetful of the King, he loses his reputation by uxorious living. Enid's regrets that this should happen waken his suspicions. After insisting that she wears the meanest dress she can find, he rides forth with her into the wilderness. Enid chooses the faded silk she wore when he brought her to Arthur's court. So we are introduced to the story of Geraint's earlier venture when he left court to avenge an insult to the Queen.

He comes to a town where everyone is busy preparing for a tourney; the only harbourage he can find for the night is the ruined castle of Yniol, whose daugher Enid he falls in love with as soon as he sees her in her faded dress. Her first suitor had been the bibulous Limours; her second, Yniol's nephew Edyrn, the 'sparrow-hawk' who had despoiled the castle and insulted the Queen. As Enid's champion, Geraint defeats Edyrn, and sends him to seek pardon at Arthur's court, where he becomes the King's faithful follower. Lost when the castle was sacked, the dress, 'All branched and flowered with gold', which Enid's mother had given her is retrieved, but Geraint prefers her to ride to court in her faded silk, knowing the Queen will clothe her 'like the sun in Heaven' for her marriage. Enid's compliance stills his suspicion, for he feared that her main objective was to escape a dreary ruin for courtly glamour. The first part of the divided story ends inartistically with their marriage at Caerleon; the sequel continues the introduction.

After days apart in the wilderness, the mistrusted wife leading the way, and some remarkable but insignificant feats of arms, Geraint and Enid reach a town, where roysterers, including Limours, the lord of the place, break into their chamber. Limours protests his love, and Enid prepares Geraint's armour for sudden encounter. Before they leave at early dawn she tells him what has happened. Limours overtakes them, and is left stunned or dead; Geraint rides wounded until he faints and falls. After tending his wound, Enid rests with him by the road until the arrival of the lawless Earl Doorm. Geraint is carried to an empty hall, where she nurses him until he wakes from his swoon; when he sees her weeping, he pretends to be dead in order to 'prove her to the uttermost'. The Earl and his men are animal-like in their growling and eating; women 'whose souls the old serpent had long drawn down' hiss at each other's ear in satisfying anticipation of Enid's humbling by their lord. After offering to share his earldom with her, he tries to make her eat and drink, then insists that she shall wear a foreign dress, thick with jewels, its lovely blue playing into green 'like a shoaling sea'. She refuses, and he slaps her cheek; her cry wakens Geraint, who leaps to his feet, decapitates Doorm, and swears he will never doubt her again. She rides behind, holding him, hands beneath heart, as they flee. They are met by Edyrn, who escorts them to Arthur's camp, telling them how he had been saved from his madness and wolf-like state. His reformation is far more wonderful to the King than if a single knight had slain a realm of robbers one by one. After admitting that he has allowed wrong to triumph, Arthur announces his intention to cleanse his realm, and sends a thousand men to till the wastes. Geraint being healed, they return to Caerleon, where the Queen clothes Enid in 'apparel like the day'. Geraint cannot regain the serenity he knew before doubting Guinevere's disloyalty, but he keeps the King's justice in his own country, and wins high esteem until he dies fighting against the heathen.

Had he continued the *Idylls* in this fashion, it might fairly be claimed that Tennyson would have employed his gifts more worthily in translating Homer's *Iliad*. The Enid stories are not without excitement, but for long periods they lack a greatly inspiring or significant subject. Imaginative evocativeness is rarely sustained, but a few ancillary images call for admiration, especially in the simile which conveys Enid's joy when at last she feels Geraint hers again: 'she did not weep, But o'er her meek eyes came a happy mist Like that which kept the heart of Eden green Before the useful trouble of the rain'. Impressions of her faded dress differ as much as a leaf in mid-November from what it was in mid-October, and the message that she must wear it, and not her golden one, falls on her 'Like flaws in summer laying golden corn'. The description of the ivy on the ruins of Yniol's castle shows close observation: monstrous stems 'Claspt the gray walls with hairy-fibred arms, And sucked the joining of the stones, and looked A knot, beneath, of snakes, aloft, a grove'. Repetition can be effective, but the stressing of Geraint's manifestly suspicious nature by making him look at Enid in each book as keenly 'As careful robins eye the delver's toil' suggests some perfunctory composition, the simile being brought forward from 'Early Spring', a poem of 1833.

'Merlin and Vivien' (to keep to final titles) has greater imaginative significance and interest. Mark, King of Cornwall (a late introduction to the *Idylls*), alluding to Lancelot and Guinevere, tells Vivien: 'Here are snakes within the grass; And you . . . can stir them till they sting.' Born of death on a battlefield, while her mother dies on her father's corpse, she has no fear, sneers at the purity of Arthur and all, and promises to bring back the hearts of the Round

Table knights when she has 'ferreted out their burrowings'.
Pretending to be menaced by Mark, she seeks protection at
Arthur's court, and is granted it by the Queen, who rides off
hawking with Lancelot. Vivien's game is 'royaller'; she is the little
rat that bores a hole in the dyke 'to let the boundless deep Down
upon far-off cities while they dance – Or dream'. She spends her
time sowing scandal, then quietly withdraws like 'an enemy that has
left Death in the living waters'. Having failed to win the attention of
'the blameless King', she aims at winning Merlin, the 'Wizard' who
created Arthur's halls, havens, and ships. The aged enchanter, as
she gains hold over him, becomes melancholy, sensing

> A doom that ever poised itself to fall,
> An ever-moaning battle in the mist,
> World-war or dying flesh against the life,
> Death in all life and lying in all love,
> The meanest having power upon the highest,
> And the high purpose broken by the worm.

(Like other short insertions, this passage was added in 1873 to
emphasize the deeper implications of the poem.) With Merlin's
final fall and enslavement, Arthur's loss of power is inevitable.

Merlin, followed by Vivien, leaves for Brittany, where he
becomes 'lost to life and use and name and fame'. In her attempt to
win the charm that will give her complete power over him, Vivien
repeats a song she heard Lancelot sing on the theme 'Unfaith in
aught is want of faith in all': 'It is the little rift within the lute, That
by and by will make the music mute.' Merlin recalls how different
was the song he heard by the same oak when he and others pursued
the hart with golden horns (the Gleam), and discussed the founding
of the Round Table 'for love of God and men and noble deeds'. Like
most of the narrative in the 1859 *Idylls*, the story of Merlin's
seduction is protracted, but it reaches an exciting climax. He knows
the danger of acceding to her will and, as she slanders Arthur and his
knights, regrets that the King's purity is not intelligible to base
minds. Hearing 'harlot' two or three times as he mutters his
indignation, she leaps from his knee, and stands stiff like a frozen
viper, 'the bare-grinning skeleton of death' flashing from her rosy
lips as she indulges murderous thoughts. By flattery and tears she re-
asserts her ascendancy until he half-believes her again. His anger
subsides, and he calls her to shelter in the hollow oak, where she

clings to him and wearies him until she wins the secret that makes
him her prisoner. The outer scene proleptically reflects the ruin of
Arthur's realm:

> and ever overhead
> Bellowed the tempest, and the rotten branch
> Snapt in the rushing of the river-rain
> Above them; and in change of glare and gloom
> Her eyes and neck glittering went and came;
> Till now the storm, its burst of passion spent,
> Moaning and calling out of other lands,
> Had left the ravaged woodland yet once more
> To peace; and what should not have been had been . . . .

The intellectual, once inspired by the Gleam in the traditional
wood of Error, has become a decadent; the music has turned to
moaning.

'Lancelot and Elaine', the story of 'the lily maid of Astolat' which
Tennyson transmuted in 'The Lady of Shalott', is much the
brightest of the early Arthurian idylls, if 'idylls' is appropriate to
such an elaborately extended subject (Gladstone questioned the
adequacy of such a title for the scope of the 1859 volume, with
reference to both parts and whole). Though turning on the
unrequited love of Elaine, it depends inauspiciously on the doom-
stricken diamonds which Arthur found before he became King, in a
glen where two brothers, one a king, had slain each other at a blow.
In misty moonshine Arthur had trodden on a skeleton, thereby
breaking the skull from the nape, and causing its crown to roll 'like a
glittering brook' down to a tarn; he had rescued it, and set it on his
head, thinking he would be a king. Lancelot, after winning one of its
diamonds at each of eight successive annual jousts, hopes to win the
last, the central diamond, and present them all to the Queen. He
misinterprets her lack of enthusiasm, and withdraws; but she,
sensitive to 'vermin voices' that sting in response to Vivien's
campaign, persuades him to enter unknown, all for glory.

Angry with himself, Lancelot loses his way among the downs
until he comes to Astolat, where he speaks of the twelve great battles
won by Arthur against the heathen. He is 'yet a living soul', his face
marred by a tormented conscience, but Elaine loves him at first
sight. He leaves her his shield, with which she lives in fantasy, while
he returns with her brother's, a blank one, and her favour, a red

pearl-ornamented sleeve, bound on his helmet. He is awarded the diamond, after his kin, alarmed that his renown should be lost to an unknown champion, have overborne him and his charger, wounding him so grievously that he rides off at once. Sir Gawain, the prince of courtesy 'with a touch of traitor in it', is commanded to find him, and present the diamond; but the King is angry to hear of Lancelot's deception, and finds it ominous that he has been wounded by his own kin. Gawain reaches Astolat with news of the victor, tries to win Elaine's love, and delights her by announcing that her shield is Lancelot's. Rebuked by the King for leaving the diamond with her and not fulfilling his commission, he retaliates by spreading news of Elaine's love, which reaches the Queen.

Elaine finds Lancelot in a hermit's cave, presents the diamond, and tends him daily until his life is saved. 'His honour rooted in dishonour', he loves her 'with all love except the love Of man and woman when they love their best', and is ready to die 'In any knightly fashion for her sake'. Elaine knows she must die if he cannot love her; and with her brothers (one of whom had accompanied him, one her, to Camelot) they return to Astolat, where, being pressed to ask some gift, the nearest to her heart, she confesses her love. When she hears he cannot return it, she swoons and is carried to her tower. As Lancelot leaves, she flings the casement back, and looks down on his sleeveless helmet; Lancelot hears, and she 'by tact of love' realizes he knows she is looking at him, though he does not look up or wave his hand – his one discourtesy. Her father tells her the court scandal, but she will not believe it and prepares for her death, making arrangements for her body's conveyance to Camelot, a queenly figure to meet the Queen. Lancelot presents the diamonds to Guinevere, but, telling him to give them to his lady-love, she flings them out of the palace window into the river; while watching listlessly, he sees the barge passing where they fell, and Elaine lying on it 'like a star in blackest night'. She is borne in by Sir Percivale and Sir Galahad. After reading the letter she carries, Lancelot declares that she loved him with a love surpassing the love of all other women he had known, though he had done nothing to encourage it. Guinevere asks him to forgive her jealousy, and the King commands that the maid of Astolat be buried like queen. He wishes Lancelot had married her; 'Free love, so bound, were freëst', he declares, and Lancelot is left wishing the Lady of the Lake who caught him from his mother's arms had drowned him in the mere, or that an angel would haul him up, bear him far, and fling him into it. The climactic scene is moving, and perhaps the most dramatically memorable in the whole of the *Idylls*.

'Guinevere', a shorter work written in about a fortnight, presents the disruptive Modred as the villain, a subtle beast, once caught spying on 'the high top of the garden-wall' by Lancelot – a reminder of Satan in *Paradise Lost* (IV. 172ff.). The Queen is fearful: grim faces come and go in the dark night; if she sleeps, she has an awful dream:

> for then she seemed to stand
> On some vast plain before a setting sun,
> And from the sun there swiftly made at her
> A ghastly something, and its shadow flew
> Before it, till it touched her, and she turned –
> When lo! her own, that broadening from her feet,
> And blackening, swallowed all the land, and in it
> Far cities burnt, and with a cry she woke.

She urges Lancelot to return to his own land, and arranges a last meeting, which Vivien ensures is observed by Modred and his creatures. Shamed for ever, Guinevere flees to the nunnery at Almesbury, hearing, she imagines, the moaning spirits of waste and weald; a croaking raven suggests 'a field of death' consequent on heathen incursions from the North. While an unknown inmate at Almesbury, she is tortured by a novice, who sings a song of too-late repentance, and babbles innocently of 'the good King and his wicked Queen', of rumours of wars, and of supernatural appearances in Lyonnesse before the sinful Queen came to Camelot. Eventually, thinking the novice a spy sent to plague her, Guinevere dismisses her angrily. As she is lost reflecting on the glorious days of Lancelot and Arthur, the King is announced. In a long speech, monotonous and hollow as a ghost's, he denounces her; her children are 'sword and fire, Red ruin, and the breaking up of laws'. He has come from war against Lancelot, and reports Modred's revolt; he will protect Guinevere 'in the wild hour coming on'. He expatiates on her sin and evil example, which has spread; he cannot allow a wife who is false, the mockery of his people and their bane, to rule his house. He forgives her grandly, though he loathes her polluted body; his 'love through flesh' has wrought so far into his life that he is doomed to love still. Perhaps, if she purifies her soul, they will meet in heaven. That is his last hope, for he is called to the great battle in the west. Grovelling at his feet, Guinevere perceives his hands blessing her in the darkness. Outside the moonlit vapour makes him look like a giant phantom until, as he moves to his doom, his grey figure dissolves in the mist. The final scene between Arthur and the Queen shows the nobler qualities of both, but its denunciatory absoluteness illustrates Tennyson's artistic problem. The King, as Guinevere reminds us, is 'the highest and most human too'. Their last meeting seems entirely human in its presentation, and by human standards Arthur seems inhumanly perfect. Like that of Modred, the parabolic role of the King is not yet adequately conveyed; at this stage it is merely emergent. Not until it is realized by the reader does the scene assume cogency; as it stands, it seems to confirm the view of George Meredith in *Sandra Belloni*: 'Alas! in our world, where all things must move, it becomes, by-and-by, manifest that an "ideal", or idol, which you will, has not been gifted with two legs.'

* * *

The next book to be written, after an interval of almost ten years, was 'The Holy Grail', which Tennyson undertook with some reluctance, under pressure from his wife and the Queen. 'The old writers *believed* in the Sangreal', he told the Duke of Argyll in 1859 (after the subject had been recommended by Macaulay), doubting whether it could be handled 'without incurring a charge of irreverence'. When he read the poem to the Bradleys he explained 'how the natural, if people cared, could always be made to account for the supernatural'. His scepticism is expressed by the homely but not unscholarly monk Ambrosius, who listens to Sir Percivale's narration, and by King Arthur. The image of the Holy Grail appears only to those in abnormal states of mind. A frustrated, oversexed girl, after becoming a nun, hears much on the subject, with the fervent hope that it will now appear and save the Round Table from its adulterous decline. She has fasted and prayed in the hope of seeing it, until she is more spirit than body. Having seen it one night, she asks other knights to fast and pray, that the world may be healed; she makes Sir Galahad her knight, her love, inspiring him with her deathless passion. The one knight who has lost his life for Christ's sake, and thereby found it, he can sit in the chair fashioned by Merlin, the Siege Perilous in the great hall. When he does so, there is a thunderstorm, and the Grail, covered by a luminous cloud, is imagined stealing down an immensely bright beam of light. No knight sees it, but each observes a glory on his fellow's face, and many swear to spend a year and a day in the hope of seeing the Grail. They forget the principle which is cardinal to Tennyson's work, 'that Man's duty is to forget self in the service of others'.

Sir Gawain, who swore more loudly than the rest, soon tires of the Quest, preferring merry maidens. Sir Bors is imprisoned countless hours within a dark cell of huge piled stones, one of which is dislodged in a storm; through the gap one clear calm night he imagines he sees the Grail, coloured as it crosses the Great Bear like fingers before a burning taper; Tennyson's note suggests it was a meteor. Galahad, on the point of death, sees it blood-red wherever he goes; (the legend ran that it contained the blood which flowed from our Lord's side, and was brought to Glastonbury by Joseph of Arimathea). Sir Percivale believes he sees it while watching from a hill above the region of death and corruption which Sir Galahad speedily crosses along bridges consumed by fire; when he reaches the great sea of eternity, across which he is swiftly conveyed in a boat, it shines over him, first appearing veiled, then redder than any rose; as the celestial city emerges from the sea, a rose-red sparkle from a star shoots towards it, and Percivale is certain that the Holy Grail is there and will never again be seen on earth.

Even more imaginatively described, and in some of Tennyson's most fluent blank verse, is the climax of Sir Lancelot's search. The sin from which he cannot be released whips him on in madness. After being driven a week over the sea, he reaches the enchanted castle of Carbonek, where he is gripped by lions and told not to doubt but go forward. Coming to a vacant hall, he sees 'only the rounded moon Through the tall oriel on the rolling sea' (words which Tennyson loved to quote for their sound). A sweet lark-like voice in the eastern tower encourages him to climb painfully a thousand steps, as if in a dream. Blasted and blinded by the glaring heat as he opens a door, he swoons, yet thinks he sees the Grail. He knows that it is veiled, and that the Quest is not for him. The externalizations give magnificent expression to the fluctuations of his mental state.

Though illusory, the Holy Grail which accompanies Sir Galahad reflects his total, utterly selfless, commitment to God. By contrast Sir Percivale and the other questers are self-seeking; he is pure in the worldly sense of the word, but it is false motivation that makes his earthly happiness and glory turn to dust; his withdrawal from the world marks his acceptance of defeat. Ambrosius, his human-hearted fellow-monk, provides a modicum of relief to Percivale's narration, especially when, after hearing of the knight's renunciation of the lady he loves, he comments regretfully on sweetness forgone, and checks himself for speaking 'too earthlywise'. Arthur's opposition to the Quest is maintained to the end. He is angry when he hears of the vows his knights have taken, tells them they will follow wandering fires, and that his Order will be maimed in consequence. Hardly a tithe returns. He tells Bors, Lancelot, and Percivale that they are blessed, unlike Gawain, in desiring to see; and thinks Lancelot exaggerates his sin. To those who hold that he too would have sworn the vow had he 'seen the sight', he replies that man has earthly duties which must be fulfilled. His views are the poet's, utterly in opposition to spiritual quests which withdraw men from everyday tasks, 'leaving human wrongs to right themselves'. Tennyson thought 'The Holy Grail' one of his most imaginative poems, because it expressed his 'strong feeling as to the Reality of the Unseen'; Arthur speaks for him at the end,[20] when he enlarges on a true visionary awareness of the spiritual reality.

'The Coming of Arthur' and 'The Passing of Arthur' (1869) are brief and complementary. They present more than the origin and conclusion of a régime; they indicate the cyclical significance of the *Idylls* as a whole, and provide the keys to its symbolism. Before Arthur's coming the land was laid waste by war; the wilderness in which 'the beast was ever more and more, But man was less and less' increased. Arthur slays the beast, fells the forest, and lets in the sun. The legendary uncertainty about his genealogical origin is insignificant (Tennyson removed a reference to the Arthur–Modred kinship at the opening of 'Guinevere'); what matters is the account given by Bleys, Merlin's master, to Bellicent. As soon as Uther died at Tintagel, the two magicians, descending the chasm in dismal darkness, saw high up, as if in the air, a ship like a winged dragon, bright with shining people, which instantly disappeared. The ninth and largest wave was aflame, and it bore a child to Merlin's feet; the wave lashed round, clothing him and the child in fire (signifying that Arthur was born of God; cf. Daniel vii. 10). When Bellicent asked Merlin to confirm the story, he concluded a riddling answer on the difficulty of ascertaining truth with the unqualified statement 'From the great deep to the great deep he goes.' These deeps, the alpha and omega, the beginning and the end, of the *Idylls*, are one, synonymous with God, as in Revelation. Representing the

Soul or the Ideal (from the Christian or the Platonic heaven), Arthur, following Christ, takes flesh to do God's work on earth. He marries Guinevere in the hope of lifting her from a land of beasts up to his throne, that they may live and reign as one, and 'Have power on this dark land to lighten it, And power on this dead world to make it live'. When he faced the foe in battle, 'the world Was all so clear about him, that he saw The smallest rock on the faintest hill, And even in high day the morning star' (an 1873 addition). The fire of God descended on him, and the heathen were defeated. It was Merlin who had Arthur crowned, the three queens who would help him at his need standing by his throne. When the Lady of the Lake presented him Excalibur to drive out the heathen, a voice from heaven (as of the waters: Revelation xiv. 2) was heard among the hymns. Leodogran's dream before he agrees to the marriage of Arthur and his daughter does not merely point to the ending of the *Idylls*. It presents symbolically *in ovo* the ultimate tragic significance of Tennyson's theme: a phantom king, now looming, now lost, on a peak while battle rages below; few remain loyal to him as the haze thickens with smoke; when it descends, the earth is blotted out, and the King is seen crowned in heaven.

The context of 'Morte d'Arthur' in 'The Passing of Arthur' adds little to this. The whole is from the story told by Sir Bedivere, 'First made and latest left of all the knights'. He hears the King lamenting that God is not found in men's ways, that the world seems to have been made by some lesser god unable to shape it as he would, and that he himself had been simple in expecting to work God's will (another 1873 addition). Arthur perishes by the people he had made, and all his realm reels back into the beast. The last battle is concluded in mist on waste sand by the waste sea. Those who fall fighting for Christ look up for heaven and see only mist, and friend slays friend unknowingly. Arthur strikes the last blow with Excalibur in killing Modred. After watching the barge which conveys him with the three queens towards the eastward horizon, Bedivere remembers the weird rhyme 'From the great deep to the great deep he goes.' As if from beyond earthly bounds, a sound like that of some fair city hailing a king returned from war is faintly heard. The speck-like barge vanishes in light, 'And the new sun rose bringing the new year'. *Idylls of the King* does not end in failure and despondency, but with a reminder that despite periodic setbacks (the 'vast eddies in the flood Of onward time' of *In Memoriam*, cxxviii) the war of soul and sense, of the ideal and man's imperfections, continues.

As the main stories of individual knights are offshoots of the main Arthurian action, it was now possible for Tennyson to insert additional books as he pleased. The next two he began were 'Pelleas and Ettarre' and 'Gareth and Lynette'. The latter created much difficulty, and was not completed until 1872, but, as it is the first of 'The Round Table' idylls (the inner ten) and antithetical to 'Pelleas and Ettarre', which belongs to the period of Arthur's fast-waning power, it may advantageously be given priority. Having concentrated on stories illustrating the forces which militated against the King's success, Tennyson must have felt obliged to choose a counterbalancing subject. Yet, though almost the longest book in the *Idylls*, 'Gareth and Lynette' is a lightweight, the most charade-like among them. It is strange to find a youth fighting against the temptations of the three ages of life in the Morning Star, Noonday Sun, and Star of Evening, much less against Death, all four representing the 'war of Time against the soul of man'. Death, laying siege to Lady Lyonors in Castle Perilous, looks huge, black, and fearful, but proves to be 'a blooming boy' over whom Gareth gains an easy victory. 'O death, where *is* thy sting?' is the obvious implication. Whether all this conveys the significance which the romance had for its author (the joy of 'victories of ascent' which lives in 'the eternal youth of goodness') is questionable. The book is spirited, and brightness prevails. Gareth's resolve and idealism are undaunted, despite the raillery of Sir Kay and the taunts of Lynette, who, incensed at being given a kitchen-knave instead of Sir Lancelot, slowly turns from scorn to admiration and love as her knight prevails against all his opponents. Lancelot is sent to watch over him from a distance; the only aid he gives is his shield and charger against Death. Tennyson uses the story to illustrate the utter conscientiousness of Arthur in rectifying wrongs, and prepares for 'The Last Tournament' by introducing the villainy of Mark, King of Cornwall.

Most important of all, near the beginning of the *Idylls*, he reinforces his parabolic drift with reference to Camelot. As Gareth approaches, its summit flashes above the mist; then the whole fair city vanishes. Its gate is amazingly sculptured, with the three queens over all, the Lady of the Lake with the emblem of Christianity over her breast, and on either side (Tennyson's description evidently indebted to Wordsworth's 'Yew-trees') 'Arthur's wars in weird devices done, New things and old co-twisted . . . so inveterately, that men Were giddy gazing there'. To Gareth the gateway seems alive, and he hears a blast from the city. An old man (Merlin) tells him that Camelot was built to music, and 'there is nothing in it as it seems Saving the King', though some think he is a shadow, and the city real. If Gareth heard music, 'like enow They are building still, seeing the city is built To music, therefore never built at all, And therefore built for ever'. Materialists may discount the spiritual, but the existence of the 'fair city' on earth depends on vision, an informing spirit which is part of the eternal reality.

Pelleas, youthful and undaunted like Gareth, becomes one of Arthur's knights after the depletion of the Round Table by the Quest. In the green-glooming twilight of a grove, this unworldly lord of many a barren isle daydreams of love, until his attention is drawn to damsel riders lost in the forest, the chief among them being Ettarre. Pelleas is abashed by her fleshly beauty, and mistakes it for beauty of soul. They all scorn him, but consent to be guided by him to Caerleon, where he fights as the lady's champion in the Tournament of Youth, and wins the golden circlet and knightly sword. Ettarre avoids him as she rides with her escort to her castle, outside which she turns her three knights against him. The lover overthrows them, but consents to be carried in, only to hear her mock his vows and the King. After watching him overthrow the knights again, Sir Gawain proposes an exchange of arms, so that he may plead his cause, after gaining entrance by claiming that he has slain Pelleas. Pelleas agrees, and is kept waiting three days. Restless and mindful of the song 'A worm within the rose', he rides to the castle in bright moonlight, finds the gates open, walks across the court and climbs up by a rose garden overgrown with brambles (an image of lawless love). At the top he finds three pavilions, the knights, red after revel, snoring in one, and Gawain and Ettarre asleep in another. He creeps out in shame, then returns tempted to slay them; remembering the vows of Arthur's brotherhood, he leaves his sword across their throats. Mounting his horse, he stares at the towers, which seem magnified in darkness as they throng 'into the moon'. He crushes the saddle between his thighs, clenches hands, and moans, wishing an earthquake would rend the towers, and Hell burst burning and bellowing up to their harlot roofs. He feels the King's vows have fooled him, and reflects sardonically that the lawless race of brutes to whom love is but lust are great and sane. Then he dashes the rowel into his horse, and vanishes through the night.

His sleep at the monastery to which Sir Percivale has withdrawn is broken by a dream in which he sees Gawain fire Merlin's hall, and the morning star (signifying the purity of dawn) reel in the smoke, burst into flame, and fall. When he learns that the Queen is false, he questions the integrity of the Round Table and the King, then vaults on his horse, rides over a hunched cripple who supplicates for alms, and drives furiously on, hill and wood streaming past until the gloom thickens. 'Black nest of rats', he groans as he sees Merlin's hall 'Blackening against the dead-green stripes of even'. Challenged by Lancelot, after clashing blindly into him, he says he is a nameless scourge to lash the treasons of the Round Table; he is 'wrath and shame and hate and ill-fame'. The Queen quails in the hall at Camelot as he hisses, 'I have no sword', and springs into the dark. Modred, the Judas-like traitor, is certain that the time is at hand (cf. Matthew xxvi. 45). How wrong was Browning when he wrote with reference to this highly charged story, probably the greatest in 'The Round Table', 'Tennyson thinks he should describe the castle, and the effect of the moon on its towers, and anything *but* the soul.' Numerous characteristics and details in outer scenes reflect Pelleas's searing disillusionment in psychological impressions which are all the more intense for being imaginatively conveyed.

Pelleas is morally shattered, and becomes the Red Knight of 'The Last Tournament', who forms a Round Table of dissolute ruffians in the North. His title, like the use of 'red' with reference to Ettarre's drunken knights (and Tristram), suggests complete abandonment of the moral and spiritual for fleshly indulgences. He flouts the King, informing him through a swineherd he has maimed that his tower is full of harlots worthier than Arthur's, for they profess to be none other. The King rides with a hundred knights to the tower in the marshes, where he is cursed and insulted by his drunken foe, who stretches forward to strike, and falls from his horse into the swamp. Maddening rage dehumanizes Arthur's knights; they also reel back into the beast as they trample their enemy's face, sink his head in the mire, and beslime themselves. They rush into the fortress, slay men and women until the floor streams with carnage, and, answering yell for yell, set fire to the building. The Red Knight's fall is graced with an admirable simile which is inappropriate for its subject:

> as the crest of some slow-arching wave,
> Heard in dead night along that table-shore,
> Drops flat, and after the great waters break
> Whitening for half a league, and thin themselves,
> Far over sands marbled with moon and cloud,
> From less and less to nothing,

Tristram is the centre of interest, however. 'The Last Tournament' begins on a treacherous note, when a babe with a ruby necklace is rescued from an eagle's nest in a half-dead oak with roots that cling to the crag as if they were a black coil of snakes. The child dies, and the carcanet becomes the honour at the Tournament of Dead Innocence. The detail of the symbolism is perfect, even to the red hand with which Tristram receives the prize, at the end of a tourney which is irregularly conducted. The wan day ends wet and glooming; somebody cries out that the white day of innocence is over, and that, with snowdrops, the world would be blank as winter. A colourful attempt to be festive fails. Tristram, playing his harp, meets Dagonet the fool, whom Gawain had made mock-knight of the Round Table, and asks him why he will not skip. He will not skip to broken music, for Tristram has broken Arthur's music in deserting his wife Isolt of Brittany for Isolt, wife of Mark, King of Cornwall. Tristram's jaunty reply is that he was late joining the Order ('The life had flown, we sware but by the shell'), and he sings a song on free love, to suit the newer day (a glance at Victorian paganism, to be resumed in 'Balin and Balan'). Dagonet tells him that swine, goats, asses, rams, and geese once trooped round a pagan harper who sang a similar song.

On his way to Cornwall, Tristram dreams that he shows both Isolts the ruby-chain, until in their struggle for it the Queen of Cornwall's hand is red. His libertinism accounts for his heartless reply to a woman who has lost her husband, as he journeys to his paramour at Tintagel. Isolt entreats him to swear, even if he lies, that he will love her in old age; 'lie to me: I believe'. She speaks bitterly of what vows had meant in Arthur's prime; Tristram says they served their time, when 'every follower eyed him as a God', but began to gall with the sullying of the Queen; he is the 'worldling of the world', and chooses to love while he may. After talking of their woodland paradise and mocking ungainly Mark, he sings to his harp and displays the carcanet he has won for her. As he bends and kisses her throat, a shadow rises behind him: 'Mark's way', said Mark, and clove him through the brain. That same night Arthur returns from his war against the Red Knight, and hears sobbing at his feet as he climbs the stairway. It is Dagonet the jester, broken-hearted like King Lear's fool before the final catastrophe; he will never make his master smile again.

'Balin and Balan' suggests a split personality. Balin, after an outburst of violent rage, is restored to favour by the King, and he and his brother Balan, his good counsellor, are introduced in a symmetrical tableau, as if the pair are one. Balan leaves to fight a demon in the wood of worldly error. Balin, emulating Lancelot, is allowed to wear a replica of the Queen's crown-royal on his shield. Overhearing these two lovers, he dashes gloomily into the woods, following Balan's track. Blind with rage, he does not notice the mouth of a dark cavern, but feels a spear shot from behind him, and catches a glint of disappearing armour. At Pellam's overgrown castle he hears slander of Lancelot and the Queen from Sir Garlon, whom he attacks; hearing the approach of men-at-arms, he escapes by vaulting through a window of the chapel by means of a long red spear which lay before the altar. Superstitions, spurious relics such as this, and Balin's difficulty in seeing Christ for figures of saints in the chapel, glance at the growth of High Anglicanism and Catholicism in England. While he is in gloom and torment over his renewed violence, Vivien with her squire rides through the woods towards him, singing 'The fire of heaven has killed the barren cold', a reference (like Tristram's 'New leaf, new life – the days of frost are o'er') to passionate protests such as those of Swinburne against Christian asceticism. When Balin tells her he has shamed the Queen's cognisance, she invents a story of Guinevere's perfidy with Lancelot. Immediately his evil spirit possesses him, and with a yell he seizes his shield, defaces it with stamping, and hurls it from him. His yell is mistaken by Balan for that of the wood-demon. The two brothers clash mortally. Before they die, Balan hears what has happened. Remaining unruffled during his visit to Pellam's castle, he has learned the truth: Garlon is the slanderer–demon of the woods, who issues from the Mouth of Hell, where he is wont to dally with Vivien. The Queen, Balan holds, is pure. Born and dying together, the brothers are one; the woodland demon is a projection of the Balin self. 'To lay that devil would lay the Devil in me', he says. Most of the story is original, and Tennyson could readily empathize with it. It is the signature-piece with which he concluded *Idylls of the King*: without losing his ultimate faith, he could be subject to violent feelings against the iniquitous state of Victorian England, as *Maud* and 'Locksley Hall Sixty Years After' show.

* * *

The inner evidence of the *Idylls* suggests, it has been estimated, a time-schedule of twelve years for the main action. If the story of 'Lancelot and Elaine', hinging on the last of nine annual tournaments, belongs to the tenth year, half the books relate to the last quarter of Arthur's reign. Very little is devoted to the early years, for Tristram is a knight when Gareth arrives at Arthur's court, and, as 'The Last Tournament' discloses, the former came late. The 'rift within the lute' begins in the third book with the rumour of the Queen's guilty love and its effect on Geraint. Arthur's victories and glory are no more than a background by which to measure forces which corrupt high moral values; through the King's idealism, Tennyson affirms with Wordsworth that national greatness cannot be achieved or sustained without spiritual strength. The chronology of rise, decline, and fall constitutes a cycle; at the beginning of Arthur's victorious campaigns, and with his ultimate defeat, 'the old order changeth, yielding place to new'.

Details of this chronology are far less significant than those of the seasonal cycle which contribute subliminally, and markedly in the closing stages, to an imaginative sense of the whole. Beginning earlier with Arthur's birth, it is summarized by Tennyson: 'The Coming of Arthur is on the night of the New Year; when he is wedded "the world is white with May"; on a summer night the vision of the Holy Grail appears; and the "Last Tournament" is in the "yellowing autumn-tide". Guinevere flees thro' the mists of autumn, and Arthur's death takes place at midnight in mid-winter.'

'I have no doubt', Tennyson told H. D. Rawnsley, 'the old order will yield place to new, and we shall find higher gods than Mammon and materialism'; 'the battle of Modred in the west will yet be fought'. If Modred connotes 'the sceptical understanding', as the poet indicated about 1833, the battle continues. Mammon and materialism, however, do not contribute noticeably to Arthur's fall; if the main cause appears to be a lax sexual morality, that is largely due to the prominence of the Lancelot–Guinevere story. Lancelot's significance is wider; to him may be applied what Tennyson said in

1887 about Zola and the need for reticence and idealism in art: 'The higher moral imagination enslaved to sense is like an eagle caught by the feet in a snare, baited with carrion, so that it cannot use its wings to soar.' Undoubtedly the poet regarded free love as a serious factor in national decline, but he would hardly have agreed with the zestful Lawrence that wholeness in marriage is the solvent for all socio-economic and international problems. The implications of the Vivien–Merlin story extend far beyond the sexual; and 'The Holy Grail' indicates how strongly Tennyson felt the disservice done to Catholic countries when large numbers of the most able are withdrawn from the community for spiritual pursuits.

For man the trial is on earth, where soul and flesh are interdependent; Arthur cannot accomplish his mission without marrying Guinevere. Criticism of his weakness to control what goes on around him is inevitable; he is not to be judged as a person. Arthur is the living spirit, and the question is how long that spirit can ennoble, how far its influence can extend, and whether it can prevail over fleshly and worldly temptations. Tennyson intended him to represent 'the Ideal Soul of Man coming into contact with the warring elements of the flesh' (the latter being most apparent in 'The Last Tournament'). The 'house' which is his doom is the body; Vivien rejoices that 'Great Nature through the flesh herself hath made Gives him the lie.' In the *Idylls* he is repeatedly designated 'the blameless King'; Merlin, disgusted with Vivien before he gives way to her, reflects:

'O true and tender! O my liege and King!
O selfless man and stainless gentleman,
Who wouldst against thine own eye-witness fain
Have all men true and leal, all women pure;
How, in the mouths of base interpreters,
From over-fineness not intelligible
To things with every sense as false and foul
As the poached filth that floods the middle street,
Is thy white blamelessness accounted blame!'

Guinevere, genuinely contrite for her sins, sees her 'great and gentle lord' as 'the conscience of a saint Among his warring senses', and regrets that, instead of looking up to his perfection, she allowed her 'false voluptuous pride' to take all its impressions from below, and yearned for the 'warmth and colour' which she found in Lancelot.

The light of Guinevere's eyes enters his life when Arthur first sees her, but she finds the King 'cold, High, self-contained, and passionless', not like Lancelot as he escorted her to him. Just as Arthur (who believes 'Man's word is God in man') and Lancelot had done on the battlefield, she, at her wedding, swears a deathless love before Christ's shrine; and the knights gaze on 'all earth's beauty in their Queen'. The 'fairest of all flesh on earth', she is associated with flowers. When Lancelot brings her to the King, they ride innocently conversing under groves blossoming like paradise, and over sheets of hyacinth like 'the heavens upbreaking through the earth'. Much later, troubled by guilty love, he meets Guinevere in the garden by Arthur's hall, entering by the lily path as she enters by the walk of roses. Balin hears them in the bower where they are concealed. Lancelot had dreamt of a maiden saint whose face was illuminated by the light which flowed from the spiritual lily she held; the Queen prefers the deep-hued rose, even more the wild-wood hyacinth and the bloom of May. She reminds him of the rides they have taken among such flowers in 'those fair days – not all as cool as these', and wonders whether he is sad or sick. Pelleas hears 'A worm within the rose' sung before the Queen, and finds Ettarre's rose garden overgrown with lawless brambles. So disloyalty in high places sets a fashion, and Merlin dreams prophetically of 'the high purpose broken by the worm'.

The earthly or fleshly role of Guinevere is not unduly obtrusive, but it inevitably creates awkward authorial equivocations. These, it should be noted, are never anti-feminist in the slightest degree; nor could any atavistic Adam-and-Eve implication be expected from the author of *The Princess*. Weaknesses of the flesh are fairly apportioned to men and women in the *Idylls*, with Lancelot and Guinevere, Tristram and Isolt, Gawain and Ettarre; and Enid and Elaine more than compensate for Vivien's feminine wiles. The import of the Vivien–Merlin episode, however, is more general than personal. Merlin is the mage who knows all the arts, and has made Camelot 'spire to heaven'; the city was built to music, 'therefore never built at all, And therefore built for ever'. Its existence is shadowy, not material; everywhere it is 'symbolic of the gradual growth of human beliefs and institutions, and of the spiritual development of man', Tennyson wrote. Merlin is inseparable from Arthur's greatness and power, as the hall he built for the King illustrates, with its four evolutionary zones: the first showing the lowest beasts prevail over men; the second, men slaying beasts; the third, 'warriors, perfect men'; the fourth, 'men with growing wings'. Regeneration must be active, among mankind; and Arthur's hall suffers irreparable damage when knights abandon his cause for the wasteful Quest. The Round Table is weakened, and Merlin is already 'lost to life and use and name and fame'; he no longer follows the Gleam. Tennyson's vision is Shelleyan, and no doubt he was influenced by *A Defence of Poetry*, published posthumously in 1840. All creators (embodied in Merlin) in this world of shadows are poets, and their vision of excellence (the Platonic Ideal) is heaven-born. Without it there can be no greatness or progress in the arts, philosophy, morals, citizenship, and government; and therefore 'poets' are 'the unacknowledged legislators of the world'.

Tennyson took issue with art-for-art's sake proponents who criticized the 1869 additions to *Idylls of the King*, and added the most telling lines to 'Merlin and Vivien' in 1875. Like Lawrence's Gudrun, Vivien is associated with destructive will-power, with nihilism, and with death (from which she is born). She reaches Camelot 'at a time of golden rest', when Arthur's court is most vulnerable, relaxing after the defeat of all his enemies. Her destructive aims are revealed in 'Balin and Balan'. Brought up in the court of Arthur's enemy Mark, she, like Tristram, believes in hedonism and free love; her sun-worship revival will 'beat the cross to earth, and break the King, And all his Table'. The chapel to which the dying Arthur is carried after the defeat of his forces is no more than 'A broken chancel with a broken cross' on a dark strait of barren land. Her influence and that of Modred, in destroying high purpose, are echoed in Tennyson's concluding lines 'To the Queen', where alarm is expressed at 'Waverings of every vane with every wind', 'fierce or careless looseners of the faith', 'Cowardice, the child of lust for gold', 'Art with poisonous honey stolen from France', and 'that which knows not, ruling that which knows'.

Medieval romances which are purely descriptive–narrative can command only a transient adult attention; and critics, using comments of Meredith and Carlyle, have been ready to dismiss *Idylls of the King* as 'Musery' with superlative lollipops by the way. Admittedly the earlier books to be written tend to be protracted. Too much space is devoted to the Enid stories, and their significance is almost inversely proportional to their length. 'Lancelot and Elaine' is pictorially attractive, and reaches a climax combining rare dramatic and poetic distinctiveness. The ending of 'Merlin and Vivien' is memorably descriptive, the elements of the outer storm being resonant with disaster not just for Merlin but for all Arthur's hopes. Had Tennyson's deeper purposiveness been more defined and creatively integrated from the outset, *Idylls of the King* might have been shorter, more vivid and concentrated, and more artistically admirable. Though intensive poetic effects are more abundant in the later additions, there are, as could be expected, graphic passages in all the books, but in none more, or at greater length, than in 'The Holy Grail'. Sometimes a surrealist impression is given, as with Guinevere's dream or the maddened, despairing, final efforts of Lancelot to find the Grail. There are imaginative overtones of two kinds: those which are psychological, where outer scenes communicate the outlook, mood, or feelings of a central character, and others, more widespread and often in frequent succession, in which images are correlated with the moral or spiritual import of the situation. 'Pelleas and Ettarre' and 'Balin and Balan' provide ample illustration of the former. The latter type of poetry, though narrative gives it greater explicitness, is akin to the more concentrated form it reaches in Eliot's *The Waste Land*, which has obvious affinities with 'The Passing of Arthur'.

Intensiveness of such kinds makes the *Idylls* more rewarding in parts than as a whole. 'Poetry is like shot-silk with many glancing colours. Every reader must find his own interpretation according to his own ability, and according to his sympathy with the poet', Tennyson wrote. Full appreciation depends on sympathy with the innermost subject or theme. It had a contemporary relevance; it is relevant today, and always will be, as long as readers are interested in the progress of civilization. There were times of depression when the poet, like Arthur, could not find God in his ways with men, rather in the universe from stars to flowers. Yet he retained his belief in man's unconquerable spirit: 'I believe in God, not from what I see in Nature, but from what I find in man', he said. This view is consonant with the spiritual tenor of the *Idylls*, and the poem concludes with the 'new sun' which brings the 'new year'. Arthur's battles do not belong solely to the past; they are depicted 'as if Time were nothing'.

17

Epistolary Poems

The truth of Wordsworth's contention that a poet is 'a man speaking to men' could hardly more gracefully be illustrated from serious verse than it is in Tennyson's epistolary poetry, occasional or dedicatory. Pope was adept in a more dramatic vein, but the conversational tone of his epistles is often checked by the see-saw bias of his heroic couplets. To achieve a conversational ease and fluency in rhymed stanzas, as Tennyson continually does, demands not only an at-homeness in the medium but also, like all intimate letters, a friendly, affectionate, or moving rapport with the person addressed. Such ease of manner has been noticed in 'The Miller's Daughter' (1832); it is the hall-mark of 'Will Waterproof's Lyrical Monologue' (1842); and it is delightfully illustrated in 'To the Vicar of Shiplake', which was written on the poet's wedding-day. Greater concentration, and occasionally, for metrical purposes, syntactical reordering, can be expected in verse, but for the most part Tennyson's manner is that of conversational prose. There are times when this is superlatively achieved in *In Memoriam*.

The style emerges first in 'To J. S.' (addressed to James Spedding in 1832, on the loss of his brother); it is found in the dedication of the 1851 edition of *Poems*, 'To the Queen', and in 'To E. L. on his Travels in Greece' (both written in the *In Memoriam* stanza), though the second opens with cumulative inversion in praise of the skill shown by Edward Lear with pen and pencil in the record of his travels:

Illyrian woodlands, echoing falls
　Of water, sheets of summer glass,
　　The long divine Peneïan pass,
The vast Akrokeraunian walls,

Tomohrit, Athos, all things fair,
  With such a pencil, such a pen,
  You shadow forth to distant men,
I read and felt that I was there:

the poet then describes how delighted he was to find his spirits 'in the golden age'.

'The Daisy', one of the poems which suggests that Tennyson excelled in this kind of poetry, was written to his wife from Edinburgh, when the poet, on finding the crushed 'nurseling of another sky' in the book she had lent him, was moved to recall the stages of their 1851 Italian tour, to the point where the flower was plucked and presented.

And I forgot the clouded Forth,
The gloom that saddens Heaven and Earth,
  The bitter east, the misty summer
And gray metropolis of the North.

Perchance, to lull the throbs of pain,
Perchance, to charm a vacant brain,
  Perchance, to dream you still beside me,
My fancy fled to the South again.

'O love, what hours were thine and mine, In lands of palm and southern pine', he begins:

What slender campanili grew
By bays, the peacock's neck in hue;
  Where, here and there, on sandy beaches
A milky-belled amaryllis blew.

So the recollections continue, to Milan and the excitement created by the singing and the architectural glory of the cathedral, to Lake Como:

Remember how we came at last
To Como; shower and storm and blast
  Had blown the lake beyond his limit,
And all was flooded; and how we past

From Como, when the light was gray,
And in my head, for half the day,
   The rich Virgilian rustic measure
Of Lari Maxume, all the way,

Like ballad-burthen music, kept
As on The Lariano crept
   To that fair port below the castle
Of Queen Theodolind, where we slept.[21]

The closeness of the language to speech tends to conceal metrical skill, a special feature of which is the quickening movement at the centre of each final line ('fled to the South', 'flooded; and how'). In style and subject, the poem is comparable to Browning's 'By the Fire-side' (written later, but also published in 1855).

The stanza, its metre 'representing in some measure the grandest of metres, the Horatian Alcaic', was modified in 'To the Rev. F. D. Maurice'. Writing from Farringford, where he watches 'the twilight falling brown All round a careless-ordered garden Close to the ridge of a noble down', Tennyson urges his old friend, after dismissal from his professorship for heterodoxy, to come and see his godson Hallam. Characteristic lines ('Making the little one leap for joy', 'Crocus, anemone, violet') open with dactyls which impart convincing life to the invitation. The only gossip his guest would hear would be that of the magpie, 'Garrulous under a roof of pine',

For groves of pine on either hand,
To break the blast of winter, stand;
   And further on, the hoary Channel
Tumbles a billow on chalk and sand;

Where, if below the milky steep
Some ship of battle slowly creep,
   And on through zones of light and shadow
Glimmer away to the lonely deep . . . .

The Crimean War was looming. They could discuss its menace and origin, or poverty and the development of 'valour and charity'. Maurice is urged to come with the spring flowers, 'Or later, pay one visit here, For those are few we hold as dear; Nor pay but one, but come for many, Many and many a happy year'.

The remaining examples of this kind of verse belong to the period

after the completion of *Idylls of the King*. 'Prefatory Poem to My
Brother's Sonnets', written at the passing of midnight on 30 June
1879, not long after the death of Charles Turner (Tennyson), and
for publication with his *Collected Sonnets* (1880), is addressed to his
brother's spirit. The cuckoo of the wet summer recalls the phantom
bird of boyhood, and midnight turns into the sunshine of sixty years
earlier, 'When all my griefs were shared with thee, As all my hopes
were thine – As all thou wert was one with me, May all thou art be
mine!' It is astonishing how much Tennyson can compass in
thought and feeling by variation of phrases in the most simple
language.

'To Virgil', written at the request of the Virgilian Academy of
Mantua, for the nineteenth centenary of the poet's death (1882),
glances at the major aspects of a writer Tennyson had loved since
boyhood. What appeals to him as a poet is mirrored in Virgil's most
eminent qualities. There is a sympathy in philosophical outlook:

> Thou that seëst Universal Nature moved by Universal Mind;
> Thou majestic in thy sadness at the doubtful doom of human
>   kind. . . .

Virgil is pastoralist, landscape-lover, and creator of vivid epic
scenes. Above all, he is 'lord of language', with 'All the chosen coin
of fancy flashing out from many a golden phrase' and 'All the charm
of all the Muses often flowering in a lonely word'. Tennyson salutes
him as the 'Wielder of the stateliest measure ever moulded by the
lips of man', and honours his 'ocean-roll of rhythm' in a wavelike
succession of trochaic hemistichs which emulate the linguistic
splendour of his exemplar.

'Prologue to General Hamley', published with 'The Charge of
the Heavy Brigade at Balaclava', and written as a token of gratitude
for confirmation of its historical accuracy, is remarkable for being
sustained in one long sentence of thirty-two lines. It begins with the
Aldworth scene and 'Green Sussex fading into blue With one gray
glimpse of sea' at the time of the general's visit, and ends, after riding
in steady climax with proud thoughts of a victory in which Hamley
had participated: 'Yet know you, as your England knows That you
and all your men Were soldiers to her heart's desire, When, in the
vanished year, You saw the league-long rampart-fire Flare from
Tel-el-Kebir Through darkness . . . .'

When Tennyson was revising 'Tiresias' for publication he

remembered Edward FitzGerald's decided preference for his earlier work, and dedicated the poem to him. 'To E. FitzGerald' refers to his vegetarianism and his 'golden Eastern lay', the *Rubáiyát* of Omar Khayyám. Not long after the dedication was written, in June 1883, FitzGerald died. Tennyson therefore wrote a codicil or epilogue, referring to the rhymes that 'missed his living welcome', like 'guests an hour too late, Who down the highway moving on With easy laughter find the gate Is bolted, and the master gone'. He questions Omar's dark philosophy of death:

> The deeper night? A clearer day
> Than our poor twilight dawn on earth –
>   If night, what barren toil to be!
> What life, so maimed by night, were worth
>   Our living out? Not mine to me . . . .

In one respect the dedication is the most notable of all Tennyson's epistles, for its fifty-six lines consist of one sentence that never tires. It begins with a recollection of the writer's stay with 'Old Fitz' at Woodbridge, and ends with the rather sad hope that his friend will welcome his gift

> Less for its own than for the sake
> Of one recalling gracious times,
>   When, in our younger London days,
> You found some merit in my rhymes,
>   And I more pleasure in your praise.

'To Ulysses', another poem whose intended recipient died before he could read it, was written early in 1888 (when 'The century's three strong eights have met To drag me down to seventy-nine') in response to F. T. Palgrave's brother's gift of *Ulysses*, a collection of essays on his travels in the East and tropical climes. Tennyson, soaking in winter wet at Farringford, contrasts the trees he loves to study, including the wellingtonia planted by Garibaldi, with 'The wealth of tropic bower and brake; Your Oriental Eden-isles, Where man, nor only Nature smiles'. 'To Mary Boyle' belongs to the following spring, when 'Our elmtree's ruddy-hearted blossom-flake Is fluttering down'. The poet urges her to come before 'all the gold from each laburnum chain Drop to the grass', and sends her a copy of 'The Progress of Spring', a poem he wrote in 'rick-fire days' that 'made an English homestead Hell'. She was in mourning. 'What use to brood?' he asks; 'this life of mingled pains And joys to me, Despite of every Faith and Creed, remains The Mystery'. As they are both close to the 'dim gate', he concludes,

> Take, read! and be the faults your Poet makes
> > Or many or few,
> He rests content, if his young music wakes
> > A wish in you

> To change our dark Queen-city, all her realm
> > Of sound and smoke,
> For his clear heaven, and these few lanes of elm
> > And whispering oak.

'To the Marquis of Dufferin and Ava' begins rather stiffly, but is memorable for its acknowledgement of the Governor-General of India's kindness to Lionel Tennyson during the illness which prostrated him before his fatal voyage. The *In Memoriam* stanza becomes more free as personal feeling enters:

> And those lone rites I have not seen,
> And one drear sound I have not heard,

> Are dreams that scarce will let me be,
> > Not there to bid my boy farewell,
> > When That within the coffin fell,
> Fell – and flashed into the Red Sea,

> Beneath a hard Arabian moon
> > And alien stars. To question, why
> > The sons before the fathers die,
> Not mine! and I may meet him soon.

'To the Master of Balliol', a dedication accompanying 'The Death of Oenone', is another poem in a single sentence; though brief, it does not run altogether as smoothly as others. Most of these epistles are not just urbane and intimate; they stir deeper chords. Such is their technical attainment that art often seems lost in an unaffected flow of language. Some of them must take their place among the most readable and rewarding of Tennyson's poems.

18
Drama

Tennyson's precocity in dramatic writing (a scene written at the age of fourteen survives, as well as *The Devil and the Lady*) does not indicate the suppression of a dramatist for a half-century of poetry. Several of his pre-marriage letters show that he was steeped in Shakespeare, but this devotion argues an interest in poetic language rather than in writing for the stage. Theatricals in which his sons took part, notably at Mrs Cameron's, probably did something to sharpen his interest in dramatic art, but his play-writing from 1874 to 1882 is accounted for, partly from the lack of a large and important subject to engross him poetically after the completion of *Idylls of the King*, more positively because, living for a period each year in London, he was able to attend stage-performances which excited his dramatic ambition. The highlights at this critical juncture were Henry Irving's performances in *Richelieu* and *Hamlet*, and Helen Faucit in *As You Like It*.

According to his son Hallam, he chose *Harold*, *Becket*, and *Queen Mary* (not in that order) 'to complete the line of Shakespeare's English chronicle-plays'. All the evidence shows that he studied the history of the periods very closely. The trilogy, Tennyson wrote, presents 'the great conflict between Danes, Saxons and Normans for supremacy, the awakening of the English people and clergy from the slumber into which they had for the most part fallen, and the forecast of the greatness of our composite race'. In *Becket* we have the struggle for predominance between Crown and Church, 'a struggle which continued for many centuries'. The subject of *Queen Mary* is 'the final downfall of Roman Catholicism in England, and the dawning of a new age: for after the era of priestly domination comes the era of the freedom of the individual'. Although it is a play of another order, Tennyson associated *The Foresters* with his more historical trilogy; in it, he wrote rather exaggeratedly, 'I have sketched the state of the people in another great transition period of the making of England, when the barons sided with the people and eventually won for them the Magna Charta.' Clearly his efforts were lifted by a great swell of national feeling.

Queen Mary was published in 1875. Sir Richard Jebb attributed to it a 'dramatic fire' unequalled in historical drama since Shakespeare. J. A. Froude, whose *History of England* had been of great benefit to Tennyson, went further; he thought it the greatest of the Poet Laureate's works. Tennyson came to believe it was the most successful of his plays in character-portrayal. A dramatized chronicle, as it was accurately described by Henry James, it was too long and unmanageable for the stage, and a curtailed version soon ended in failure. Like all Tennyson's plays, however, it is worth reading; they merit consideration for radio, if not television, broadcasting, some in their complete text. Had Tennyson taken a more Aristotelian look at the problem of stage-presentation, avoiding the chronicle form and a proliferation of scenes (which was possible on the Elizabethan but not on the lavishly set Victorian stage), he would probably have been much more successful, though his general inability to maintain dramatic heightening in speech and situation would have militated against him.

Aware of the degree to which anti-Catholicism had been provoked by Tractarianism, Tennyson was at pains in *Queen Mary* to be historically thorough and impartial. In dramatizing historical movements he neglected the dramatic action of the play as a whole; he expected the stage to accommodate crowd scenes and grand spectacle; he presented interesting minor characters, but allowed insufficient room for the development of his leading figures, who come to life intermittently, in flashes or relatively brief passages. Act I presents the religious conflict, centred in the Queen's determination to marry Philip of Spain. The second act comprises Wyatt's revolt and its failure; Sir Thomas White, Lord Mayor of London, supports the Queen, who defends her policy (ii). Most speeches move at a pedestrian pace, with occasional phrases of dramatic intensity and more frequent recourse to simile. When Act III opens, the Queen and Philip are married; Lady Jane Grey (her end movingly described by Bagenhall) has been executed. The awakening of the babe within her womb rouses Mary to a magnificat; she sees her star rising with the coming of the defender of the Faith, the second Prince of Peace, who will put heretics to the sword, and cause the ghosts of Luther and Zuinglius to fade (ii). She sits between Philip and Cardinal Pole when Gardiner, Bishop of Winchester, makes a smooth submission to the latter as papal representative; and Bagenhall, refusing to bow the knee to Rome, is sent to the Tower. Elizabeth, in banishment at Woodstock, finds consolation in philosophizing, and wishes she were a milkmaid, after hearing one sing outside; the blank verse continues, rather line by line, in studied, not stirring, composition. Act IV is almost a play within a play: Cranmer, condemned to death despite his recantation, retracts in St Mary's, Oxford, after hearing that his burning testifies to God, and will be rewarded in Paradise. The final act shows the decline of the Queen: the people hate her; she loses Calais; the husband on whom she had doted despises her. 'Bride of the mightiest sovereign on earth', she knows it, knows too that the only child she will bear is death. Yet in her frenzy she wishes she had done more to follow his lead:

> There are Hot Gospellers even among our guards–
> Nobles we dared not touch. We have but burnt
> The heretic priest, workmen, and women and children . . . .
> We have so play'd the coward; but by God's grace,
> We'll follow Philip's leading, and set up
> The Holy Office here – garner the wheat,
> And burn the tares with unquenchable fire!

At the point of death she says,

> Open my heart, and there you will find written
> Two names, Philip and Calais; open his, –
> So that he have one, –
> You will find Philip only, policy, policy, –
> Ay, worse than that – not one hour true to me!
> Foul maggots crawling in a fester'd vice!
> Adulterous to the very heart of Hell.

She leaves her throne to Elizabeth, whom her politic, lecherous husband hopes to marry. Tennyson did not sympathize with her cause, but there is no doubt about his sympathies with the Queen, whom he thought much misunderstood. Her religious mania is interpreted in terms of a tormented passion which ultimately (at the most moving stage of the play) she knows is wasted.

In preparation for his next play, *Harold* (1876), which he called his 'tragedy of doom', Tennyson studied many recent plays; it contains no more than half the number of scenes and characters in *Queen Mary*. He also re-read Aeschylus and Sophocles; and it is interesting to note that his friend Aubrey de Vere observed everywhere in the new play 'a sort of Aeschylean strength' which made the simplicity of its characters and plot seem heroic. Longfellow found it like 'Boädicea', 'a voice out of the Past, sonorous, strange, semi-barbaric'; he did not know where to look for anything more masterly than the fifth act.

The play is more successful than *Queen Mary*, though too much of it follows the chronicle pattern. Half the drama is completed before Harold succeeds to the throne, and the action preceding the fatal climax is swift. The first part is doom-laden (including a ghastly Grecian kind of play on words when Harold tells his Norman warder to keep out of earshot while still keeping him in eyeshot). In conventional Shakespearian style the play opens with the heavens blazing forth the doom of England, premonitions of which are reinforced by dreams, Harold's persistence in going to France, and the melodrama of Aldwyth's eavesdropping and of the soliloquy in which this ex-Queen of Wales outlines the means whereby she will become Queen of England. A grand stage climax in which the ill-fated hero finds he has testified before the bones of saints from the holiest of Norman shrines dramatizes the ruthlessness of Count William in extracting promise of support for his claim to the English throne. A believer in the Welshman's saying 'The Truth against the World' (Tennyson's adopted motto), Harold is repeatedly compelled to be false to himself. Aldwyth entices the superstitious Edward the Confessor to insist that Edith shall remain a vestal virgin as a redemptive measure against the breaking of his pledge by her lover Harold when he succeeds him as King of England. All Aldwyth's machinations prosper, and she becomes Queen. The previous Queen, Harold's sister, sympathizes openly with her banished brother Tostig, who, supported by the King of Norway, leads a rebellion in the north of England. When Harold mourns his death in the battle at Stamford Bridge, Aldwyth tells him he is too kindly, and admonishes him for allowing so many Normans to leave the country: 'Thy fierce forekings had clench'd their pirate hides To the bleak church doors, like kites upon a barn.' Before the final battle, Harold speaks strongly for England against the Papacy: God is nobler than the saints. Within a tent overlooking the field of Senlac (> Sanguelac, lake of blood) scenes continue before and during the battle. Harold's self-analysis, after dreams in which Edward, his

own brother Wulfnoth (kept as a hostage in Normandy), Tostig, and
the Norman saints pronounce his doom, shows the integrity of his
troubled conscience:

> dreams – where mine own self
> Takes part against myself! Why? for a spark
> Of self-disdain born in me when I sware
> Falsely to him, the falser Norman, over
> His gilded ark of mummy-saints, by whom
> I knew not that I sware, – not for myself –
> For England – yet not wholly – . . . .

Edith enters; he tells her she is his true bride, and he leaves England
his 'legacy of war against the Pope' until 'the Pope be Christ's'. She
tells him he is the first of a line of kings coming from the people and
chosen by the people. The authorial emphasis is patent. How next
could the battle be presented? Tennyson's achievement here is far
more imaginative and dramatically acceptable than the typical
apologetic Shakespearian rendering. The Archbishop enters, and
the chanting of canons without and the prayers of Edith within
alternate with his vivid reporting, as he answers her anxious
questions in an admirably sustained blending of the lively and
solemn. The final scene has its interest, not so much in the search of
Aldwyth and Edith for the King (Edith proving she is his true wife
when she finds his corpse and their marriage ring on his finger,
before dying theatrically with him) as in the change which William
assumes when he becomes King of England by might. The 'fox–lion'
of the past is made to speak briefly for Tennyson:

> never yet –
> No, by the splendour of God – have I fought men
> Like Harold and his brethren, and his guard
> Of English. . . . Of one self-stock at first,
> Make them again one people – Norman, English;
> And English, Norman.

His more extended imperial vision, fleetingly indulged, reveals his
ruthless hoof.

How thorough was the preparation for *Becket*, which was not
finished until 1879, may be judged from the historian J. R. Green's
remark that his researches had not disclosed as vivid a conception of

Henry II and his court as he found in Tennyson's play. It opens more promisingly than either *Queen Mary* or *Harold*. A prologue set in Normandy foreshadows the main drama, Henry and his friend Becket, whom he had raised from low estate to the Chancellorship, playing chess, with king and bishop in decisive moves, Becket foreseeing a clash between 'God's favour and king's favour' if he becomes Archbishop, the King revealing where his 'true heart-wife' Rosamund de Clifford is hidden, and Queen Eleanor engaging Fitzurse against her and Becket. The confrontation of Church and Crown is not deferred: Act I opens with Becket as Archbishop of Canterbury asking whether he is the man for the position and hearing God's reassurance. A spectacular scene in the hall of Northampton Castle, in which he thwarts the King, is followed by one emphasizing Becket's regard for the destitute and impoverished. The composer Stanford, impressed by the contrast it drew between the traitorous splendour of the nobles and the homely loyalty (and humour) of the maimed, halt, and blind, thought Irving's omission of it a mistake. Tennyson was too inclusive, however. So much of the play between the opening and final acts is devoted to the Rosamund legend that insufficient movement is allowed for the main conflict. Hallam Tennyson found the germ of the play in 'Rosamund's Bower', a short dramatic lyric which his father (whose partiality for the subject appeared in 'A Dream of Fair Women') had written before 1842, and this disproportioning leads to a long diversion (reaching a climax when Becket saves Rosamund from Eleanor's dagger) where the central tension needs dramatic development. The pace is too leisurely; the jester–commentator William Map's wit is as tedious as the long-windedness of Margery at the Bower. More to the point is John of Salisbury's counsel before the catastrophe, when he tells Becket that God's war against the King may have an admixture of private spite. 'Clothed with the full authority of Rome', Becket is immovable, believing the martyrdom of his dream is God's will. Significantly it is Eleanor's jealousy of Rosamund that leads to his murder in Tennyson's play: after angering Henry with taunts that he is ruled by Becket, she tells him that the Archbishop is now lord of his amours, having committed Rosamund to Godstow nunnery; it is then, before the knights whom she has prepared to strike, that the enraged monarch unleashes the fatal call, 'Will no man free me from this pestilent priest?' Significantly, too, Rosamund witnesses Becket's death, and is seen at the very end, as lighting flashes through the cathedral, kneeling by his body. *Becket* follows the chronicle style, and contains powerful and spectacular scenes. How little Tennyson had studied stagecraft, however, may be gauged by comparing it with Eliot's *Murder in the Cathedral*, which may be indebted to *Becket* for some of its insights, but achieves more in a disciplined, predominantly classical style of presentation, without melodrama or romance.

The Falcon, a lively one-act embroidering of a Boccaccio story (*Il Decamerone*, V. ix) which was first commended for the English stage by Hazlitt, was concluded in November 1879, and enjoyed a moderately successful run at St James's Theatre almost immediately afterwards. A count, after beggaring himself to win the love of a lady, is so destitute that, when she pays a surprise visit to his cottage, he has to kill his prized falcon in hospitality to her, not knowing until the repast is over that she comes at the request of her spoilt boy, who, after being allowed to hawk with it, thinks he will recover from his illness if it is his. The climactic revelations are artistically delayed, and the widow's confession of love, in defiance of her brother's veto, provides a happy ending, unlike Boccaccio's. Other differences suggest Tennyson's resourcefulness: acting as servants, the count's foster-brother and his old nurse (to some degree reminiscent of the nurse in *Romeo and Juliet*) supply a humorous commentary; a withered wreath plays a part almost as important as that of the falcon; and poetry and song come from Count Federigo.

The Cup, a tragedy in two acts from Plutarch's *The Bravery of Women* (xx), was suggested by a paragraph in Lecky's *History of European Morals*. Finished in 1880 in response to Irving's recommendation of a shorter play (after rejecting *Becket* on the pretext that it would prove too costly), it was lavishly produced at the Lyceum, with Ellen Terry as Camma, wife of the Tetrarch of Galatia. At the end of Act I he is stabbed to death by Synorix, the previous Tetrarch, an unpopular designing Tarquin type, who had sent her a cup, rescued from a burning shrine of Artemis, in the hope of seducing her. She takes refuge in the Temple of Artemis, where, 'for her beauty, stateliness, and power', she becomes the Priestess. Act II takes place within this temple, cheers outside announcing the public coronation of Synorix. Still wishing to marry her, he sends her a crown, 'diadem of the first Galatian Queen', which she accepts. Preparations are made for the King's entry. Synorix calls on the life-giving, Camma on the life-destructive, to bless their marriage. According to custom they drink from the same cup as a symbol of marriage unity. It is the gift of Synorix, and the potion is poisoned.

Tennyson makes the most of his classical subject; there are fine verse passages, and grandeur of spectacle enhances the heroics.

The Foresters is a romantic tale of Robin Hood and Maid Marian. Their ultimate happiness depends on her father's ability to pay the heavy debts incurred by raising a ransom for his son, a prisoner of the Moors, and on the defeat of the combined villainy of King John and the Sheriff of Nottingham, which is brought to pass with the arrival of Richard the Lionheart. All ends well in a rapid succession of events, finally with the return of Marian's brother and of the money sent for ransom. Though there is some emphasis on Robin Hood as the protector of England against the 'Norman tyranny' of the arrogant, dissolute John, the play lacks the serious historical import Tennyson claimed for it. Robin refers to the 'vice-king John', and adds 'True king of vice – true play on words'. The wit is never sprightly; Friar Tuck tells the unrecognised Richard that fighting with Robin Hood will give him a new zest for dinner, 'though thou wert like a bottle full up to the cork, or as hollow as a kex, or the shambles-oak, or a weasel-sucked egg, or the head of a fool, or the heart of Prince John, or any other symbol of vacuity'. The foresters' song 'There is no land like England' was adapted from one published by Tennyson in 1830, its anti-Gallic strain being removed; and Robin's dream of the fairies was added not very inspiredly on Irving's recommendation. The play was written quickly, and contains little of high quality. Its drama resides almost wholly in externals, and is more appropriate to the world of opera; most adult readers would find T. L. Peacock's *Maid Marian* more entertaining.

The Promise of May is much more interesting. In it Tennyson strove 'to bring the true drama of character and life back again', presenting 'one leaf out of the great book of truth and nature'. Rejected by Irving and by the producers of *The Falcon*, it had a short run at the Globe at the end of 1882, and was hurriedly withdrawn from the press; at an early performance the Marquis of Queensberry protested that it was a caricature of free-thinking. The subject is a village tragedy begotten by a self-deluding contemporary intellectual who accepts a hedonistic philosophy for his own ends. It is like the invasion of Arcadia by Tennyson's Tristram in modern dress, or by a distant cousin of Fitzpiers in Hardy's *The Woodlanders*. If the after-life is a 'lost gleam', does one join St Paul and Edward Young in accepting the philosophy of self-indulgence without moral restraints? This was the question inevitably raised by FitzGerald's version of the *Rubáiyát*, and by Swinburnian protests against the excessive, rather hypocritical, preaching of Victorian Christianity. Edgar, the hero–villain of *The Promise of May*, argues that, if his pleasure breeds another's pain, it follows nature; a progressive in his own estimation, he believes that marriage and churches are outmoded, that conventional vice is virtue, and that evolving man, 'following his own instincts as his God, Will enter on the larger golden age'. A gentleman–artist, disinherited after an amorous 'frolic', he comes into the country and seduces Eva, one of Farmer Steer's daughters. There are some delightful rustic scenes, with Farmer Dobson instinctively suspicious of the visitor. At the outset, the antithetical components of the song by Eva's sister Dora foreshadow the theme, 'red fire' waking in the heart of a town and changing joy to grief in a rural community; (with Queen Mary's tragic song 'Hapless doom of woman happy in betrothing', this is one of the most impressive lyrics in Tennyson's plays).

When Edgar returns disguised and remorseful five years later, he blames heredity for his wrong-doing; more interesting is his renunciation of Socialism, Communism, Nihilism, and such 'Utopian idiotcies' after inheriting his uncle's large estate. When Eva ran away, she indicated that her body would be found in the river, and Farmer Steer, blind and broken, now believes she drowned herself. She returns, and is concealed by Dora, who is on the point of marrying the disguised Edgar. Eva recognises him and, after saying that she will forgive him if he makes Dora happy, falls dead. He curses this 'world of mud', 'its idiot gleams Of pleasure', and 'all the foul fatalities That blast our natural passions into pains', but is spurned by Dora, who sees more good in Farmer Dobson, and recalls Eva in 'the promise of her May', at fifteen when Edgar 'came on her'. The melodramatic ending concludes on a note of forgiveness. The play has obvious weaknesses, but is astonishingly forward-looking in conception. Just over ten years later 'Ibscene drama' became the sensation of London theatre-goers. Could Tennyson have addressed himself to the study of stagecraft as Ibsen did, his drama would have been incalculably different.

19
Popular Dramatic Monologues

Far more popular than his published plays or *Idylls of the King* were the stories and sketches which Tennyson versified with ready and sometimes not over-subtle art, especially in his later years. Technically expert, but with a worrying dearth of major inspiring subjects, the Poet Laureate adopted, almost by force of habit, the dramatic monologue form, and long heavily stressed lines, caesurally divided to make for balance and easy reading. His subjects vary from the amusing to the heroic, and were obviously well suited for the readings and recitations which had become fashionable.

'The Flight', published in 1885 but written fifty years earlier, presents a situation similar to those in 'Locksley Hall' (written about the same time and imagined in a similar Lincolnshire setting) and *Maud*. A motherless girl is betrothed for her father's advantage to one she scorns: 'These ancient woods, this Hall at last will go – perhaps have gone, Except his own meek daughter yield her life, heart, soul.' Stock Tennysonian associations are introduced: she feels sacrificed like Jephthah's daughter; if she is mad, she is like Scott's Lucy of Lammermoor, the 'mad bride who stabbed her bridegroom on her bridal night'. Her feelings, as she talks to her sister, after waking early on her bridal day, are expressed in the moaning of the sea that sounds as if it would burst the shore. With thoughts of her lover Edwin at sea, among the islands of the Blest, and of the happy singing of the birds that love their mates, the poem does not escape the sentimental. It ends with the two sisters preparing for flight; the world cannot be as harsh as the speaker's fate if she remains, for 'every heart that loves with truth is equal to endure'.

With 'The Grandmother' we come to the period which immediately follows the 1859 *Idylls of the King*. The subject was
recommended by Benjamin Jowett, and the poem first appeared in
Once a Week with an illustration by Millais. The talkative old lady
lives in the past, and is at peace with the world; her eldest son Willy
has died not far short of seventy, and she cannot weep. She tells her
grandchild Annie that there was a time when she could, as she did
when the man she married walked out with her slanderer Jenny, or
when their first child was born dead (Tennyson recalls his own
sorrow in the babe that 'fought for his life'). All her children are
dead, but they live around her, Harry in the five-acre and Charlie
ploughing the hill, or they sing to their team, or hover about her
chair and bed. She hears Annie, who died at two, pattering over the
boards, and sees Willy still ruddy and white and strong on his legs.
She rarely grieves; often she is back at her father's farm, laughing
and gossiping with her neighbours. There is no sentimentality in the
poem, which ends as it began, with a mother-in-law's remark:
'Willy's wife has written; she never was over-wise.'

'Northern Farmer' (Old Style) and 'Northern Farmer' (New
Style) present contrasting moods, both situations being devised
around memorable Lincolnshire statements, the first of which
Tennyson heard when his great-uncle at the age of eighty told him
about the death of a farm-bailiff: 'God A'mighty little knows what
He's about, a-taking me. An' Squire will be so mad an' all.' The
crusty old man on his death-bed, after visits by the doctor and the
parson, berates his nurse for being away so long, and tells her
(contrary to the doctor's advice) to get him his ale as usual. Having
held her attention until he has said all he wishes, he dismisses her
brusquely: 'Git ma my aäle I tell tha, an' if I mun doy I mun doy.'
The parson reads a sermon once a week, but he (the speaker) has
made Thurnaby waste productive. To think that God is taking him,
'Wi' aäf the cows to cauve an' Thurnaby hoälms to plow!'; it will be
a relief not to know what happens to his land when he is dead, for he
couldn't bear to see it.[22]

The second poem arose from the sentence 'When I canters my
'erse along the ramper [highway] I 'ears "proputty, proputty,
proputty".' Catching sight of the parsonage, the farmer of the new
generation brings to a standstill the horse whose trotting echoes his
obsession, and addresses his son Sam, who has confided his love for
the parson's daughter:

An' I went wheer munny war: an' thy muther coom to 'and,
Wi' lots o' munny laaïd by, an' a nicetish bit o' land.
Maäybe she warn't a beauty: – I niver giv it a thowt –
But warn't she as good to cuddle an' kiss as a lass as 'ant nowt?

At one point the horse is restive, and Sam is asked to break some ash twigs from the hedge to protect the horse's head from bees. What are beauty, love, gentility, the farmer continues, without money? He and his wife agree that Sam is an ass. He surveys the scene, points out how his property has grown, and where he intends it to extend. He then talls Sam flatly that if he marries a 'good un' he will inherit the land; if he marries a 'bad un', it will go to his brother. The poems are complementary; the farmer of the departed era leaves his land in good heart; the new farmer is a heartless mercenary. The second monologue may be regarded as a pendant to 'Aylmer's Field', which was completed probably a year or so earlier.

One of Tennyson's Farringford neighbours called his attention to the *Leisure Hour* account which led him to write 'Rizpah' (cf. II Samuel xxi. 8–10), first plainly entitled 'Bones'. It presents another death-bed scene, an old woman living so intensely (thinking aloud) in the exploit of a wild dark night when she rescued her son Willy's bones from the gibbet, and secreted them at home before burying them in the churchyard (at Old Shoreham in the 'Old Brighton' story),[23] that she is startled to find she has been overheard by a lady who has come to pray with her, and who listens to her revelations. Her boy had been dared to rob the mail-coach; she had pleaded in vain for his life. His last cry had driven her out of her mind. When she was released from her asylum, she stole the bones: 'My baby, the bones that had sucked me, the bones that had laughed and had cried – Theirs? O no! they are mine – not theirs – they had moved in my side.' She had kissed and buried them. She asks, ironically, to be read a verse on the Lord's compassion and mercy, and, on hearing that her son died unrepentant, declares she has no wish to be saved if he is not in heaven; her interlocutor has never borne a child, and is as hard as a stone. The loud call of Willy in the wind makes it difficult to hear what is said to her. The night is clear: he does not call from the gibbet, but from the church; and she is going. There is pathos in her final illusion, and the poem has a touch of the macabre; yet it appeals insistently through the elemental passion of a mother's love which rises above the discriminations of sectarian morality.

'The First Quarrel' was founded on what Tennyson's Isle of

Wight doctor was told when he attended a widow in childbirth. After the birth of her boy, the woman tells the doctor her life story: how Harry, her companion from childhood, had worked for a farmer relative in Dorset, then married her, but had to seek employment across the Solent. During his absence she found a letter from him to a Dorset sweetheart. When he returned, she quarrelled with him because he made light of it; at the moment of his departure, when she was near her time, she told him she would 'sooner be cursed than kissed'. He wrote to say that he had always been true to her, had just found work in Jersey, and was leaving by boat that night. The dramatic opening sustains the straight narration, which ends with tragic finality:

An' the wind began to rise, an' I thought of him out at sea,
An' I felt I had been to blame; he was always kind to me.
'Wait a little, my lass, I am sure it 'ill all come right' –
An' the boat went down that night – the boat went down that night.

Two Lincolnshire monologues are interesting rather than stirring, though each is dramatically rounded off. 'The Northern Cobbler' was suggested by the poet's recollection of a man who 'set up a bottle of gin in his window when he gave up drinking, in order to defy the drink'. When a sailor who has returned from the tropical zone is refused a drink, and points to the bottle of gin, he hears how his host the cobbler, after behaving badly to his wife, had turned teetotaller, and had the bottle placed there in the name of the Lord, so that he could look his enemy in the face. He chose a quart bottle rather than a pint, believing that the bigger the temptation, the stronger his resistance. It is to stand there until his death, and be buried with him, so that he can take it 'afoor the Throän'.

'The Village Wife' is the only one of the Lincolnshire dialect poems that presents a portrait 'in any way' drawn from life; and this seems to be the old Squire rather than the Mrs Poyser-like speaker who has supplied the Hall 'wi' butter an' heggs for huppuds o' twenty year'. The old Squire and his son, to whom the estate had been entailed, die about the same time, and the new Squire has only just arrived. The village gossip knows nothing about him, but what she doesn't know about 'the owd Squire an' 'is gells' isn't worth knowing. He is the centre of interest, a bookish man and a collector, who gets into debt, which cannot be paid off when his books are sold, because 'the lasses 'ed teärd out leäves i' the middle to kindle the fire', as they did with some of the valuable books in Bennet Langton's library, near Somersby.[24]

Two subjects were suggested by Gladstone's daughter Mary, the first being based on a true, published story. 'In the Children's Hospital' is told by a loving, religious nurse who interprets the surgeon's scepticism as a proof of his indifference to suffering. She tells how Emmie, thought to be asleep, overheard the doctor's remark that she couldn't live through the operation, and asked her companion Annie what she should do. How could the Lord know her fróm other children, she asked when Annie counselled her to cry to Jesus. She must put out her arms, and tell the Lord that she is 'the little girl with her arms lying out on the counterpane'. The storm and the bleat of a motherless lamb heard by the nurse on the first night she is off duty cannot lift the story above sentimental piety. The Lord hears; the child who is thought to be asleep, with her long, lean, little arms stretched out before her, when the surgeon arrives with his 'ghastly tools', is dead.

The second touched deeper chords in Tennyson. 'Despair' is a perfervid address by a crazed man to the preacher who three days previously had saved him, but not his wife, from suicide in the sea. Their faith had been destroyed by family misfortunes and modern science, in violent reaction to the preacher's Calvinist teachings on 'a God of eternal rage' and 'Hell without help'; his 'know-all' chapel looks over the sand. Enlightenment had brought no hope: why live in grief and torment, and what matters morality or vice, if death is the end of all? The preacher protests against blasphemy when he hears that the God of Love and of eternal Hell is a contradiction, and, if there be such a God, may the Great God curse and destroy him. Having lived three more days in godless gloom, the speaker makes clear his suicidal intention. Tennyson voices not only his own anti-Calvinism but his morbid depression when confronted by the apparent bleakness of scientific philosophy: 'these are the new dark ages' of the popular press, when 'Doubt is lord of this dunghill', and life on this homeless planet can be expected to cease, with the last worm fleeing from the dead fossil skull 'in the rocks of an earth that is dead'.

Three monologues were composed, or completed, during 1884. 'The Spinster's Sweet-Arts', entirely the poet's invention, is a light Lincolnshire subject, mainly a portrait of the speaker, who has become accustomed to identifying her cats with suitors of her youth, and treats them accordingly, two favourites receiving most of her attention. 'Tomorrow' is the story of Molly Magee, whose lover on his way to England was swallowed in an Irish bog, and discovered years later when she was old and crazed. She was about to enter chapel for mass when she saw his well-preserved body laid out for identification. He had kept his word; 'He said he would meet me tomorra', she remarked, and dropped dead over him. The story was told by Aubrey de Vere, and Allingham helped Tennyson with the dialect. 'The Wreck' has inner connotations. A young woman seeks refuge in a nunnery after her life has been wrecked. A lover of the arts, she was married to a handsome but haughty Philistine financier whom she could not love; when she bore him a girl, he looked coldly at it and said, 'Pity it isn't a boy.' She left him, after falling in love with an intellectual, with whom she took ship for his home on a West Indian island. One day a bird fell from the shrouds and died, making her think of the child she had left. As the storm rose, she heard her in the wailing wind, and the thunder of ocean and heaven emphasized her maternal guilt. Her lover and all on deck, except one man tied to the mast, were washed overboard; she was rescued as the ship was sinking. After passing the Needles, and Alum Bay with its coloured sand, she landed in England, and learned that her child had died on the day of the storm. The story undoubtedly had a strong sensational appeal, far greater than it is likely to have today; the dramatic context of its narration is hardly more than a device to quicken interest, and is soon forgotten.

The narration in 'Owd Roä' is much more dramatic, developing a sense of solid character, and suggesting that Tennyson was still very much at home imaginatively in the rural world of his youth. The idea for the poem came to him when he read in a daily paper how a child was rescued from a burning house by a black retriever. 'The details in this story are of course mine', he wrote. His narrator recalls Rover's feat ten years earlier, when the importation of corn some time after the repeal of the Corn Laws threatened the livelihood of British farmers. Interest is heightened because the rescued babe is now the listener whose appetite for refreshments late on Christmas Eve needs checking. 'The Church-Warden and the Curate', also in the Lincolnshire dialect, presents a memorable character. It was invented around two sayings (ll. 16, 49–50) which were brought to the poet's notice by H. D. Rawnsley, who received such advice after his ordination, when he returned to Halton Holgate, his father Drummond Rawnsley's parish. The churchwarden found it paid to leave the Baptists, whom he can no longer bear,

'Fur they weshed their sins i' *my* pond, an' I doubts they poisoned the cow'. If the parson sticks to the churchwarden, the Church is not in danger. The young curate is advised to speak out against the Baptists, but not against 'the faults o' the Squire': 'if tha wants to git forrards a bit . . . creeäp along the hedge-bottoms, an' thou'll be a Bishop yit'.

'Happy' was published in 1889 as a companion poem to 'Forlorn'; it was suggested when Tennyson read in an Isle of Wight newspaper how lepers were sometimes followed into banishment by their faithful wives. Unfortunately a story in the period of the Crusades is given a Victorian melodramatic turn, the faithful leper's bride recalling how the Count her tempter (whom she in her jealousy allowed to kiss her brow) was killed by lightning from God. The attempt to present the higher spiritual beauty at the expense of the body, 'This coarse diseaseful creature which in Eden was divine, This Satan-haunted ruin, this little city of sewers', may be dramatically apposite to one who can think God, 'in His loving care for both', has made her husband a leper that they 'might cling together, and never doubt each other more'. It does not reflect a sane, healthy mind; and Tennyson's handling of the subject seems as questionable as the credibility of his fiction.

'Charity', said to be founded on a true story, is more credible, though it blends a rather Hardyan situation of chance with narrative more typical of the Victorian novel. The woman tells the man who solicits her hand that she needs no 'wages of shame' in 'this pitiless world of ours'; she tends the grave of her betrayer's widow, whom he had married for wealth. The man she addresses had been his friend. The widow had discovered her husband's perfidy, come unknown to the woman's house, nursed her through pregnancy, and provided for her, before dying 'of a fever caught when a nurse in a hospital ward'. Technically this is one of Tennyson's most successful short dramatic monologues, the situation in the present holding interest throughout, and being inextricably linked with the past. His last, 'The Bandit's Death' (1891) is based on 'Death of El Bizarro' in Sir Walter Scott's *Journal* (Naples, 15.iv.32). It is a suspenseful, romantic, Judith–Holofernes story, but the poet's dramatic introduction is too revelatory to produce a strong conclusion.

Some of these monologues reveal the Victorian penchant for the sentimental, the pious, and the melodramatic. They have other weaknesses. The pronounced swing of the verse tends to counteract the speech effects, and occasionally the sense has to be broken by the caesura to preserve metre and linear balance (e.g. 'Haven't you eyes? I am dressing/the grave of a woman with flowers' or 'Knowing the Love we were used/to believe everlasting would die'). In the most artistic dramatic monologues, one usually finds the interest of a developing situation with reference to the speaker (the drama of the present) in addition to revelations of the past or of hopes and intentions, the whole presenting facets of character and outlook. By such criteria Tennyson succeeds in 'St Simeon Stylites' and 'Ulysses'; Browning, more often, in 'My Last Duchess' or 'Andrea del Sarto', for example. A few of Tennyson's minor monologues, notably 'The Spinster's Sweet-Arts' and 'The Church-Warden and the Curate', do not attempt stories; usually the story is to the fore, so much so in some that the drama of the present is sketchily limited to the introduction and ending, and is soon forgotten. Drama in the present, such as obtains in 'Northern Farmer (New Style)' and 'Despair', undoubtedly gives life to the situation in which the speaker finds himself, thereby intensifying the general effect. So indispensable is this kind of drama to the completion of the whole in 'Charity' that its presentation vitalizes and sustains interest in a rather hackneyed kind of story.

20

A Miscellany

The miscellaneous character of Tennyson's more important poems in his later years is hardly surprising, if we take into account his absorption in *Idylls of the King* and the eight years he devoted to dramatic works, though it reinforces the impression that, as a poet, he continued to be dependent on casual inspirations. Only the metrician or historian can find sustained interest in the experimental verse of 'Boädicea', which Tennyon came to believe would 'come all right' if it were 'read straight like prose'. More popular and still a favourite in schoolboy anthologies is 'The Revenge: A Ballad of the Fleet', in irregular paragraphic stanzas and metre, with lines varying from two to six stresses. How much more subtly, by comparison with the general tempo of Tennyson's monologue stories, the verse conforms to its changing subject is well illustrated at the close, with the rising wind, the impact of the gale on the shot-shattered Spanish fleet, and the foundering of the *Revenge*. The details of Sir Richard Grenville's heroic battle came from Arber's 'English Reprint', and it is possible, as Christopher Ricks points out, that Tennyson was struck by his description of it as 'the Balaclava charge of that Spanish war'.

'Lucretius' (begun in 1865) is the most successful of these incidental poems, though FitzGerald, with unrelenting prejudice and astonishing myopia, instantly branded it as a failure (15.v.68), asserting that it was 'Exactly what Lucretius is not; nothing but Art. I am sure dear old Alfred should write no more – of his own, I mean. He could now translate for us some Sophocles!' Apart from its narrative introduction and ending, it is a soliloquy which voices the thoughts of Lucretius (with close reference to the philosophy and imagery of *De Rerum Natura*) at a time when he was distraught to madness in consequence of intensely sexual dreams induced by the love philtre which his jealous wife had given him. The philosopher who believed in Epicurean calm as the *summum bonum* of life is seen in a most unLucretian mood. He is crazed by dreams, one of the universe in chaos again before the emergence of a new order, its flaring atom-streams 'Ruining along the illimitable inane' (reflecting his own thought – 'Of and belonging to me'; 'inane' also hints at the emptiness of the materialistic conception of the universe for Tennyson). Others are sexual: Hetairai, 'Hired animalisms', circling round him and yelling as they close in on him, or the breasts of Helen, a sword pointing at them and sinking shamed by their beauty, until they emit the fire of Ilion, and the dreamer is wakened by its scorching.

Scientifically minded, he appeals to the Venus of nature, not of mythology; how could he have offended her if she lives a life of eternal calm with the Gods, who are indifferent to the affairs of mortals? So his master Epicurus taught, but, if his own atomic theory is correct, are not the Gods dissoluble according to natural law? And if they are carefree, why need he care for them; why not end his life to avoid the 'prodigies of myriad nakednesses', the abominable 'twisted shapes of lust', and the foul fleeting phantoms of his universe, which blast his peace and fill him with 'animal heat and dire insanity'? If only he had Nature's powers, and could be serene after cloud and storm! Another sexual vision comes, and he realizes his participation: 'How should the mind, except it loved them, clasp These idols to herself?' After fearing that the oread pursued by the satyr will fling herself shameless on him, he cries instinctively, 'Catch her, goat-foot', and the conflict of sexual repulsion and attraction continues. He had thought he was like the Gods, with 'Nothing to mar the sober majesties Of settled, sweet, Epicurean life'. It is as if he, like the satyr, is 'twy-natured'; beastlike as he finds himself, why not manlike end his life, letting Nature, 'womb and tomb of all', renew his life in her blind metempsychotic processes? (Tennyson's memorable phrase was transferred from Nature to night, with further adaptation and enrichment, by Gerard Manley Hopkins in 'Spelt from Sybil's Leaves'.) At best human life is crowned with a flower or two before it ends; 'momentary man', 'no more a something to himself', vanishes 'atom and void' in the unseen for ever. Before committing suicide, Lucretius trusts he will know that pure Tranquillity which is beyond pain and pleasure. His reflections on human finiteness may have Victorian Positivist overtones; if so, they are slight. By its imaginatively psychological re-creation of a classical situation, the poem underlines the inadequacy of a philosophy which excludes an essential part of nature; sexual repression in the pursuit of tranquillity ultimately drives Lucretius mad.

The dramatic monologue of 'Columbus' (from Washington Irving's *Life*) was written to preserve one of the great ironies of history. The discoverer, bedridden, cast off, and starving, tells the courier who is astonished to see his chains that he is ready to prove his loyalty to Ferdinand by making another voyage; better still, by leading a last crusade against the Saracens. God had sent him a dream in which the first island he discovered on his first voyage appeared like the New Jerusalem, thereby reminding him of the resolve he made that whatever wealth he brought back from the West should finance another crusade and the freeing of the Holy Sepulchre from the Saracens. He recalls the opposition he met from scholars when he insisted that the earth was round, prejudice against him as a Genoese, and how he and his men were chained by a commissioner sent out to judge between him and his slandered self. Perhaps it would have been better had the West not been opened to a flood of Spanish atrocities. He takes comfort in the thought that he is like the Son of God in being the victim of slander. He has kept his chains; they hang on his bed, and he wishes to be buried with them. It is said that the truth will make us free, but Columbus has grown to recognise that it is never welcome to the established order. Historical particulars not only illustrate a general truth; they even symbolize it.

Suppression of truth in the name of heresy is central to 'Sir John Oldcastle, Lord Cobham', which raises the perennial question asked by Shaw, in the very same words, at the end of *St Joan*: 'How long, O Lord, how long!' Tennyson had thought of writing a poem on Oldcastle (traditionally but falsely associated with Prince Hal) in 1858, but his Catholic friend Sir John Simeon had dissuaded him on the ground that the subject was too contentious. He presents the thoughts of Wycliffe's follower after his escape from the Tower into Wales. The discomposure which results from his being alone and fearful of arrest, combined with onsets of abhorrence at the thought of Church iniquities, is conveyed in broken, sudden verse movements. He thinks of adulterous living within the Church, sanctuary given to criminals, and the extermination of men who uphold the teaching of the Gospel in the mother-tongue to common people regarded as swine – the swine who, God willing, will 'outlearn the filthy friar'; he thinks also of the heresy of declaring that God's work with humanity is holier than the worship of images, or of refusing to believe that consecrated bread is God's body. The friend he expects arrives with no bread; he knows that he will not die for lack of it, but is destined to be burnt at the stake.

'The Voyage of Maeldune' is a tale of fantasy, hyperbole, humour, satiety, quarrelling, and slaughter, with a dominant urge for revenge; it glances at a perennial, localized historical truth. An island chief, supported by his fellows (each looking like a king, and boasting that he springs from the oldest race on earth), seeks to avenge his father's death, but, on approaching his enemy's island, is blown across a boundless sea. They reach the Silent Isle, then the Isle of Shouting; the Isle of Flowers (where 'the topmost spire of the mountain was lilies in lieu of snow') and the Isle of Fruits (the mountain peak composed of the hugest apples ever seen, so red that they set the sunset aflame); the Isle of Fire, and an island of Paradise under the Sea; the Bounteous Isle (which they hate, for there is no enemy near); the Isle of Witches; the Isle of Double Towers (which cause disputes, as a result of which 'one half slew the other'); and the Isle of a Saint who asks them to remember how vengeance had continued from generation to generation, before urging them to return to their island. They do so, and there is the enemy, and his life is spared. Returning with only a tithe of his men, the avenger of old is weary of travel and strife and sin; he has learned wisdom through incalculable craziness, suffering, and loss. In this elaboration of an old Irish legend 'intended to represent in his own original way the Celtic genius', Tennyson supplied most of the detail as well as islands to form the antitheses. It succeeds, glancing *en passant* at a number of Irish characteristics. The poem is an adroit parable, of which the lesson has yet to be learned: 'Go back to the Isle of Finn and suffer the Past to be Past.'

The situation of 'The Sisters' ('They have left the doors ajar') is contrived, and the interest of this dramatic monologue lies principally in the speaker's character. After being engaged to Edith, he had married her younger sister Evelyn; now a widower with two children, Edith and Evelyn, he is anxious that the young suitor he is interviewing shall make the right choice of partner; he makes much of his daughters' differences, even their voices as they are heard singing, assuming that the young man will weigh them in the finest scales. His own marriage suggests a man who, with illusions of love, acts by careful processes of judgment. After being engaged to Edith, it occurs to him that she is not Plato's Ideal; when he declares his love he is on the stairs of Paradise. Just then the wheels announcing the return of Evelyn from Italy are heard, and he is soon in love with her. He wins her in Edith's absence. She is Evelyn's bridesmaid but, on the night of the wedding, is found knocking witless at the door of the church where the ceremony took place. (The climactic details of this sensational story were based on actual events remembered by Tennyson.) The speaker talks of her as the 'great Tragedian' whose 'brain broke With over-acting'. He is not prepared to sacrifice his family name, which is older and more venerable than that of the youth's family. The suitor has inherited his fortune from an uncle who longs for the alliance. The question arises whether the father is more akin to the speaker in 'My Last Duchess' or to the world of Henry James. In the end he weighs one daughter against the other; both are 'Dearest of all things', but, if 'Most dearest' be a true superlative in love, he thinks he also loves Edith 'most'. A finical humbug, he dreams that the sisters smile on him from the grave, but does not know which he loves more.

'The Ring', based on a legend reported by J. R. Lowell 'of a house near where he had once lived', and already made use of in Henry James's 'The Romance of Certain Old Clothes', unfolds its story in dramatic duologue form. In accordance with his dead wife Miriam's wishes, the father gives his daughter the ring as she makes final preparations for her wedding. He bought it in Venice, being told that it would bind the love of the maid to whom it was given, and would bring death or madness to anyone who stole it. It was sent to Miriam, but claimed by her cousin Muriel. On his return and at his request, Miriam removed it from Muriel's finger. They were happily married, but she died on the day of the second Miriam's birth, insisting that her daughter, not Muriel, should inherit the ring. The father eventually acceded to Muriel's request that she should take charge of Miriam for the sake of the child's health; she told him she had loved him ever since the ring arrived, and gratitude made him marry her. Soon she dropped her maternal mask, and demanded the ring. After stealing the key for the chest containing it and other 'sacred relics', she was found dead alongside it, a red mark on her finger suggesting she had wrenched off the ring, which lay beside her. The father is sure the ghost of Miriam's mother had guarded it; her spirit is now free, hovering by the church where they were married, and where she waits to see her daughter arrive like a queen. There are many minor *frissons*, but it is strange that Tennyson could have devoted so much labour to such a story,

unless (as his grandson Charles suggested) he had been infected by
Frederick's spiritualist enthusiasm in 1887.

When Tennyson agreed to his son Hallam's request that he
should write a poem on Demeter, he said it was 'no use giving a mere
réchauffé of old legends'; such 'an antique' had to be endowed with
modern significance. 'Demeter and Persephone' is the most pictorial and tender of the later poems, and Tennyson, without undue
elaboration, makes the most of his classical subject and setting. Its
philosophical thought is simple. In her search for Persephone,
Demeter finally sees a shadow pass, crying,

> 'The Bright one in the highest
> Is brother of the Dark one in the lowest,
> And Bright and Dark have sworn that I, the child
> Of thee, the great Earth-Mother, thee, the Power
> That lifts her buried life from gloom to bloom,
> Should be for ever and for evermore
> The Bride of Darkness.'

She is ill-content when Zeus allows her daughter to return to her for
nine months of the year. Younger Gods will come, she trusts, under
whose reign plague and famine will be halted, noon will enter
darkness, Pluto's halls will admit the sun, and Persephone will
remain 'the whole bright year' with her. Stripped of its classical
terms, this dramatic monologue ends with a yearning for the reign of
Love, when evil is banished from the earth.

'The Death of Oenone' seems to be no more than a pendant to
'Oenone'; it provides readers with the less familiar ending of the
heroine which is hinted at in that poem, and is written with a Greek
simplicity which is more effective and commendable than the
highly wrought luxuriance of its youthful predecessor.

Suggested by one of the FitzGerald letters (29.viii.42) which were
published in 1889, 'Romney's Remorse' is one of the most dramatic
of Tennyson's monologues. The painter, believing in Sir Joshua
Reynolds' statement that 'marriage spoilt an artist', left his wife
in the north of England (cf. ll. 18–21) soon after their youthful
marriage. 'Old, nearly mad, and quite desolate', he returned to her,
and she 'received him and nursed him until he died', FitzGerald
wrote, with the comment, 'This quiet act of hers is worth all
Romney's pictures!' Tennyson shows him emerging from his

delirium until he recognises Mary, 'The truest, kindliest, noblest-hearted wife That ever wore a Christian marriage-ring'. His fame gives him no comfort when he thinks of the wrong he had done. The world would be the loser if one such as his wife should vanish unrecorded; he had dreamt of the scene when he painted her and their baby girl by Windermere, and he wishes to paint her again. The attempt soon fails, and he exclaims, 'This Art, that harlot-like Seduced me from you, leaves me harlot-like, who love her still, and whimper, impotent To win her back before I die.' He will be condemned by posterity and God for deserting his wife and children. Thoughts of damnation for the sake of Art excite him: 'I am wild again! The coals of fire you heap upon my head Have crazed me.' He remembers Claudio's saying in *Measure for Measure* that the miserable have no other medicine but hope, and believes, as his wife soothes him, that her forgiveness will touch heaven and be reflected with light upon him.

The subject of 'St Telemachus' was provided by F. W. Farrar. The narrative tells how Telemachus, after watching blood-red sunsets glare against the cross he had reared on the ruins of a pagan temple, felt the call to travel west to Rome. When he entered this Christian city, he moved with the brawling crowd to the Colosseum, where he found eighty thousand Christians enjoying the spectacle of man murdering man in gladiatorial combat. The shock gave him strength, and he did not stop until he had flung himself between the combatants, calling on them to forbear for Christ's sake.

> A silence followed as of death, and then
> A hiss as from a wilderness of snakes,
> Then one deep roar as of a breaking sea,
> And then a shower of stones that stoned him dead,
> And then once more a silence as of death.

(The excerpt is a poem in itself, perfectly rounded with climax and repetition of more tragic weight.) Telemachus's deed woke the world until Honorius ordained that Rome 'no more should wallow in this old lust' of paganism. The repeated 'Vicisti Galilæe!' suggests a rejoinder to Swinburne's indictment of Christianity in 'Hymn to Proserpine': 'Thou hast conquered, O pale Galilean; the world has grown grey from thy breath.' The record of a step forward in history is interesting, but its versification, admirable as it may be, does not make it an important poem.

The majority of the incidental poems which Tennyson wrote for more literary readers in his later years impress, however, not only by artistic attention to detail (which continually lights up new significances, as all great poetry will) but by the variety and import of their subjects. From 'Lucretius' to 'Columbus' and 'The Voyage of Maeldune', for example, compasses an enormous range of experience. Story and character-analysis may have no overtones in some; others present correlatives, particularly from history, which are instinct with 'truths that wake, To perish never', though usually passing unrecognised under changing forms from age to age. 'Demeter and Persephone', like Keats's *Hyperion*, invests a classical subject with evolutionary faith, and is related to a final group among the poems of Tennyson's last years.

2 1

The Gleam

Belief in human evolution on earth and its spiritual continuation after death had supported and heightened Tennyson's recovery of faith during his *In Memoriam* period. Later he believed he had been too optimistic. A more pessimistic view of life without loss of faith became the higher directing force in the completion of *Idylls of the King*. Yet his faith was troubled; although he had long recognised that religious belief was beyond the finite realm of intellectual proof, he longed for an assurance of life after death. So often did he find such conviction in his thinking and reading that he was apt to assume it as a fact; it became his sheet-anchor, leading him to assert in his Epilogue to 'The Charge of the Heavy Brigade':

> And though, in this lean age forlorn,
>   Too many a voice may cry
> That man can have no after-morn,
>   Not yet of these am I.
> The man remains, and whatso'er
>   He wrought of good or brave
> Will mould him through the cycle-year
>   That dawns behind the grave.

Life without such an assurance, he would declare with irrational vehemence, is not worth living. 'What matters anything in this world without full faith in the Immortality of the Soul and of Love?' he wrote on the manuscript of 'Vastness'.

Here, perhaps, is Tennyson's greatest defect as a thinker: it is not just a failure of nerve: it is a blindness in humanitarian imagination which makes him empathize with the crazed mind of the would-be suicide in 'Despair', and associate Positivist assumptions with the unworthwhileness of life for Lucretius. This is more astonishing because Tennyson repeatedly insists, nowhere more than in 'The

Holy Grail', that the test of religion is what it does for the betterment of humanity. In 'Vastness' he reaches an utterly defeatist conclusion:

> What the philosophies, all the sciences, poesy, varying voices of
>   prayer?
> All that is noblest, all that is basest, all that is filthy with all that is
>   fair?
> What is it all, if we all of us end but in being our own corpse-
>   coffins at last,
> Swallowed in Vastness, lost in Silence, drowned in the deeps of
>   a meaningless Past?
> What but a murmur of gnats in the gloom . . . ?

Influenced by Positivistic views, Hardy sees life less morbidly when the single existence of his heroines in *Desperate Remedies* and *Tess of the d'Urbervilles* is threatened with tragic mischance; brief as it is in the sum of things, it is like that of gnats irradiated or glorified in the sunshine of love or the zest for living. Tennyson's poem, though it contains some attempt to balance evil with good, suggests a man whose light is extinguished; uncertainty about immortality fills him with a gloom that infects the world; the voice is undoubtedly that of 'Locksley Hall Sixty Years After', without the mask. The depression lifts when he thinks of Hallam: 'Peace, let it be! for I loved him, and love him for ever: the dead are not dead but alive.'

In December 1867, when he talked about 'all-pervading Spirit being more understandable by him than solid matter', he was more confident. On this he wrote three short poems, the first a forerunner, in the metre of revival hymnology, of 'The Higher Pantheism', where the division between God and the solid world of the individual, who sees no more than 'broken gleams' of Him, is Shelleyan and markedly unWordsworthian. God is inseparable from natural law, but sense-perception is misleading; he is beyond eye and ear, but 'Spirit with Spirit can meet – Closer is He than breathing, and nearer than hands and feet.' 'Wages' shows a more equable mind than 'Vastness', though it asks whether Virtue would 'have heart to endure for the life of the worm and fly': she seeks no rest beyond this life, but only 'the wages of going on' undyingly. 'Flower in the crannied wall' poses in simple lyrical form the question elucidated by Wordsworth with reference to the 'vast chain of Being' in 'The Primrose of the Rock'. The source of all life remains a mystery: '*if* I could understand What you are, root and all, and all in all, I should know what God and man is'. 'The Voice of the Peak' (begun during Tennyson's Alpine holiday in 1873) is 'The Higher Pantheism' in another guise. The voice is heard in the roar of the streams as they make their way to the deep, but none of these forms is eternal. There is 'A deep below the deep, And a height beyond the height! Our hearing is not hearing, And our seeing is not sight.'

'De Profundis', begun at the birth of Hallam Tennyson and not finished until 1880, is in two parts, one relating to the biological world, the other to the spiritual, the 'true world within the world we see, Whereof our world is but the bounding shore' (a metaphor recalling Wordsworth's 'Intimations of Immortality'). It combines the circumambient image of *Idylls of the King* with the evolutionary idea that brings *In Memoriam* to a close, that the child is 'prophet of the perfect man'. Its spirit comes from the deep which is beyond the million aeons of a vast waste dawn, and which works 'Through all this changing world of changeless law' ('the law within the law' of 'The Two Voices') and through 'every phase of ever-heightening life'. After death it proceeds to 'that last deep where we and thou are still'. All that Tennyson adds on the divisible–indivisible, the numerable–innumerable, or the finite–infinite, illustrates an inability to take the subject further. His cry is beyond this world of shadows to the 'Infinite Ideality'. 'Crossing the Bar' repeats the deep-to-deep image with prospective reference to the poet's own death: 'When that which drew from out the boundless deep Turns again home'.

'The Ancient Sage' (1885), though written after reading the Chinese philosopher Lao-tsze (on the recommendation of Jowett, who hoped it would provide 'a subject for Alfred'), presents Tennyson's own views. In this poem of two voices, he counters contemporary thought, his ancient pausing beside waters issuing from a cave, to comment on the verses of his companion, a younger man who honours him but disagrees with his philosophy of life. Those who believe there is no Power beyond the natural world should dive into the temple-cave of self to learn that the Nameless has a voice (the elder insists), for 'Knowledge is the swallow on the lake That sees and stirs the surface-shadow there', but has never reached 'The Abysm of all Abysms' in nature at large and in the infinitesimal, however much it is divided.[25] The Reality of all life is beyond proof. The Nameless is timeless; only mortals in this dream-world of passing shadows break 'the Eternal Now' into 'Thens' and 'Whens'. None but Gods could build 'this house of ours', imperfect though it is and will be until 'That which knows' descends on 'this half-deed' and shapes it to his will. (The thought is comparable to that pronounced in 'Demeter and Persephone'; it differs from Hardy's Unfulfilled Intention in postulating that the Nameless is aware of nature's imperfections.) The answer to a pessimistic vanity-of-vanities philosophy is that the darkness may be in man, and that in time he will acquire 'the last and largest sense' which will show that 'the world is wholly fair'.

When he reads hedonistic counsel (recalling Omar's) the sage looks beyond 'the black negations of the bier'. He remembers (Tennyson writes, not very convincingly, from his own experiences) the passion of the past, when gleams of 'far, far away' came like intimations of immortality in boyhood, and how the sound of his own name could transport him out of self into the Nameless. He advises his gloomy friend to cease wailing, and help his fellow-men, sending the day into the darkened heart. With the thought that outlook or philosophy will influence action, and a glance at possibilities of moral decline such as are illustrated in the later books of *Idylls of the King*, the sage concludes with full affirmation of Tennyson's faith:

> Do-well will follow thought,
> And in the fatal sequence of this world
> An evil thought may soil thy children's blood;
> But curb the beast would cast thee in the mire,
> And leave the hot swamp of voluptuousness
> A cloud between the Nameless and thyself,
> And lay thine uphill shoulder to the wheel,
> And climb the Mount of Blessing, whence, if thou
> Look higher, then – perchance – thou mayest – beyond
> A hundred ever-rising mountain lines,
> And past the range of Night and Shadow – see
> The high-heaven dawn of more than mortal day
> Strike on the Mount of Vision!

The grey magician who declares he is dying in 'Merlin and the Gleam' is Tennyson; the setting is the Isle of Wight, and the poem was written about the time of his eightieth birthday. Most of it relates to phases of his poetry, without keeping quite to their chronological order: in his boyhood (ii); the effect of criticism, probably Croker's, though J. H. Buckley thinks the allusion is to Christopher North (his familiar in _Noctes Ambrosianae_ being a raven), who 'instigated Croker's attack' (iii); early poetry (iv); English idylls (v); the Arthurian epic which Tennyson had in mind (vi); the death of Arthur Hallam, the 'wintry glimmer' alluding to 'Morte d'Arthur' (vii). The magic of the legendary Merlin was connected with the arts, including poetry. Tennyson indicated that the Gleam signifies 'the higher poetic imagination'; and 'higher' suggests, as it did for Wordsworth, 'Faith in life endless, the sustaining thought Of human Being, Eternity, and God' (_The Prelude_, xiv). This belief in life endless had been with Tennyson from 'The Mystic' onwards, being strengthened by questioning in 'The Two Voices' and _In Memoriam_. 'All but in Heaven', the Gleam hovers over 'the border Of boundless Ocean' (viii), and he urges the young Mariner to follow it, 'ere it vanishes Over the margin'. His spirit is that of Ulysses' unending quest, 'To follow knowledge like a sinking star, Beyond the utmost bound of human thought'. (The relatedness of this to T. S. Eliot's spiritual goal is evident in the imagery from 'Ulysses' which appears in the original script of _The Waste Land_.)

Knowing Tennyson's interest in Eastern philosophy, Jowett sent him several books, hoping he would find an Indian subject for a poem. The result was 'Akbar's Dream', a dramatic monologue rather more learned than alive, but valuable as an indicator of Tennyson's undogmatic faith. It was the tolerance of the great sixteenth-century Mogul of India that appealed to him. Allah is Love, yet 'every splintered fraction of a sect' clamours '_I_ am on the Perfect Way'; the narrower the sectarian cage, the greater the formalist's fury. Akbar hears the 'clash of tides that meet in narrow seas', not the Great Voice of the true Deep; he hates the rancour of caste and creed. The only miracle he recognises is the universe; all else is form and ritual, varying with the tribe. He does not despise forms, but knows they should be used with politic care, as they vocalize the 'silent Alphabet-of-heaven-in-men'. His mission is to spread the divine faith like calming oil on stormy creeds, and alchemize old hates into the gold of Love. He had dreamt of a non-sectarian temple, lofty, simple, open-doored to every breath of heaven, a dwelling for Truth, Peace, Love, and Justice. Then came a schismatic jeer; gradually the stones of the temple were loosened, and from the ruin arose the shriek and curse of trampled millions, until an alien race 'fitted stone to stone again, and Truth, Peace, Love and Justice came and dwelt therein'. This allusion to the 'greatness of Christianity'[26] is a sad example of Tennyson's insularism; it cannot be dissociated from English colonialism, and inevitably provokes thoughts of a schismatic history incompatible with the creed-transcending tenor of the poem, and with the juxtaposed hymn to the sun as a symbol of the one universal God.

Tennyson's faith was still shored up by evolutionary theory. 'By an Evolutionist' begins:

> The Lord let the house of a brute to the soul of a man,
>   And the man said 'Am I your debtor?'
> And the Lord – 'Not yet: but make it as clean as you can,
>   And then I will let you a better.'

It ends retrospectively with the thought that old age has 'starved the wild beast' linked with the soul of man at birth, and that he has lived to stand 'on the heights of his life with a glimpse of a height that is higher'. 'The Dawn', after glancing at bloody cannibalism and its counterpart in contemporary civilization (the murder of Truth), draws the conclusion that 'We are far from the noon of man', and asks when the ghost of the brute will be laid, and what *our* children will be 'a hundred thousand, a million summers away'.

The uncertainty of 'Our Playwright may show In some fifth Act what this wild Drama means' in 'The Play', a mere quatrain, has different resolutions in 'The Making of Man' and 'Faith', two poems written at the end of Tennyson's life. The first is clearly defined:

> Where is one that, born of woman, altogether can escape
> From the lower world within him, moods of tiger, or of ape?
>   Man as yet is being made, and ere the crowning Age of ages,
> Shall not aeon after aeon pass and touch him into shape?
>
> All about him shadow still, but, while the races flower and fade,
> Prophet-eyes may catch a glory slowly gaining on the shade,
>   Till the peoples all are one, and all their voices blend in choric
> Hallelujah to the Maker 'It is finished. Man is made.'

The second is Tennyson's answer to 'Despair'; adverting to the unProvidentiality of nature, and the inadequacies of human creeds, it reserves the perfecting of man to a higher world: 'Through the gates that bar the distance comes a gleam of what is higher. Wait till Death has flung them open, when the man will make the Maker Dark no more with human hatreds in the glare of deathless fire!' The poet's fear that his 'tiny spark of being' will wholly vanish at death in a myriad Lucretian world is stilled in 'God and the Universe'. 'The Dreamer', the last poem he finished, shows that, despite the setbacks and scepticism of his age ('a Voice of the Earth'), he still followed the Gleam. The 'all is well' of *In Memoriam* becomes 'all's well that ends well'; the Earth should 'Whirl, and follow the Sun'. Where Tennyson could not prove, he could only believe; his ultimate belief consisted of 'broken lights', and he could express them only in symbols.

22

Epilogue

As 'The Passion of the Past' which Tennyson recalls in 'The Ancient Sage' relates to the boyish enchantments of 'Far-Far-Away', his reported use of the phrase with reference to the poem 'Tears, idle tears' has helped to foster a recent critical trend to the effect that the key to Tennyson's most significant poetry is a recurrent frustration or despair which makes him long for the days that are no more. He told his son Hallam that 'Tears, idle tears' did not express 'real woe', 'rather the yearning that young people occasionally experience for that which seems to have passed away from them for ever'. There can be little doubt that, occurring as it did to him at the same place and about the same time as the writing of the poem on his deeper anguish for the loss of Arthur Hallam (*In Memoriam*, xix), its generalized subject emanated from the more immediate personal grief which he found inexpressible. Yet Tennyson's statement confirms other indications that the passion of the past belongs to his youth. His relating it in a discussion with Knowles to the charm which distance in time or landscape always had for him does not suggest any abnormality or the perpetuation of a melancholic temperament. More paramount in his poetry, almost from first to last, is his visionary assurance of the reality and truth of the spiritual world, the source of a faith which, in the words of 'The Ancient Sage', 'sees the Best that glimmers through the Worst'. From the early stages of *In Memoriam*, in *The Princess*, and even in *Idylls of the King*, he is forward-looking; he follows the Gleam.

He did not share Wordsworth's reverential conviction that Heaven lies about us in our infancy; there was, in fact, much in his early years he was glad to forget. He suffered from anxieties and morbid depressions in his early manhood, but his marriage proved to be exceptionally happy and stable. Whatever his son Hallam excluded from his *Memoir*, nothing suggests that the frequent testimony to his boyish, lovable nature and geniality is seriously misleading. The state of England could upset him, but by temperament he was not commonly disposed to repine. His innumerable friendships, his humour, his ready conversation on an immense variety of subjects (FitzGerald regretted he had not been his Boswell), his wide and ever-active interest in nature, science, the world, and its history and literature, and his faith in 'Aeonian Evolution, swift or slow', surely indicate the contrary.

By judicious selection from the volumes of such a multifarious poet as Tennyson it is not difficult to support conflicting interpretative theories. Outside *In Memoriam* (in which regret 'Becomes an April violet, And buds and blossoms like the rest') , his most lyrical poems on the loss of friends or relatives are neither long nor numerous. 'Break, break, break' and 'In the Garden at Swainston' are notable, but the most hauntingly musical are 'In the Valley of Cauteretz' and 'Frater Ave atque Vale'. 'In the Valley of Cauteretz' is not a poem of 'Death in Life', like 'Tears, idle tears', but of the living dead; it is not elegiac in tone. Apart from moving rhythm and effective alliteration, its most obvious feature is repetition. Tennyson resorts to it frequently for emphasis, but never more than here: 'all along the valley' in every alternate line (five in all) stresses his sustained communion with Hallam, but more remarkable is the incidence of the repetition in the last three lines, where the inner pairing of 'the voice of the dead' within the opening and final 'living voice to me' presents the overriding thought; the key note, first and last, is one of joyful assurance which subdues regret. In 'Frater Ave atque Vale' regret for the death of Charles Tennyson is secondary to the recollection of Catullus's mourning and his association of beautiful Sirmio with the 'Lydian laughter' of Lake Garda. Such a balance of contrarieties is enhanced by the recurrence of long 'hollow oes and aes', the one contributing to a sense of almost breathless delight in beauty ('So they rowed, and there we landed – "O venusta Sirmio" – . . . groves . . . glow'), the other deepening the communication of grief ('"Frater Ave atque Vale" . . . Garda'). The grief, however, is subordinate to literary expression, past and present; Tennyson's interest is predominantly aesthetic and technical.

Assessed in all its aspects, the evidence is insufficient in quality as well as in quantity and chronology to substantiate such generalizations as those of T. S. Eliot, that Tennyson is 'the saddest of all English poets' and 'had nothing to which to hold fast except his

unique and unerring feeling for the sounds of words'. Tennyson had
a faith that looked through death; if it was shaken occasionally, he
soon recovered. Influenced by Harold Nicolson, Eliot was convinced that Tennyson suffered from 'emotion so deeply
suppressed . . . as to tend rather towards the blackest melancholia
than towards dramatic action'. If we add to this the illogically
expressed statement that he had 'the finest ear of any English poet
since Milton', we can see how unoriginal Auden was when he wrote,
'he had the finest ear, perhaps, of any English poet . . . there was
little about melancholia that he didn't know'. The addition 'there
was little else that he did', and 'he was also undoubtedly the
stupidest' of English poets, indicates Auden's mood at the time of
writing. Whatever reservations one may have on the conclusions
reached by Tennyson, from the interaction of unconventional
Christian thought and evolutionary theory, he probably considered
the scientific and philosophical problems of his own era more deeply
than any succeeding British poet has considered those of his own.
The Prologue of *In Memoriam* presents unusual integrity and
wisdom. 'Believing where we cannot prove' may be truer to the
whole of one's experience than disbelief which is equally un-
verifiable. 'Sea Dreams' and 'The Ancient Sage' testify to
Tennyson's recognition that the creeds of Churches are relatively
ephemeral, and that everything relative to the Ultimate or
Nameless is beyond proof.

Like Wordsworth, he believed not only that this Reality or Truth
is outside the dimensions of science, but that all truths discovered by
scientists are an essential part of the world in which the imaginative
poet can be expected to move. With his sons he discussed 'the great
facts and discoveries' in astronomy, geology, botany, and chemistry,
'and the great problems in philosophy', helping them to understand
the laws governing the universe and the 'law behind the law.'
Thomas Huxley said the scientists of his time claimed Tennyson 'as
having quite the mind of a man of science'; he was the only modern
poet, perhaps the only poet since Lucretius, he wrote, who had
taken the trouble to understand the work and methods of men of
science.[27] Sir John Denham (1615–69) in his poem 'On Mr
Fletcher's Works' sees Nature and Art ('Skill') as the two tops of the
ancients' Parnassus: in his 'Parnassus' Tennyson (without reference
to the perennial truth of this traditional but comprehensive view)
presents the new 'terrible' Muses, Astronomy and Geology; for the
modern philosopher–poet they are taller than all the others, and

'huger than all the mountain'; they point to those 'awful' Carlylean 'eternal verities', beside which theological disputations are like the threshing of straw. History continually shows regression as well as progress, and 'The Dawn' proclaims no facile evolutionary assurance: 'We are far from the noon of man' but 'if twenty million of summers are stored in the sunlight still . . . there is time for the race to grow'.

One hypothesis drawn from scientific speculation was anathema to Tennyson: he could never consider with philosophic calm the possibility that life ceases with death; it made him regard Time as 'a maniac scattering dust', and Life as 'a Fury slinging flame', his irrationality on the subject convincing him that, but for belief in a future life, man would sink to a brutish level (*In Memoriam*, l; cxx). He could even say that without such a belief he would commit suicide. His prevailing faith was based partly on the argument that 'God, Who is Love, would be far more cruel than any human being' were Immortality denied, and that 'The Good, the True, the Pure, the Just' are eternal.[28] From 'The Mystic' to Ida in *The Princess* and late poems such as 'De Profundis' and 'The Ancient Sage', it is clear that the bias of his religion is Platonic.

In drawing conclusions on Tennyson's views, the distinction between poetic imagination and personal empathies needs to be observed discriminately; insufficient attention is sometimes given to the dramatic quality of his poems. This explains the excessive ascription of morbidity or melancholia to the younger poet, who asserts time and time again that he longs for more life and greater accomplishments. The conventional but crude Victorian dichotomy of soul and body permeates Tennyson's evolutionary belief, the 'working out' of the beast for 'ever nobler ends' in this life and beyond; but, whether or not 'This Satan-haunted ruin, this little city of sewers' is appropriate to the leprous body as it is regarded by the spiritually exalted wife in 'Happy', it is certainly not an expression of the poet's carnal disgust. Nor is the latter to be found in the allegorical scene when the Ideal in Arthur expresses a loathing for Guinevere; without her (soul and body in union) he could never have achieved anything in this world. The moral significance of their relationship extends far beyond the physical, but the evidence of *Idylls of the King* as a whole confirms that on the question of sexual morality Tennyson is at one with Lawrence in his abhorrence of infidelity and licentiousness. Although he does not write explicitly on the subject with the zeal of Browning or Meredith, his 'statelier

Eden' when woman assumes her rightful role does not thwart 'fiery Passion', but is fulfilled in 'The single pure and perfect animal' (*The Princess*, vii. 136–291). There was no puritanism in Tennyson, as his remarks on *The Song of Solomon* and his admiration of Marvell's 'To his Coy Mistress' disclose;[29] nor was there any primness in his marriage, as may be seen in his comments on the publication of the oread and satyr passage in 'Lucretius': 'With respect to the Oread please yourself, but send the full passage to America. They are not so squeamish as we are', and 'My wife is copying *Lucretius*. . . . She says she does not think it will shock people.'

In this age of slim anthologies it is hardly surprising that earlier poems which Tennyson revised assiduously for publication or re-publication in 1842, with two or three songs from *The Princess*, are still his most widely known, and that scant attention in usually paid to his major works, even *In Memoriam* and *Maud*, much less to *Idylls of the King*. Yet, for those who read widely, the volume of his poetry combining high artistic merit with interest and significance is considerable, including much from his main poems, and shorter works such as 'The Brook', 'Lucretius', 'Columbus', 'The Voyage of Maeldune', 'Locksley Hall Sixty Years After', 'Romney's Remorse', in addition to stories, verse epistles, and lyrics. Their variety is as striking as their number. Those who accept Eliot's absolute, 'But for narrative Tennyson had no gift at all', should read and re-read 'Pelleas and Ettarre'. For vivid blank verse narration, it would be difficult to find finer passages than that describing Sir Lancelot's search for the Holy Grail and Sir Percivale's account of its course (as he imagines it) above 'the great Sea' as Sir Galahad crosses to the heavenly city.

Yet, for all the splendour and admirable qualities that may be found in Tennyson's poetry, one cannot overcome a feeling of disappointment. Much of his earlier poetry could be aptly charac-terized by the comment of Charles Sumner on the 1842 poems: 'I am struck with the melody of his verse, its silver ring, and its high poetic fancy; but does it not want elevated thought and manliness?' A richer warmth of imaginative experience is to be found in the best of Keats or the poetry of Milton's early manhood. Tennyson's formative years were sheltered and bookish; his development at Cambridge was more intellectual than aesthetic. Cultivating traditional styles or resorting to classical models for subject, presentation, and metrical experiment, he became too conservative to revitalize English poetry. One advantage of this devotion to our literary heritage is the enrichment of his style with echoes, which are frequently deliberate, as may be seen in the change from 'many' to the 'thousand' of *Hamlet* in the 'thousand shocks that come and go' of *In Memoriam*, cxiii, and in the undisguised recall of a wish to commune with the dead (Webster, *The Duchess of Malfi*, IV.ii.18–20) which 'Oh! that 'twere possible' announces at the outset. Given the kind of courage and initiative which kindled the verbal creativity and wit of G. M. Hopkins, however, he would have found many more poetic subjects around him on which to concentrate his technical skills.

Wisdom is based on knowledge, and in the light of his day the more mature Tennyson often shows judgment which has stood the test of time; his manly strains, prompted by what George Eliot calls 'the generous leap of impulse' for humanitarian causes, could be intentionally provocative. When impelled to write, he usually composed with great rapidity, but spent much time revising and polishing, his major concern being with euphony and the elusive *mot juste*. Despite its initial absolutism, there is truth in Lascelles Abercrombie's reservation: 'Tennyson's life was wholly given to his art . . . . That is certainly one reason why his poetry is so good in its kind. Perhaps, too, it may be a reason why his is not one of the supreme kinds of poetry.' 'Great things are done when men and mountains meet', and James Spedding, after reading the 1842 volumes, had reason to think what astonishing results would follow if his friend could 'find a subject large enough to take the entire impress of his mind'. A writer who devotes his whole life to poetry usually finds that great subjects to which he can fully respond are not often found by searching. Never having deeply felt, as Keats did, that he must bid farewell to his youthful prepossessions for the nobler life wherein are found the agonies and strife of human hearts, Tennyson remained imaginatively handicapped by living a life that, despite frequent meetings with intellectuals and admirers, was too retiring, exclusive, bookish, and comfortable to provoke the sustained intensely creative thought from which great poetry can grow.

The major poetic works of his later years, *Maud* and *Idylls of the King*, developed from earlier inspirations. Many of his poems, often brief, arose from a philosophical obsession with the spiritual world and life after death, but his poetry depended too much on chance, suggestions coming from his reading, and just as often from friends, all ready, on the encouragement of Emily Tennyson, to recommend 'a subject for Alfred'. Although FitzGerald's tastes became nostalgically reversionary at an early age, his discernment is undeniable. He steadfastly believed that Tennyson reached his poetic peak in 1842, and it was then, he wrote thirty years later, that he told him he needed 'some active employment that would keep his soul stirring, instead of revolving in his own idleness and tobacco smoke; and now he is sunk in coterie worship, and (I tremble to say it) in the sympathy of his most lady-like, gentle wife. . . . I mourn over him as over a great man lost – that is, not risen to the greatness that was in him.'[30] Despite its injustice, one can sympathize with the same critic's comment on *The Holy Grail and Other Poems*: he recognised how pure and noble was the principal work, but read on until 'The Northern Farmer' drew tears; he was 'got back to the substantial rough-spun Nature' he knew, and found 'the old Brute, invested . . . with the solemn humour of Humanity' (like Shakespeare's Shallow), a more 'pathetic Phenomenon' than Alfred's knights. Had Tennyson been gifted with more vigorous creative originality, his variety and output would have been greater, and he might have developed both the dramatic lyric and the dramatic monologue more subtly than he did. It is not to be wondered at that he felt much better 'spiritually, mentally, and bodily, while engaged on some long poem'; at such times he could concentrate his powers where they were most effective, not so much on the whole design as on successive passages and incidental imagery.

The creative shortcomings incidental to Tennyson's temperament and habits inevitably affected the design of his more ambitious works. When *The Princess* appeared FitzGerald grieved that the poet's self-indulgence debarred him from writing a heroic poem like Dante's or Milton's. He described it as 'this grotesque abortion', thinking perhaps of Dante's design, which is at the other extreme from the conveniently aggregative and fanciful structuring of *The Princess*. Though not failing to emphasize its originality, 'its fine blank verse, and the many good things in it', Tennyson spoke of it with regret in 1869, and dismissed it as, 'after all, only a medley'. *In Memoriam* grew, and was arranged; *Idylls of the King* grew, probably with varying aims, within a loose accommodating plan, the result being agglomerative and disproportionate. One can apply to him the criticism levelled at contemporary poets by Matthew Arnold in the preface to his 1853 *Poems*: Shakespeare knew 'what constituted a poetical action'; they thought they could emulate him by concentrating their gifts on the 'accessories', in which he excelled, forgetting the truth of Goethe's dictum that 'what distinguishes the artist . . . is *Architectonicè* in the highest sense; that power of execution, which creates, forms, and constitutes: not the profoundness of single thoughts, not the richness of imagery, not the abundance of illustration.

'No poet in English, not even Milton, is so consistently Sublime' as Tennyson, writes Harold Bloom, using 'Sublime' with reference to passages indicative of sexual repression.[31] In its more usual sense, defined by Longinus as 'the note which rings from a great mind', it is much more applicable to Wordsworthian heights than to Tennyson's. Religion made him reflect, but it never raised such lofty thoughts as those of Wordsworth in 'Lines composed a few miles above Tintern Abbey' or at several points in *The Prelude*. Nor, on the subject of national independence and liberty, does he ever approach Wordsworth's grandeur of thought and language in a number of sonnets. Tennyson's failure with the sonnet is evident; he thought highly of 'Montenegro', probably because its vocal values are effectively sustained; there is more live feeling is his apology to Sophy Rawnsley, 'To thee, with whom my best affections dwell'. His most extended successes are in blank verse and in the stanza commonly associated with him, that of *In Memoriam*; in both there are laboured . passages (sometimes versifying prosaic thoughts) where liveliness and flexibility are lost in that mannered or 'Parnassian' style which (as G. M. Hopkins defines it) is written '*on and from the level* of a poet's mind' when he is not creatively inspired. Lacking freshness and surprise, it soon palls. Tennyson's ability to write competently in the simple, rather Biblical, style of 'Dora', without attaining a real and moving language like Wordsworth's in much of 'Michael', justifies Arnold's criticism in the last of his *On Translating Homer* lectures, after his comparison of the 'distilled thoughts in distilled words' of Tennyson's blank verse with Homer's poetry, which is 'all natural thoughts in natural words'. Among the passages he quotes to illustrate Tennyson's 'heightened and elaborate' style is one from 'The Marriage of Geraint' (ll. 74–8) where a 'standing' arm muscle slopes like 'a wild brook o'er a little stone, Running too vehemently to break upon it', a visual observation which, however distracting, has more to recommend it at a point of inaction than one of the best of Tennyson's seascapes at a critical point in the action of 'The Last Tournament' (ll. 454–70).

Pictorial and auditory passages, especially of the sea, are so frequent and evocative in Tennyson that they are often listed as samples of his most perennial art. In poetry they are most enriching when harmoniously subordinated to higher ends, as in Keats's *Hyperion* or (usually) in *Idylls of the King*. Though often more creative, such recognisable imagery is on the same poetic plane as the 'democratic art' or 'revelation of the poetry . . . in common things' which Kingsley went out of his way to praise in *Alton Locke* (ix), taking as his examples, inaccurately and confusingly, 'the desolate pools and creeks' of 'The Dying Swan' and 'the silvery marsh mosses' of the moat in 'Mariana'. Tennyson's exactness of observation is the subject of Mr Holbrook's enthusiasm in *Cranford* (iv), where he misquotingly refers to a cedar that 'spreads his dark-green layers of shade' and 'More black than ashbuds in the front of March' in 'The Gardener's Daughter'. The lengthened simile, however exact, cannot have the immediate imaginative effect of the metaphorical glance, memorable examples of which can be found in most of Tennyson's poetry, from the fields of barley and of rye that 'clothe the wold and meet the sky' and the little breezes that 'dusk and shiver' in 'The Lady of Shallot', 'the wrinkled sea' of 'The Eagle', and 'shoals of puckered faces' in *In Memoriam*, to the 'living gold' and 'naked strength' of 'The Oak', a poem 'clean-cut like a Greek epigram' which indicates how far the aged poet had moved from the luxuriant tendencies of youth. If recognition of common things in poetry is a test of democratic art, it would be hard to find a more magical instance of it than the bird-song of 'The Throstle', another poem of 1889, unless it be the inexpressibly kinetic image of 'The long light shakes across the lakes' in 'The splendour falls', the song which links the third and fourth sections of *The Princess*.

Like the hyperbole of Dante Gabriel Rossetti when he said in old age that he would rather have written 'Tears, idle tears' than the whole of his own poetry, Tennyson's preference of Gray's 'Elegy' to the whole of Wordsworth's poetry (and even his own) should not be taken very literally. Whatever its oversights, it expresses inclinations, one supported by his remark to Edmund Gosse that it is not the thought that makes poetry live, but 'the expression, the form'.[32] Testimony to his memorable gift for language is afforded by the number of his expressions which have become household words, from the telling phrase which has not lost its poetic strength ('The home of woe without a tear' or 'a handful of dust' – better known from *The Waste Land*) to statements of truths so honoured by succeeding time that they have been reduced to triteness. Tennyson

has often been compared to Virgil, and one could apply to much of
his poetry part of Johnson's epitaph on Goldsmith, 'Nullum quod
tetigit non ornavit' ('Whatever he touched he adorned'), but, as can
be expected, his style varies according to subject and mode; it is
often astonishingly plain and simple, basic at times as if he were
consciously on the side of Wordsworth against 'poetic diction'. He
could never have supported Gray's claim that poetry 'has a
language peculiar to itself', yet, drawn to classical subjects, and
imitative of classical forms in idyll and epistle, he would admire
Gray's formal perfection and relish his classical echoes. To assume
from his appreciation of the 'Elegy' that he adopted Pope's view of
excellence in writing, 'What oft was thought but ne'er so well
expressed', would be misleading, however. His classical subjects are
usually correlatives of significance for all time, and most of his
important poetry raised questions of live concern for his own age.

Whatever its limitations, the volume of Tennyson's high poetic
achievement is large. There was little decline in his later years:
monologues such as 'Columbus' and 'Romney's Remorse' are more
dramatic, more humanly alive and moving, than 'Ulysses'; more
imaginative vitality will be found in the later additions to *Idylls of the
King* than in the earlier portions. The many-sidedness of Tennyson's
genius is being recognised again, though it can never be the same as
it was for Grant Allen in 1892. The tide of disparagement has
receded, but modern taste will inevitably be affected to some degree
by the anti-Victorian revolt led by Lytton Strachey in the period of
disillusionment and cynicism which were engendered by the first
'World War'. In the early half-lights of this disenchanted era two
studies of Tennyson appeared. Hugh I'Anson Fausset had no doubt
that Alfred's false morality and high-mindedness were much to
blame for the 1914–18 holocaust; Nicolson's judicial analysis
exerted a stronger, more insidious, pervasive, and prolonged influence. Convinced that Tennyson's poetry had been *devastated* by 'the
requirements of his contemporaries', he aimed at salvaging 'organic
growth' from 'parasitic', 'the lyric poet' from 'the civic prophet'
who moved 'a little clumsily at times within his sacerdotal
vestments'. His 'essential inspiration', Nicolson concluded, 'was the
inspiration of fear'. The result was Tennyson's romantic reduction
to the lyrist of the Lincolnshire Wolds, 'a morbid and unhappy
mystic' with a frightened soul crying out 'like some wild animal
caught in the fens at night-time'. Misreadings and exaggeration
have led to creative or fictional criticism. As if the rest (nine-tenths

at least of Tennyson's poetry) were silence, Nicolson's patently restricted study ends: 'Let us recall only the low booming of the North Sea upon the dunes; the grey clouds lowering above the wold; the moan of the night wind on the fen; the far glimmer of marsh-pools through the reeds; the cold, the half-light, and the gloom.'

Nicolson's own age predetermined his affinity with the half-light and the gloom, but his predilections may have owed something to FitzGerald, who, missing 'the old vintage' (the champagne flavour) of Tennyson's 'earlier days', steadily lost patience with all his poetry after 1842, and thought his decline due to the loss of whatever virtue 'caused the long roll of the Lincolnshire Wave to reverberate in the measure of Locksley Hall'. To ascribe the swing of the 'Locksley Hall' measure to the wave-rhythm of the Lincolnshire coast is a fanciful analogy; whatever its origin, the 'roll' was not lost; it continued to reverberate in several late poems, including 'Locksley Hall Sixty Years After'. Nor is it subtle or indicative of genius; it came too readily and too often.

Nicolson's influence helped T. S. Eliot to one of his blinder judgments: though an instinctive rebel, Tennyson was 'the most perfect conformist'; he became 'the surface flatterer of his own time'. Yet no poet spoke out more vehemently against the injustices and horrors of an age that created 'two nations', with little done to bridge the gap between heartless mammonism and the degradation of the poor. Only a Balin–Balan complex can explain the abhorrence of social evils which exists conjointly with the art of dramatic control in *Maud* and 'Locksley Hall Sixty Years After'. The 'two voices' of Tennyson in the second half of the nineteenth century reveal a man more deeply moved by man's inhumanity, and more philosophically mature, than he had ever been in inner debates and resolutions of doubt. His evolutionary hopes, though unextinguished, had become far more qualified and distanced. On the one hand we find the gloomy thought that 'some lesser god' had made the world offset by belief in the eventual triumph of altruism or Johannine love: 'I believe in God, not from what I see in Nature, but from what I find in man.' Against that is the categorical statement that 'mankind is as yet on one of the lowest rungs of the ladder, although every man has and has had from everlasting his true and perfect being in the Divine Consciousness'.[33] Tennyson was convinced that the dim, weird battle of the west would continue; he anticipated some of the worst fears expressed by Yeats in 'The Second Coming' and by Eliot in *The Waste Land*. His eyes were not closed to most of the major issues of his age, nor did he usually take refuge in shallow optimism. On the role of art, on women's emancipation and the factors that promote civilized progress, on science and its relatedness to religion, and on practical and philosophical religion, he offers much that is relevant to modern times. Nor will the variety and vividness of his presentations, and his rare and sustained mastery of melodic language, lose their appeal.

Notes

Mem. Hallam Tennyson, *Alfred Lord Tennyson: A Memoir* (2 vols), London and New York, 1897

RBM R. B. Martin, *Tennyson: The Unquiet Heart*, New York and Oxford, 1980

Ricks Christopher Ricks (ed.), *The Poems of Tennyson*, London, 1969

1. On the poetic association with which Baumber's Farm is wrongly credited, Tennyson wrote, 'The Moated Grange is an imaginary house in the fen; I never so much as dreamed of Baumber's farm as the abode of Mariana, and the character of Baumber was so ludicrously unlike the Northern Farmer, that it really makes me wonder how any one can have the face to invent such stories' (Mem. I.4–5).

2. She gave him £100 p.a. until long after his marriage (RBM. 60).

3. The hexameters of Leonine verse are divided equally, the word before the caesura rhyming with the last word of the line.

4. 'As for "The Lover's Tale", that was written before I had ever seen a Shelley, though it is called Shelleyan', Tennyson told his son Hallam (Mem. II.285). Hallam states that the poem was written in 1827, when Tennyson was seventeen (Mem. I.48, II.239), but the evidence that it was written in his nineteenth year (1827–8) and worked on at various times until 1832 (Ricks, 300) seems more convincing. Shelley's poetry was discussed at the Cambridge Union in May 1829; the Apostles' debate on his poetry took place on 21 November that year, and five days later Sunderland, Hallam, and Milnes travelled to Oxford to argue the superiority of Shelley's poetry to Byron's in an inter-university debate that evening (Peter Allen, *The Cambridge Apostles: The Early Years*, Cambridge, 1978, p. 50). The fact that little was known about Shelley by the Oxford students lends support to Tennyson's statement.

5. In *Maud* (II.iv) the invocation is to Christ, as if Tennyson recalled the old lyric 'Westron winde, when wilt thou blow, The smalle raine downe can raine? Crist, if my love wer in my armis, And I in my bed againe.'

6. W. L. Paden, in *Tennyson in Egypt: A Study of the Imagery of His Earlier Work*, Lawrence, Kan., 1942, p. 157, refers to three peaks that, according to G. S. Faber, were characteristic of holy mountains, and hence of lands of the blest, in mythology. There could be an allusion to the Trinity.

7. Told by William Hazlitt in *Sketches of the Principal Picture-Galleries of England* (Complete Works, ed. P. P. Howe, vol. X. 68–9).

8. See the note written by Wordsworth on 'The Thorn' for the 1800 edition of *Lyrical Ballads*. The reference is to Judges v.27, the second of the three passages he quotes.

9. For the narrators, see the opening of section i, the passage which follows the song 'Thy voice is heard' and introduces section v, and the cancelled passages: Ricks, 751, 801, 1768–9.

10. The statement made by Tennyson late in his life, denying personal feeling in this lyric (Mem. II.73), suggests that he had forgotten how closely connected it was with regret for Hallam's death. See p. 22 of 'Tennyson's Life' and p. 233 of 'Epilogue'.

11. Undoubtedly a recollection of 'the casement at the dawn of light, Began to show a square of ghastly white' when Hero is about to leap into the sea and join her drowned lover, at the end of Leigh Hunt's 'Hero and Leander'.

12. Tennyson told S. E. Dawson in 1882 that these songs were not an afterthought: 'Before the first edition came out, I deliberated with myself whether I should put songs in between the separate divisions of the poem; again I thought the poem will explain itself; but the public did not see that the child, as you say, was the heroine of the piece, and at last I conquered my laziness and inserted them.'

13. See E. F. Shannon, *Notes and Queries*, June 1959. The poem has a Lincolnshire setting, but is 'a simple invention as to place, incidents and people' (Mem. II.379).

14. For this and other details, see P. G. Scott, *Tennyson's 'Enoch Arden': A Victorian Best-Seller*, Lincoln (The Tennyson Society), 1970.

15. The Offences against the Person Act [D. J. Palmer (ed.), *Tennyson* (Writers and their Background), London, 1973, p. 157n].

16. See 'Wordsworth, Tennyson, and Browning; or, Pure, Ornate, and Grotesque Art in English Poetry', *The National Review*, November 1864, or Walter Bagehot, *Literary Studies* (vol. 2).

17. Mem. II.89–90. He had begun a poem on Merlin, and composed another on Lancelot's quest for the Holy Grail without writing it down (Charles Tennyson, *Alfred Tennyson*, London, 1949, p. 297).

18. See Mem. II.126–7. For the 'house' metaphor as the body of the soul, cf. Tennyson's poem 'By an Evolutionist'.

19. See Mem. II.124–5 for the five-act scenario (or Ricks, 1461–2).

20. Compare Tennyson's declaration of January 1869 (Mem. II.90).

21. See Virgil, *Georgics*, ii.159–60. The castled port was Varenna.

22. For the farmer and his abhorrence of 'steäm-kettles' (steam-engines of any kind), see Hallam Tennyson, *Tennyson and his Friends*, London, 1911, p. 271.

23. For details see Mem. II.249–51.

24. Cf. Mem. II.253.

25. On this Tennyson had speculated from boyhood; cf. *The Devil and the Lady*, II.i (Ricks, 30).

26. Mem. II.388–9.

27. This was written after Tennyson's death – Sir Alfred Lyall, *Tennyson* (English Men of Letters), London, 1902, p. 68.

28. See Mem. II.35, 457, and 'Locksley Hall Sixty Years After', ll.71–2.

29. Mem. II.51, 500–1.

30. Quoted by Nicolson in his *Tennyson*, London, 1923, pp. 199–200, with one correction, from T. Wemyss Reid, *Richard Monckton Milnes*, 1890, vol. II, pp. 264–5.

31. H. Bloom, *Poetry and Repression*, New Haven, Conn., 1976, p. 154, or Elizabeth

A. Francis (ed.), *Tennyson* (Twentieth Century Views), Englewood Cliffs, N. J., 1980.

32. The evidence for this is in the British Library (RBM. 562, 614).

33. See Mem. I.314, 324 and II.374, as commentary on 'Forward, till you see the highest Human Nature is divine' near the end of 'Locksley Hall Sixty Years After'.

Appendixes

A. FAMILY TREE

1.

Michael Tennyson = Elizabeth Clayton

George Tennyson = Mary Turner
1750–1835   1753–1825

| Elizabeth | Mary | GEORGE CLAYTON | Charles |

2.

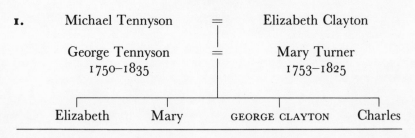

George Clayton
Tennyson
1778–1831
= Elizabeth Fytche
1781–1865

George	1806 (d. 1806)
Frederick	1807–98 = Maria Giuliotti
Charles	1808–79 = Louisa Sellwood
ALFRED	1809–92 = Emily Sellwood
Mary	1810–84 = Alan Ker
Emily	1811–89 = Richard Jesse
Edward	1813–90
Arthur	1814–99 (married twice)
Septimus	1815–66
Matilda	1816–1913
Cecilia	1817–1909 = Edmund Lushington
Horatio	1819–99 (married twice)

3.

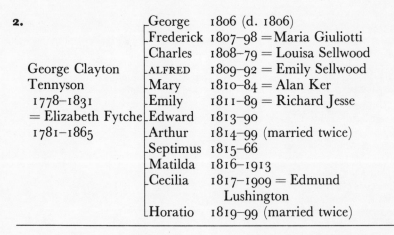

Alfred Tennyson = Emily Sarah Sellwood
1809–92   1813–96

Hallam = Audrey Boyle   Lionel = Eleanor Locker
1852–1928   1854–86

248

B. GLOSSARY

a he
addle, earn
adit, access
affiance, trust
allow, approve
an, if
anew, enough
asthore, dear (Irish)

baculinum, with a rod
bara, bread (Welsh)
barne, child
battle-twig, earwig
baulks, beams
beäl, bellow, bawl
belt, built
blow, bloom
boggle, phantom, goblin
boor-tree, elder tree
boughts, folds
brewis, broth
brig, bridge
broach, roasting-spit
bublin', unfledged bird
burn, born; stream
butter-bump, bittern
buzzard-clock, cockchafer

casselty, casualty, chance
Caucasian, Indo-European
chouse, deceive, dupe
clat, mess; dirty (verb)
claumbs, climbs
clem, clutch
clench, fasten
clerk, cleric
clomb, climbed
clump, sole
conceit, reasoning
costrel, bottle hung from the waist
cotched, caught

crathur, liquor (Irish)
curiously, with care and attention to detail

decent, having the required qualities
Dim Saesneg, No English (Welsh)
doffed, took off (his hat)
doom, judgment

eglatere, eglantine
eld, old age
embattail, arm for battle
'enemies, anemones
eyne, eyes

far-weltered, lying on its back (sheep)
fealty, loyalty
(in) fee, (as a) rightful and undisputed possession
fell, fierce
fere, companion
fewmets, droppings
flayflint, skinflint
forrards, forward, on
frith, firth, estuary
frore, frozen, icy-cold
fun', found
fust, first; fast, firmly fixed

gaudy-day, holiday
(a-)gawming, staring vacantly
ghostly man, priest
glimmer-gowk, owl
gnarr, snarl
goodly, handsome
gossoon, lad
graff, graft
gride, scrape, grate

haft, handle
hallus, always

happt, wrapped
hawmin', lounging
hern, heron
(h)erse, horse
hesp, fasten
hest, bidding, command
hight, named
hoickt, lifted (freed)
hopple, hobble, tie
housel, Eucharist
howry, dirty
huck, hip
huzz, cause to hum or buzz

ivin, ivy

kennel, gutter
knave, boy, servant

langued gules, red-tongued
leal, loyal
let, hinder, prevent
lether, ladder
lief, dear
liefer, liever, rather
lig, lie
lightly, quickly
lurdane, heavy

maät, maäze, confuse, bewilder
malkin, mawkin, wench, slut
manchet, finest wheaten bread
mander, manner
mash, smash
midders, meadows
moänt, mustn't
moästlins, generally
moiled, worried
morions, steel helmets
mowt, might, could
mun, must
murphy, potato

na, than
nathless, nevertheless
nebulones, idle rascals
nim, steal
nobbut, only
nor, than

Norland, belonging to the North
nowt, Nowt, nothing, Nonentity

offices, duties
offset, offspring
or, gold tincture
ouzel, blackbird
oyer et terminer, hear and determine
owd-farraned, old-fashioned
owt, anything

parcel, part
passing, surpassing
periscelides, garters
pight, pitched
pike, peak
platan, plane tree
poach, trample
punctum saliens, beating heart of an
     incipient foetus

quid, plug of tobacco

raäte, rates paid for the maintenance of
     Church of England buildings
raäve, cut, break up
rathe, early
ravin, ravenous
reboant, rebellowing
reck, care
reckling, very small babe
remble, clear, remove
respectant, looking back
roky, misty
round, quick, brisk

saäme, lard
sacring, consecration
scran, luck
screeäd, shrieked
seed, saw
sen, self
sennight, week
sewer-ly, surely
shebeen, grog-shop (Irish)
(get) shut (on), (get) rid (of)
siege, seat
'siver, however (howsoever)
sloomy, dispirited, sluggish

slot, trail
snaggy, ill-tempered
spence, the monks' buttery
squad, mud
squench, put out
straitly, strictly
stub, break up, cultivate
stunt, obstinate
Stylites, ascetic living on top of a pillar
subjected to, lying below
suggest, tempt
summun, someone

talbot, heraldic hound
tale, number (complete, all told)
tew, disturbed state
thack, thatch
thruf(f), through
tight, neat
tilt, waggon-covering or awning
toäner, one or the other

toättler, teetotaller
tued, tired

unhappiness, mischance
unheppen, ungainly, awkward

valve, door (from the Latin)
virtue, manliness, courage

weäred, spent, wasted
weird, fateful
wersens, ourselves
whilome, formerly
windle, drifted snow
wots, knows
wud, mad

y-clad, clad
yield, reward
younker, youngster
yow(e), ewe

C. THE STORY OF *THE PRINCESS*

(I) Rejected by the princess to whom he had been betrothed in childhood, a Northern prince whose father had threatened a war in reprisal steals away with his friends Cyril and Florian, confident of success after seeing Gama, her father, king of the South. From him he learns that, moved by two widows, Lady Psyche and Lady Blanche, to believe that women are men's equals though treated like children, she had withdrawn to his summer palace, near the prince's frontier, to found a university for women. Returning north, the three young men disguise themselves as women, and reach the college entrance at midnight. After inquiring about tutors' merits, they leave a written request that three ladies of the Northern empire should be admitted as Lady Psyche's students, and then retire to bed.

(II) At dawn academic silks are brought, and they are escorted to Princess Ida, who shows them the statues in the hall, not of women such as men desire, but of brave heroines. They must drink knowledge deeply, and learn to be noble, not slaves. Statutes have been read to them, prohibiting for three years correspondence with home, departure from the king's domain ('the liberties'), and conversation with men. They join Psyche's class, and Florian recognises her as his sister; her baby Aglaïa sleeps near her, as she lectures on women's evolution from prehistoric times and on various forms of their subjection to men. She looks forward to the time when women and men will be 'Two heads in council' at home, in the affairs of the world, in science and the arts. At the end of the lecture she beckons the three, recognises Florian, and asks how he had missed the inscription over the entrance, LET NO MAN ENTER IN ON PAIN OF DEATH. The prince discloses himself and his purpose, and he and Florian appeal movingly to her kinship with the North. The secular emancipation of half the world depends on her, she answers, but she promises help if they will leave as soon as possible. She admits that it was duty which made her speak as she did, and they are busy with family recollections before discovering that Lady Blanche's daughter Melissa (who promises not to tell) has overheard

252

all. The prince and his friends then attend lectures on classical poetry (with its 'jewels five-words-long That on the stretched forefinger of all Time Sparkle for ever') and all that is known of man and nature. Cyril (who admires Lady Psyche) admits that he is smitten by Cupid's shaft. After dinner, and a stroll in the gardens (where they overhear students say their May is passing, that they wish to marry, and men hate learned women), they attend chapel with six hundred maidens in purest white, and hear the great melodious organ accompanying psalms and litanies, composed by Ida, beseeching Heaven to bless her work.

(III) Melissa warns that her mother, jealous of Psyche, suspects the truth, and Cyril gains time by offering Lady Blanche advantages at the Northern court. The three masqueraders are invited to join the princess on an academic expedition, and the prince takes the opportunity on the way to plead his own cause. She scorns the suggestion that her work may prove vain after sacrificing love, children, and happiness. She would do anything to expedite the accomplishment of women's freedom, but accepts the succession of events in the shadow of Time, though she believes that 'all creation is one act at once' and 'was, and is, and will be, are but is'. After pitching their tent on flowery levels beneath a crag, they engage in geological research near the heights, Cyril with Psyche, Florian with Melissa, and the prince with the princess.

(IV) At sunset they descend to the tent, where a maid sings 'Tears, idle tears' in response to Ida's request for a song. The princess has no time for the past, and invites the prince to sing a song of promise, to which he responds with 'O Swallow, Swallow'. She prefers songs for great ends, wishing mock-love and mock-Hymen were 'laid up like bats' until men regard women, not as vassals or babes to be dandled, but as 'living wills', whole in themselves and 'owed to none'. When a song on Northern women is requested, Cyril begins a tavern-catch which embarrasses the ladies and makes the prince interject 'Forbear, Sir', and strike him. The ladies flee, intent on taking to their horses, but are checked when the princess misses a plank and falls into the stream. After rescuing 'The weight of all the hopes of half the world', the prince meets Florian in the college grounds, and learns that Melissa, on being questioned whether she or her mother or Lady Psyche was aware of their deceit, had neither affirmed nor denied. They are caught and taken before Princess Ida, who dismisses Blanche, after listening to her voluble complaints in self-defence. Psyche has fled, and Ida decides to take charge of the infant Aglaïa. Letters arrive, indicating that Ida's father has fallen into the hands of the prince's father, who intends to keep him as a hostage for his son, and threatens war unless the latter is returned. The prince pleads love and her father's letter of introduction in excuse for his actions. Students pour in, announcing the enemy's approach, but the princess is resolute; she thanks the prince for saving her life, but has him and Florian ejected.

(v) They soon reach the Northern camp, and change their female attire for armour. Cyril has already arrived with Psyche, whom he had overtaken. She laments their breach of faith, even more the loss of Aglaïa. Finding his father bent on war, the prince urges gentleness; their opposition reflects their attitudes to women. Gama, now freed, urges him to discuss the position with his son Arac, leader of the Southern army. The result is a decision for arbitrament by combat, fifty against fifty. Ida agrees, her answer being carried to the prince, whose life she asks Arac to spare: he risked his life for her, and his mother still lives. Plumed and empanoplied, the mounted combatants fight in the lists, Arac overcoming all he meets, finally Florian, Cyril, and the prince, who falls unconscious.

(vi) Holding Aglaïa, Ida hails the victors from the palace roof; she then descends with a band of students to tend those patriots who have been wounded for her cause. By chance she passes near the unhelmeted prince, lying pale with his father by him. The king, his beard stained with his son's blood, holds up the picture and tress of the princess which the prince had worn round his neck since their betrothal. Ida asks permission to have him tended with her countrymen in the palace, and Psyche implores her to return her child. Her champion Cyril adds his entreaties, and the princess reluctantly assents. In response to Arac and her father, she forgives Lady Psyche. Again she asks the Northern king to let her tend his son; then, reminded of other wounded, she orders the palace doors to be opened to friend or foe. The prince is taken to a remote upper chamber, where he will not be disturbed. All students except some of the sagest return home until happier times, and great lords from both armies walk in and out as they please.

(vii) The college has become a hospital, and a kindlier influence reigns. Princess Ida's world, as she gazes alone from the roofs on the armies that darken 'her female field', seems blank and waste, however, until she comes down and finds peace among the sick. Blanche has gone, leaving Melissa, who attends Florian frequently with Lady Psyche. Love strikes at will on man and maid in the sacred halls, and Ida yields to the prince's plea that she kiss him ere he dies. Her dilemma is solved when she discovers that in ceding to love she has won a whole-hearted supporter of her cause.

D. SELECT BIBLIOGRAPHY

Works

(a) POEMS

Christopher Ricks (ed.), *The Poems of Tennyson*, London, 1969. Includes *The Devil and the Lady*.

(b) PLAYS

Hallam Tennyson (ed.), in the Eversley Edition of Tennyson's Works, London, 1908.

Letters

C. Y. Lang and E. F. Shannon (eds), *The Letters of Alfred Lord Tennyson*, vol. I, 1821–50, Cambridge, Mass., 1981. The first of three volumes. The editing is particularly useful for biographical detail.

Biography

Hallam Tennyson, *Alfred Lord Tennyson: A Memoir* (2 vols), London and New York, 1897. Supplementary:
Hallam Tennyson (ed.), *Tennyson and his Friends*, London, 1911.
Norman Page (ed.), *Tennyson: Interviews and Recollections*, London, 1983.

Charles Tennyson, *Alfred Tennyson*, London, 1949. Supplementary:
Charles Tennyson and Hope Dyson, *The Tennysons: Background to Genius*, London, 1974. Corrects several important details relative to Tennyson's early years and antecedents.

R. B. Martin, *Tennyson: The Unquiet Heart*, Oxford and New York, 1980. Most informative and up-to-date.

Critical Works

Alfred Lyall, *Tennyson* (English Men of Letters), London, 1902.

A. C. Bradley, *A Commentary on Tennyson's 'In Memoriam'*, 3rd edition, London and New York, 1910.

Harold Nicolson, *Tennyson: Aspects of his Life, Character, and Poetry*, London, 1923. Historically the most influential and perhaps the most misleading work on Tennyson, it provides excellent reading but demands wary evaluation.

J. H. Buckley, *Tennyson: The Growth of a Poet*, Cambridge, Mass., 1960. More consistently reliable than most works on Tennyson.

Valerie Pitt, *Tennyson Laureate*, London, 1962.

John Pettigrew, *Tennyson: The Early Poems*, London, 1970.

Christopher Ricks, *Tennyson*, New York and London, 1972.

F. E. L. Priestley, *Language and Structure in Tennyson's Poetry*, London, 1973.

John D. Rosenberg, *The Fall of Camelot: A Study of Tennyson's 'Idylls of the King'*, Cambridge, Mass., 1973.

A. Dwight Culler, *The Poetry of Tennyson*, New Haven, Conn., and London, 1977.

Critical Essays

A. C. Bradley, in *A Miscellany*, London, 1929.

Lascelles Abercrombie, in *Revaluations* (ed. A. C. Ward), London, 1931.

E. D. H. Johnson, in *The Alien Vision of Victorian Poetry*, Princeton, N. J., 1952.

Basil Willey, in *More Nineteenth Century Studies*, London, 1956.

Kathleen Tillotson, 'Tennyson's Serial Poem' in Geoffrey and Kathleen Tillotson, *Mid-Victorian Studies*, London, 1965.

Eugene R. August, 'Tennyson and Teilhard: The Faith of *In Memoriam*', *PMLA*, March 1969.

Geoffrey Tillotson, in *A View of Victorian Literature*, Oxford, 1978.

(COLLECTIONS)

Charles Tennyson, *Six Tennyson Essays*, London, 1954.

J. Killham (ed.), *Critical Essays on the Poetry of Tennyson*, London, 1960.

John D. Jump (ed.), *Tennyson, The Critical Heritage*, London, 1967.

Isobel Armstrong (ed.), *The Major Victorian Poets: Reconsiderations*, London, 1969.
D. J. Palmer (ed.), *Tennyson* (Writers and Their Background), London, 1973.
Elizabeth A. Francis (ed.), *Tennyson* (Twentieth Century Views), Englewood Cliffs, N. J., 1980.
Hallam Tennyson (ed.), *Studies in Tennyson*, London, 1981.

Bibliography

Lionel Madden, 'Tennyson: A Select Bibliography' (in D. J. Palmer, above), 1973.
J. D. Hunt, 'Tennyson' in A. E. Dyson (ed.), *English Poetry* (Select Bibliographical Guides), Oxford, 1971.

Index

Abercrombie, Lascelles   238, 257
Aberystwyth   26
Acton, Lord   54
Albert, Prince Consort   32, 37, 38, 42,
    157, 159, 173
Aldworth   46, 47, 50, 57, 59
Allen, Dr   26, 27, 151, 162, 163
Allen, Grant   242
Allingham, William   34, 43, 47, 215
America (the U.S.A.)   50, 56, 155
'The Apostles'   14–16, 17, 88, 99, 245
The Arabian Nights   74, 149
Arber, Edward   218
Argyll, the Duke and Duchess of   38, 39,
    40, 42, 56, 59, 181
Arnold, Matthew   38, 105, 239–40, 240
Ashburton, Lady   33, 36
Auden, W. H.   235
Austen, Jane   20, (Louisa Musgrove)
    47, 58, 63
Austin, Alfred   59

Bacon, Francis   155
Bagehot, Walter   168–9
Bamford, Samuel   31
Baring, Rosa   23–4, 103, 144
Barmouth   26, 127, 134, 136, 139
Barnes, William   47
Baudelaire   55
Bayons Manor   6–7, 9, 12, 13, 23, 24–5,
    28, 38
Beech Hill House   *see* High Beech
Bennett, Sterndale   157
Benniworth   7, 10
Blakesley, J. W.   25
Bloom, Harold   240, 246
Boccaccio   80, 207
Bonchurch   30, 31, 34, 39
Boulogne   22
Boxley   3, 27
Boyd, Robert   17

Boyle, Audrey and Mary   55, 56, 199–
    200
Bradley, Granville and Mrs   41, 43, 45,
    58, 59, 181
Brittany   43
Brontë, Branwell   12, 63
Brookfield, W.   24
Browning, Elizabeth and Robert   30, 34,
    36, 37, 43, 45, 51, 53, 56, 58, 187;
    (poems) 96, 133, 144, 197, 217, 222, 236
Buckley, J. H.   230, 257
Bulwer-Lytton, Edward   28–9, 37, 52
Burke, Edmund   67
Burne-Jones, Edward   37, 60
Butler, Montagu   43, 60
Butler, Samuel   155
Byron, Lord   5, 11, 66, 68, 245

Caistor   6, 23, 25
Cambridge   13, 14, 17, 20, 25, 39, 57, 75,
    87, 93
    St John's College   8, 12, 15
    Trinity College   12–13, 14, 17, 18, 39,
    51
    University of   16, 17, 41, 77, 127, 138,
    237, 245
Cameron, Mrs Julia   37, 40, 42, 43, 48,
    51, 53, 201
Canada   50, 54, 159
Carlyle, Jane   28, 30, 36
Carlyle, Thomas   6, 26, 28, 30, 33, 36,
    43, 51, 53, 108, 141, 152, 156, 165, 193,
    236
Catullus   54, 234
Cauteretz   17, 42, 51
Chambers, Robert   29, 131
Chatterton, Thomas   157
Chaucer   47, 59, 90
Cheltenham   12, 28, 31, 34, 162
Clare, John   26
Clevedon   21, 33, 124

Clough, Arthur Hugh   35, 41, 42, 165
Coleridge, Hartley   22
Coleridge, Samuel Taylor   11, 15, 22, 86, ('The Ancient Mariner') 95
Collins, Churton   57
Coniston   33, 38, 39
Cornwall   30–1, 40, 41, 57, 58
Coventry   26, 109
Cowell, E. B.   29
Crabbe, George   11, 165, 169
Craik, G. L.   59
Crimean War, the   4, 35, 145, 151, 157, 197
Croker, J. W.   20, 28, 83, 230
Cumming, Dr J.   31, 162

Dakyns, Graham   41–2, 44
Dante   14, 35, 47, 55, 78, 96, 123, 133–4, 142, 239
Darwin, Charles   41, 47–8, 130
Denham, Sir John   235
Denmark   56
Derbyshire   42, 55
de Vere, Aubrey   27, 30, 33, 204, 215
Dickens, Charles   30, 38, 49, 165
Disraeli, Benjamin   52
Dodgson, C. L.   38, 39
Dresden   44
Dufferin, Lord   39, 50, 57, 58, 59, 200

Eliot, George   5, 37, 50, 143, 162, 238
Eliot, T. S.   79, 129, 138, 234, 237, 243; *Murder in the Cathedral*   93, 207; *The Waste Land*   194, 230, 241, 243
Emerson, Ralph Waldo   30
Emma, Queen of the Sandwich Islands   44
Epping Forest   25, 106
Eton College   10, 12, 14, 47, 106

Farnham   31, 46
Farrar, F. W.   224
Farringford   34–5, 36–7, 38, 39, 42, 44, 45, 46, 47, 50, 144, 197, 199
Fausset, Hugh I'Anson   242
FitzGerald, Edward   16, 22, 25, 26, 29, 30, 35, 52, 55, 56, 93, 165, 223, 234; the *Rubáiyát* of Omar Khayyám 199, 208–9; impressions of Tennyson and his poetry   31, 49, 136, 218, 239, 243
Fox, W. J.   83, 113

Franklin, Catherine   24, 31
Franklin, Lady   45, 51
Franklin, Sir John   24, 52, 97
Frazer, J. G.   58
Froude, J. A.   43, 51, 60, 202

Garibaldi   43, 199
Gaskell, Mrs   31, 165, (*Cranford*) 241
Gilbert, W. S.   115
Gilchrist, Mrs   45, 47
Gladstone, Mary   214
Gladstone, W. E.   14, 25, 28, 37, 44–5, 45, 48, 50, 52, 53, 54, 55, 55–6, 57, 59, 158, 178
Goethe   35, 44, 47, 124, 160, 240
Gosse, Edmund   57, 241
Grasby   23, 24, 26, 27, 34, 38, 53
Gray, Thomas   65, 78, 130, 241, 242
Green, J. R.   205–6
Greville, Mrs   53, 55
Grimsby   6, 7, 10, 24
Guest, Lady Charlotte   174

Hallam, Arthur   14ff., 22, 30, 39, 44, 47, 49, 55, 69, 80, 84, 96, 245; in Tennyson's poetry   97, 98, 99, 103, 115, 120, 122ff., 145, 172, 227, 230, 233, 245
Hallam, Henry   14, 16, 18, 19, 20, 21, 22, 28
Halton Holgate   13, 25, 215
Hamley, General   198
Hampstead   43–4
Hardy, Thomas   58, 60, 130, 131, 208, 216, 227, 229
Harrington Hall   23, 144
Harrogate   43
Haslemere   45, 46, 50
Hawker, Stephen   30–1
Hawthorne, Nathaniel   38
Hazlitt, William   207, 245
Herbert, George   54
High Beech   3, 25, 26, 123, 128
Holland   27
Homer   11, (Ilion) 20, 26, 34, 55, 73, 91, 176, 240
Hopkins, Gerard Manley   173, 219, 238, 240
Horace   10, 34, 63, 67, 197
Horncastle   7, 23, 26
Houghton, Lord   *see* Milnes, Monckton
Howitt, Mary and William   28
Hunt, Holman   37, 38, 41, 43
Hunt, Leigh   21, 246

Huxley, Thomas   44, 235

Ireland   27, 30, 53
Irving, Henry   52, 54, 55, 58, 59, 201, 206, 207, 208
Irving, Washington   220
Italy   14, 16, 28, 34, 51, 54, 196–7

James, Henry   53, 58, 202, 222
Jesse, Richard   22
Joachim, Joseph   53
Johnson, Samuel   10, 114, 130, 242
Jones, Sir William   66, 142
Jowett, Benjamin   35, 36, 37, 39, 40, 41, 42, 43, 44, 50, 59, 60, 63, 200, 211, 228, 230

Keats, John   18, 18–19, 20, 35, 65, 69, 71, 74, 78, 81, 86–7, 225, 237, 238
Kemble, John   14, 15, 17, 19, 20, 21
Kinglake, A. W.   157
Kingsley, Charles   33, 34, 45, 141, 241
Knowles, (Sir) James   46, 47, 48, 122–3, 129, 233

Langton, Bennet   10, 214
Lao-tsze   228–9
Laurence, Samuel   25, 49
Lawrence, D. H.   89, 114, 116, 191, 193, 236
Lear, Edward   31, 33, 39, 40, 44, 195–6
Lecky, W. E. H.   54, 207
Lewes, George Henry   45, 50
Lincoln   7, 26, 67
Little Holland House   37, 39, 42–3, 51
Liverpool   17, 38, 142
Locker, Frederick   48, 52
Lockhart, John   20
Longfellow, H. W.   47, 204
Longinus   240
Louise, Princess   58, 59
Louth   3, 7, 9, 10–11, 11, 12, 13
Lowell, J. R.   222
Lucretius   91, 218–19, 232, 235
Lushington, Edmund   25, 27, 35, 50, 127, 129, 132
Lushington, Franklin   35
Lushington, Henry   49
Lyell, (Sir) Charles   126
Lyme Regis   47
Lymington   34, 57

Mablethorpe   12, 20, 26, 27, 30
Macaulay, T. B.   40, 181

Macmillan, Alexander   39, 56
Macmillan, Frederick   59
Malory, Sir Thomas   12, 89, 99, 172, 173
Malvern   31, 34
Manchester   17, 38, 142, 155
Market Rasen   6
Marlborough College   41, 45, 47
Martin, R. B.   6, 245, 247
Marvell, Andrew   106, 147, 237
Mason, William   67
Maurice, F. D.   15, 33, 37, 197
Meredith, George   58, 181, 193, 236
Merivale, Charles   14
Mill, John Stuart   22, 113
Millais, John   35, 49, 211
Milnes, Monckton (Lord Houghton)   14, 15, 25, 27, 33, 45, 53, 56, 245
Milton, John   11, 34, 64, 65, 66, 67, 68, 77, 78, 83, 237; *Paradise Lost* 65, 180
Mitford, Mary   87, 105, 110
Monteith, Robert   21, 25, 31
Moxon, Edward   19, 21, 27, 29, 30, 31, 36, 38, 39, 48

Napoleon (Buonaparte)   12, 153
Napoleon, Louis   34, 155
New Forest, the   39, 57
Nicolson, (Sir) Harold   235, 242, 243, 246, 257
'North, Christopher'   *see* Wilson, John
Norway   4, 39

Old Shoreham   212
Osborne   37, 42, 45, 55
Ossian   11, 65
Oxford, University of   36, 41, 245

Paden, W. L.   245
Paget, (Sir) James   43, 60
Palgrave, Francis   64
Palgrave, F. T.   31, 34, 39, 41, 42, 43, 45, 47
Palgrave, W. G.   199
Paris   12, 13, 16, 18, 21, 34, 48, 50, 51
Park House   27, 28, 30, 33, 109
Pater, Walter   136
Patmore, Coventry   30, 31, 33, 35, 37, 38
Paul, Kegan   44, 53
Pindar   34, 98
Plato   50, 65, 69, 117, 236
Plutarch   207
Pope, Alexander   11, 28, 63, 195, 242
Portugal   4, 39

Pritchard, Charles   44, 48
Pyrenees, the   41–2, 52, 127, 165; *see* Cauteretz; Pyrenean scenery in Tennyson's poetry   17, 42, 84–5, 91

Rawnsley, Drummond (son of T. H.)   31, 35, 195, 215
Rawnsley, H. D. (son of Drummond)   190, 215
Rawnsley, Sophy   23, 25, 144, 240
Rawnsley, T. H.   13, 19, 25
Reynolds, Sir Joshua   223
Ricks, Christopher   218, 245, 246, 256, 257
Ritchie, Emily   48
Rogers, Samuel   21, 28, 33
Rollin, Charles   66, 67
Romney, George   223–4
Rossetti, Dante Gabriel   36, 37, 38, 150, 241
Ruskin, John   36, 37, 40, 48
Russia   7

Sappho   72–3, 84, 86
Scotland   21, 31, 34, 38, 39, 55–6
Scott, Sir Walter   11, 55, 58, 63, 66, 77, 141, 216; *The Bride of Lammermoor*   66, 146, 210
Seaford   34
Sellwood, Emily   23, 25, 26, 27, 31–2, 113   *see* Tennyson, Emily
Sellwood, Henry   23, 24, 25, 26, 31–2
Sellwood, Louisa   23; (Mrs Charles Turner)   26, 31–2, 38, 50, 53
Shakespeare   26, 29, 78, 114, 201, 204, 205
   As You Like It   106
   Cymbeline   59, 77
   Hamlet   145–6, 238
   King Lear   151, 189
   Measure for Measure   74, 224
   Romeo and Juliet   147, 207
   The Winter's Tale   57
Shaw, George Bernard   220
Shelley, P. B.   15, 65, 69, 73, 78, 79, 80, 88, 108, 117, 132, 193, 227, 245
Sherwood Forest   55
Shiplake-on-Thames   31–2, 33
Sidgwick, Henry   130
Simeon, Sir John   36, 38, 47, 49, 145, 220
Skegness   12
Smith, Goldwin   36, 151
Somersby   7, 9, 10, 14, 16, 18, 19, 21, 25, 59, 75, 76, 110, 123, 125, 127, 128, 137,

138;   Holywell glen   9, 10, 11, 23
Southey, Robert   28, 174
Spedding, James   18, 19, 22, 25, 27, 33, 35, 37, 43, 53, 92, 195, 238
Spenser, Edmund   (*The Faerie Queene*)   67, 91, 173
Spilsby   10, 13, 21, 23
Stanford, C. V.   159, 206
Sterling, John   15, 17, 27, 28, 30, 111, 172
Stevenson, R. L.   58
Strachey, Lytton   242
Strahan, Alexander   48, 51
Stratford-on-Avon   26
Sumner, Charles   237
Sunderland, Thomas   16, 245
Sutherland, the Duchess of   43
Swift, Jonathan   (*Gulliver's Travels*)   97
Swinburne, Algernon   39, 45, 52, 55, 173, 189, 209, 224
Switzerland   16–17, 30, 48, 50, 51

Tasso   173
Taylor, (Sir) Henry   37, 43, 48
Tealby   6, 18, 23, 25
Tennant, Laura   157
TENNYSON, ALFRED (LORD):
   appearance   13, 24, 28, 38
   and biography   5–6
   and Christianity   131, 165, 167, 189, 212, 230–1, 235
   and class distinction   103, 106–7, 107–8, 109, 111, 141, 147–8, 151–2, 169–70, 243
   flesh and spirit   79–80, 177, 183–5, 190–1, 236–7
   and France   34, 109, 153, 154, 155
   and poetic inspiration   65, 78–9, 86
   politics   17, 18, 19, 68, 110, 152–61; British colonialism   50, 158, 159–60, 160, 230–1
   and reason   16, 86, 95–6, 130–1, 226
   reading   11, 34, 35, 41, 44, 58, 63ff. *passim*
   and Romanism   155, 156, 189, 191, 202, 204, 220–1
   and science   29, 235–6
   and war   157, 158, 160
   women's rights   107–8, 113–14, 119–21

(*For poems and plays see the references which follow the general index.*)

Tennyson, Arthur   28
Tennyson, Cecilia   24, 25, 27;   (Mrs Lushington)   28, 50, 123, 132
Tennyson,   Charles   (uncle: Charles Tennyson d'Eyncourt)   7, 9, 12, 13, 18, 22, 24–5, 26, 28, 38, 56, 148
Tennyson,   Charles   (brother: Charles Turner) 9, 10, 11, 12, 13, 16, 18, 21, 23, 25, 26, 27, 31–2, 34, 38, 50, 53, 54, 63, 127, 128, 129, 198, 234
Tennyson, (Sir) Charles (grandson)   6, 32, 144, 162, 223, 246, 256, 257
Tennyson, Edward   13, 23, 24, 28
Tennyson, Elizabeth (aunt: Mrs Russell) 7–8, 13, 19, 148
Tennyson, Elizabeth (mother)   7, 10, 13, 23, 24, 31, 33, 43–4, 63, 73, 113–14, 162
Tennyson, Emily (sister)   17, 18, 21, 22, 24, 28, 103
Tennyson, Emily (wife)   33, 34, 35, 36–7, 38, 39, 42, 44, 45, 46, 51–2, 56, 58, 59, 60,   144,   169,   237,   238–9   see Sellwood, Emily
Tennyson, Frederick   9, 10, 12, 12–13, 16, 19, 24, 27, 28, 34, 57, 59, 136, 223
Tennyson, George (grandfather)   6–7, 9, 10, 18, 19, 22–3, 24
Tennyson, George Clayton (father)   7, 9, 10, 11, 12, 13, 14, 16–17, 18, 26, 73, 92, 113
Tennyson, Hallam   24, 34, 36, 38–9, 41, 44, 45, 45–6, 48, 50, 51, 52, 53, 55, 56, 57, 58, 59, 155, 197, 201, 206, 223, 228, 233, 246;   *Memoir*   6, 60, 233–4, 245–7, 256
Tennyson, Lionel   35, 38, 41, 44, 45, 46, 47, 48, 51, 52, 53, 57, 58, 143, 200
Tennyson, Mary (grandmother)   6, 23
Tennyson, Mary (aunt: Mrs Bourne)   9, 25, 66
Tennyson, Mary (sister)   20, 24, 25
Tennyson, Matilda   21
Tennyson, Michael (great-grandfather) 6
Tennyson, Septimus   26, 28
Terry, Ellen   54, 207
Thackeray, Annie (Lady Ritchie)   43, 48
Thackeray, William Makepeace   25, 35, 37, 43, 45, 52, 58
Theocritus   34, 85, 102, 106, 107, 111, 163
Thomson, James (1700–48)   11, 63, 91

Tintern Abbey   22, 47
Titian   21
Torquay   26, 107
Torrijos, General   17
Trench, R. C.   16, 17, 88
Trumpington   87
Tunbridge Wells   3, 26–7
Turgenev   50
Turner, Charles   *see* Tennyson, Charles
Turner, J. M. W.   80
Turner, Samuel   23
Twickenham   33, 43–4
Tyndall, John   44

Ulloa, Antonio de   65, 67, 68
Umberslade Hall   30
Usselby   22, 24

Venice   54
Vestiges of Creation   *see* Chambers, Robert
Victoria,   Queen   33, 38, 42, 50, (Vicky) 56, 57, 59, 60, 158, 159, 160; *see* Osborne
Vienna   21, 128, 132
Virgil   34, 55, 59, 197, 198, 242, 246

Ward, W. G.   51, 52
Warninglid   33
Warwick   26
Waterloo   44, (Hougoumont) 159
Watts, G. F.   37, 39, 51
Webster, John   238
Wellington, the Duke of   4, 12, 34, 156
Westminster Abbey   45, 49, 52, 53, 56, 58, 59–60
Wharfedale   27
White, Gilbert   46
White, James   30, 34
Wilson, (Professor) John   19, 20, 230
Wimpole Street   19, 20, 124, 128
Wollstonecraft, Mary   113
Woolner, Thomas   31, 37, 38, 40, 41, 42, 43, 45, 162, 165, 169, 170
Wordsworth, William   22, 27, 28, 32, 69, 94, 105, 106, 146, 194, 233, 235, 242
his poetry   51, 69, 75, 78, 96, 110, 111, 157, 169, 185–6, 227, 228, 230, 240, 241
and politics   18, 68, 160–1, 190

Yeats, W. B.   243
York   7, 28

Zolaism   143

TENNYSON'S POEMS AND PLAYS

Adeline   72
Akbar's Dream   58, 230–1
Alexander   83–4
Amphion   106
Amy   71–2
Anacaona   77
The Ancient Sage   228–9, 233, 235, 236
Antony and Cleopatra   67
Armageddon   14, 65, 68, 69
Art for Art's Sake   48–9
Audley Court   26, 107
Ay me! those childish lispings roll   77, 78
Aylmer's Field   42, 43, 108, 162, 169–71, 212

Babylon   66, 171
The Ballad of Oriana   16, 77
Ballads and Other Poems   4, 54–5
The Bandit's Death   216
Beautiful City   153
Becket   4, 53–4, 58, 59, 201, 205–7
Boädicea   43, 204, 218
Break, break, break   100–1, 125, 234
The Bridal   66
The Bridesmaid   23
Britons, Guard Your Own   155
The Brook   110–11
Buonaparte   153
The Burial of Love   113
By an Evolutionist   231, 246

A Character   16
The Charge of the Heavy Brigade at Balaclava   157, 198
    Epilogue   157, 226
The Charge of the Light Brigade   35, 68, 157
Charity   216, 217
The Church-Warden and the Curate   215–16
Claribel   71
The Coach of Death   65
Columbus   220, 225, 242
Come down, O maid, from yonder mountain height   30, 116
Compromise   158
Crossing the Bar   58, 60, 228
The Cup   4, 55, 57, 207–8

The Daisy   196–7
The Dawn   231, 236
The Day-Dream   105

De Profundis   228, 236
The Dead Prophet   5
The Death of Oenone   85, 200, 223
The Death of Oenone, Akbar's Dream, and Other Poems   4, 59
The Defence of Lucknow   53, 158
The Dell of——   67
Demeter and Other Poems   4, 58
Demeter and Persephone   58, 223, 225, 229
The Deserted House   77
Despair   214, 217, 226, 231
The Devil and the Lady   4, 63–4, 201
Did not thy roseate lips outvie   67
A Dirge   77
Dora   22, 105–6, 111, 240
A Dream of Fair Women   90–1, 206
The Dreamer   232
The Druid's Prophecies   65
The Dying Swan   241

The Eagle   241
Early Spring   176
Early Verses of Compliment to Miss Rose Baring   144
Edwin Morris   26, 107–8, 114
Eleänore   72–3
English Warsong   153
England and America   50
Enoch Arden   42, 43, 162, 165–9
Enoch Arden, and Other Poems   4, 43
The Epic   99, 104–5, 172
Epilogue   *see* The Charge of the Heavy Brigade at Balaclava
Exhortation to the Greeks   68
The Exile's Harp   66
The Expedition of Nadar Shah into Hindostan   66

Faith   231–2
The Falcon   4, 54, 207, 208
Far-Far-Away   11, 233
Fatima   84
The First Quarrel   212–13
The Fleet   158
The Flight   210
Flower in the crannied wall   227–8
For the Penny-Wise   155
The Foresters   4, 55, 57, 58, 201–2, 208
Forlorn   84, 216
A Fragment   77–8
Frater Ave atque Vale   54, 234

Freedom   154–5
From sorrow sorrow yet is born   96

The Gardener's Daughter   18, 103–4, 107–8, 241
Gareth and Lynette, etc.   4
God and the Universe   232
Godiva   109
The Golden Year   108, 109–10
The Goose   154
The Grandmother   43, 45, 210–11

Hail Briton!   135, 153, 154
Hail, Light, another time to mortal eyes   78
Hands All Round   159
Hands All Round!   55, 155
Happy   216, 236
Hark! the dogs howl!   122
Harold   4, 52, 153, 201, 203–5, 206
The Hesperides   69, 86
The High-Priest to Alexander   66
The Higher Pantheism   47, 227
The Holy Grail and Other Poems   4
How gaily sinks the gorgeous sun   67

I loving Freedom for herself   154
I wander in darkness and sorrow   66
The Idealist   69
An Idle Rhyme   111
Idylls of the King   37, 39, 40, 42, 47, 48, 50, 51, 80, 120, 138, 172–4, 181, 183–4, 184–5, 190–4, 226, 228, 229, 236, 239, 242
    Balin and Balan   4, 51, 56, 172, 173, 189–90, 193, 194
    The Coming of Arthur   172, 183–4, 190
    Dedication   42, 159
    Gareth and Lynette   50, 185–6
    Geraint and Enid   37, 39, 173, 174, 175–6, 193
    Guinevere   39, 45, 50, 174, 180–1, 183, 190
    The Holy Grail   40, 47, 48, 108, 132–3, 181–3, 190, 194, 226–7, 237, 239
    Lancelot and Elaine   39, 174, 178–80, 190, 193
    The Last Tournament   50, 187–9, 190, 191
    The Marriage of Geraint   37, 39, 173, 174–5, 176, 190, 193, 240
    Merlin and Vivien   27, 37, 39, 174, 176–8, 192, 193, 193–4

The Passing of Arthur   172, 183, 184–5, 194
    Pelleas and Ettarre   185, 186–7, 194, 237
    To the Queen   50, 159, 193
Ilion, Ilion   71
In deep and solemn dreams   75, 77
In Memoriam A. H. H.   3, 29, 31–2, 36, 42, 76, 79, 95, 96, 97, 98, 100, 120, 122–39, 153, 172, 195, 226, 228, 230, 233, 234, 235, 237, 239, 240
In the Children's Hospital   214
In the Garden at Swainston   49, 234
In the Valley of Cauteretz   42, 234
Inscription by a Brook   86
Inverlee   66
Isabel   73

Jack Tar   156
June Heather and Bracken   58

Kate   73
King Charles's Vision   67
The Kraken   73

Lady Clara Vere de Vere   102, 103
Lady Clare   102
The Lady of Shallot   89–90, 178, 241
Lamentation of the Peruvians   66
Leonine Elegiacs   71
Life   78
Lilian   71
Lines (Here often, when a child, I lay reclined)   20
Lines on Cambridge of 1830   17
Lisette   71
The Little Maid   111–12
Locksley Hall   108, 111, 141–2, 160, 210, 243
Locksley Hall Sixty Years After   57, 143–4, 160, 227, 243, 246, 247
Locksley Hall Sixty Years After, etc.   4
The Lord of Burleigh   102–3
The Lotos-Eaters   17, 67, 73–4, 78, 80, 91–2, 96, 127, 166
Love   78
Love and Duty   26
Love thou thy land   154
The Lover's Tale   4, 16, 19, 80–2, 103, 121, 245
Lucretius   47, 218–20, 225, 226, 237

Madeline   71
The Maid of Savoy   67
The Making of Man   231

Margaret 72
Mariana 74–5, 85, 241, 245
Mariana in the South 84–5, 85
Marion 72
Maud 25, 36, 37, 50, 75, 108, 144–52, 156, 169, 210, 238, 243
Maud, and Other Poems 4
The May Queen 84, 102
Me my own Fate to lasting sorrow doometh 75, 78
Memory, dear enchanter 76
Merlin and the Gleam 58, 97, 99, 101, 172, 177, 229–30
The Mermaid 73
The Merman 73
Midnight 65–6
Midnight – in no midsummer tune 53
The Miller's Daughter 87–8, 102, 195
Mine be the strength of spirit 83
Mithridates Presenting Berenice with the Cup of Poison 67
Montenegro 240
Morte d'Arthur 22, 31, 97, 99–100, 172, 184, 230
My life is full of weary days 83
The Mystic 79, 230, 236

National Song 153
The New Timon, and the Poets 29
The Northern Cobbler 213
Northern Farmer (New Style) 211–12, 217
Northern Farmer (Old Style) 43, 45, 211, 239, 245
Now sleeps the crimson petal 116

O Darling Room 28, 83
O Swallow, Swallow, flying, flying South 116, 253
The Oak 241
Ode on the Death of the Duke of Wellington 34, 152, 156
Ode Sung at the Opening of the International Exhibition 157–8
Ode to Memory 9, 76
Oenone 17, 85–6, 91
Of old sat Freedom on the heights 154
Oh! that 'twere possible 25, 100, 122, 145, 238
Oh! ye wild winds 65–6
On a Mourner 96
On One Who Affected an Effeminate Manner 120
On Sublimity 67, 69

On the Jubilee of Queen Victoria 159, 160
Opening of the Indian and Colonial Exhibition by the Queen 159
Our enemies have fallen, have fallen 116
Over the dark world flies the wind 100
Owd Roä 215

The Palace of Art 65, 88–9, 89, 90
Parnassus 235–6
The Penny-Wise 155
Perdidi Diem 79
Persia 66
The Play 231
Poems (1832) 20, 83, 88
Poems (1842) 27, 111, 158
Poems by Two Brothers 3, 12
Poems, Chiefly Lyrical 3, 16, 18, 83, 113
The Poet 78–9, 86, 98, 101, 170
The Poet's Mind 78, 86
Poland 83
Politics 158
Prefatory Poem to My Brother's Sonnets 198
The Princess 3, 28, 30, 31, 36, 73, 108, 109, 113–21, 144, 172, 192, 236, 237, 239, 252–5
The Progress of Spring 87, 199–200
Prologue to General Hamley 198
The Promise of May 4, 55, 57, 59, 208–9

Queen Mary 4, 52, 201–3, 204
The Queen of the Isles 158

Recollections of the Arabian Nights 74
Remorse 66
The Revenge 53, 218
Rifle Clubs!!! 155
Riflemen Form! 156
The Ring 222–3
Rizpah 212
Romney's Remorse 223–4, 242
Rosamund's Bower 206
The Roses on the Terrace 144
The Ruined Kiln 86–7

St Agnes' Eve 25, 94
St Simeon Stylites 93–4, 96, 217
St Telemachus 224
Sea Dreams 162–5, 235
The Sea-Fairies 73
Sense and Conscience 79–80

She took the dappled partridge 78
The Silent Voices 60
Sir Galahad 94
Sir John Franklin 52
Sir Launcelot and Queen Guinevere 90
Sir John Oldcastle, Lord Cobham 220–1
The Sisters 84
The Sisters (They have left the doors ajar) 221–2
Song (A spirit haunts the year's last hours) 74–5
Sonnet (Alas! how weary are my human eyes) 83
Sonnet (Blow ye the trumpet) 83
Sonnet (Check every outflash) 78
The Spinster's Sweet-Arts 214–15, 217
The splendour falls on castle walls 30, 117, 241
Suggested by Reading an Article in a Newspaper 155–6
Supposed Confessions of a Second-Rate Sensitive Mind 75–6, 94
Sweet and Low 31, 116

The Talking Oak 106
Tears, idle tears 22, 115, 233, 234, 253
There is no land like England 208
The Third of February, 1852 155
Thou camest to thy bower, my love 66
Three Sonnets to a Coquette 144
The Throstle 241
Timbuctoo 14, 68–9, 86
Time: An Ode 67
Tiresias 98–9, 109, 153, 198–9
Tiresias and Other Poems 4, 56
Tithon 97–8
Tithonus 43, 98
To——, After Reading a Life and Letters 5
To Christopher North 19
To E. FitzGerald 199
To E. L. on his Travels in Greece 195–6
To J. S. 92, 195

To Mary Boyle 199–200
To Poesy 69–70
To the Marquis of Dufferin and Ava 200
To the Master of Balliol 200
To the Queen 158–9, 195
To the Queen *see Idylls of the King*
To the Rev. F. D. Maurice 36, 197
To the Vicar of Shiplake 121, 195
To thee, with whom my best affections dwell 144, 240
To Ulysses 199
To Virgil 198
Tomorrow 215
The Two Voices 22, 94–6, 97, 98, 101, 114, 122, 228, 230

Ulysses 22, 78, 80, 96–7, 98, 100, 101, 217, 230, 242

The Vale of Bones 66
Vastness 226, 227
The Village Wife 10, 213–14
The Vision of Sin 80, 134
The Voice of the Peak 228
The Voyage 101
The Voyage of Maeldune 221, 225

Wages 98, 227
Walking to the Mail 106–7
We meet no more 65
A Welcome to Alexandra 42
Will 156–7
Will Waterproof's Lyrical Monologue 106, 195
Woe to the double-tongued 84, 154
The Wreck 215
Written by an Exile of Bassorah 66
Written during the Convulsions in Spain 68

You ask me, why, though ill at ease 135, 154
Youth 101